1975

Teaching Science
IN ELEMENTARY
AND MIDDLE SCHOOLS

Teaching Science
IN ELEMENTARY AND MIDDLE SCHOOLS

Nathan S. Washton

Queens College of the City University of New York

David McKay Company, Inc., New York

Design by Bob Antler

To my wife, Sylvia

PREFACE

This text is designed to serve as a basic, concise guide that will help the prospective and in-service teacher select, organize, plan, teach, and evaluate science activities for children in kindergarten through grade eight. Regardless of the science curriculum used in a particular school, the teacher makes decisions and judges the worth of various learning activities. Such judgments are usually based on the latest learning theories, current scientific information, science-education research, and especially the needs of our children in a changing technological society.

In making adequate provisions for learning science, the teacher wishes to feel a sense of accomplishment that the pupils are learning science. The children also need to experience a sense of achievement in understanding and interpreting natural phenomena in their surroundings. Of what import is science to children today? Scientific literacy is not enough. Changing technology requires that our young people make decisions with respect to their dynamic environment. Pupils need to understand the social, economic, and political implications of science as well as the impact of science on society.

No one book can purport to meet all these requirements. Hence, the teacher needs guidelines for using succinct science concepts that begin with the concrete and develop to the abstract. The children are given many varied demonstrations, problem-solving activities, experiments, field experiences, resources, audiovisual aids, and reading materials to supplement their everyday living experiences. The teacher supplements the daily learning activities by helping children relate science to the social sciences.

Part 1 of this text represents a synthesis of the current writings in science-education research and my own experience in training teachers. Part 1 also serves as a philosophical and educational background for part 2. The teacher develops a philosophical approach to science teaching as a result of experiencing and understanding school and community relations, pupil-to-pupil and pupil-teacher interaction, objectives of science teaching, planning and organizing curriculum materials with appropriate methods of teaching, audiovisual technology, and evaluation of instruction. The first part of the text serves as *how to teach*, which is integrated in part 2 with *what to teach*.

The values of the teacher will no doubt influence the educational objectives of teaching science. The geographic location and administration of the school; the specific make-up of the children in terms of their personalities, interests, and needs; and parental aspirations will also influence the kind of science to be taught by the teacher. The degree with which teachers are actively involved in determining the science curriculum can determine the kind of successful learning experiences provided for children.

Part 2 provides concrete science concepts for three arbitrary levels: kindergarten through grade two, grades three to five, and grades six through eight. No scientific basis indicates that a particular science concept must be taught at a given grade level. Although we have no answers to these and other pedagogical questions, Cronbach writes:

> Somewhere between the drill approaches—demonstrate, exercise, reinforce—and the exploratory approaches—enrich the environment and let development occur—there would logically seem to be some optimal curriculum of experiences, arranged in some predetermined sequence, with intervention and instruction systematically regulated by the teacher.[1]

It is my intent that this text provide such science experiences to be arranged by the teacher as suggested by Cronbach. The concepts listed are not the end products of learning. They provide the basis for *development from the concrete to the abstract*. Concrete experiences should be active; hence, throughout part 2 emphasis is placed on problem-solving activities and experiments both in and outside of school. Piaget emphasizes: "Learning is possible only when there is active assimilation."[2] He explains that in order for children to know an object, they require an understanding of how the object is constructed, modified, and transformed. The rationale for the variety of learning activities in part 2 is given in part 1. Concepts are dynamic, and a spiral curriculum in which new experiences are introduced in later stages of pupils' development can result in effective learning and longer retention.

[1] L. J. Cronbach, "Learning Research and Curriculum Development," *Journal of Research in Science Teaching* 2 (September 1964): 207.
[2] Jean Piaget, "Development and Learning," *Journal of Research in Science Teaching* 2 (September 1964): 185.

The teacher may find the related science concepts at different grade levels helpful not only for purposes of articulating instruction but also for observing the development of science concept formation and the process of assimilation by children. Piaget indicates that for learning to be retained, there must be a "state of equilibrium" for the remainder of the children's lives. One purpose of this text is to aid teachers in making that state of equilibrium in learning science concepts by children a greater reality.

In discussing concept formation at different stages or age levels, and how differences are to be expected because of educational, experiential, personality, and intellectual backgrounds, Ausubel writes: "Thus a certain amount of overlapping among age groups is inevitable."[3] The extended meanings assigned to the concepts from a lower to a higher grade level are listed at the beginning of each chapter in part 2. The teacher can avoid unnecessary repetition except when needed to develop concepts from the concrete to the abstract. This development, rather than mere repetition, is part of the dynamic assimilation process where pupils continue to extend their meanings and understandings of concepts at different stages.

Wherever possible, the nature of the learning activities in part 2 involves *active* participation by pupils in order to develop cognitive as well as behavioral objectives. It is difficult to isolate completely behavioral from cognitive objectives of learning science. To be able to bring an object into focus under a microscope is a psychomotor or behavioral skill. Yet, to achieve this skill the learner must have the cognitive skill to recognize that the one-celled paramecium under focus is not a piece of dirt. Likewise, the affective domain,

[3] David P. Ausubel, "The Transition from Concrete to Abstract Cognitive Functioning: Theoretical Issues and Implications for Education" *Journal of Research in Science Teaching* 2 (September 1964): 262.

such as attitudes, is always influenced either positively or negatively as the learner responds to the teacher, the nature of the topic, the school, and other environmental factors.

During the past two decades we have observed many changes in the teaching of science. One end of the spectrum moved from very little or no science instruction, to occasional, informal or nonsyllabus science instruction, to the development of hard, scientific fact curricula, to the "alphabet curricula" stressing how scientists think and do, process–product, discovery or inquiry science and scientific literacy, to the present technological, humanistic aspects of science in a changing society.

The alphabet curricula in the sciences were initiated in 1956 with the Physical Science Study Committee (PSSC) to improve the teaching of the physical sciences in the secondary schools. Other science curricula to be developed were Biological Science Curriculum Survey (BSCS) for high schools and Elementary Science Study (ESS), Science Curriculum Imporvement Study (SCIS), and other elementary science programs. These are described under the heading "Alphabet Curricula" in chapter 4.

The humanistic, interdisciplinary approach to science and its relation to society emphasizes socioeconomic aspects of science. This appears to be gaining momentum in many schools. The environment with inherent pollution problems, technology, mixed attitudes toward science and its values by our citizens serve as very real challenges in teaching science to children in the next decade. An understanding of science, the role of scientists and their social responsibilities, and the intelligent participation by all citizens in using knowledge from all disciplines can serve as the springboard for solving society's technological problems.

ACKNOWLEDGMENTS

Many thanks are due to a great number of people for suggestions given me in the development of this text. When I participated in the meetings of the National Science Teachers Association, The Association for the Education of Teachers in Science, The National Association for Research in Science Teaching, American Educational Research Association, and The Intitute of Environmental Sciences, numerous ideas were exchanged as to what kind of science education should be given to teachers.

Although the names of my colleagues are too numerous to mention, the following may serve as an illustration. At a series of meetings over the course of a year, I received suggestions from colleagues at City University of New York: Charles Tanzer, William Reiner, and Harold Tannenbaum of Hunter College; Archie Lacey of Lehman College; William Goins,

Jr., of Brooklyn College; Harold Spielman and Dave Sarner of City College. I am most grateful to my colleagues in elementary, early childhood, and secondary education at Queens College for their inspiration on what and how children learn in science.

For a critical reading of the manuscript and invaluable suggestions, I would like to express my thanks to Kenneth E. Anderson of the University of Kansas. Thanks are due also to Clarence Boeck of the University of Minnesota for his suggestions. Responsibility for any errors should be attributed to me. Phyllis Huff of Purdue University and Charles M. Emslee of Graceland College were helpful in submitting their students' lesson plans for publication in this text.

I appreciate the cooperation of the following people for their assistance in obtaining photographs: Robert Kirsch, assistant superintendent for instruction, Long Beach Public Schools, New York; Robert Seaman, chairman of science, Manhasset Public Schools, New York; A. Campbell, chairman of science, Weber Junior High School, Port Washington Public Schools, New York.

Along with the publisher of this book, I would also like to thank the following organizations and photographers for their kind permission to reproduce their work:

American Forest Products Industries, photo, page 366; Philip A. Biscuti, courtesy of Connecticut College Alumni News, photo, page 258; Alan D. Cruickshank from the National Audubon Society, photo, page 189; Ron Curbow from the National Audubon Society, photo, page 188; Gale DuBrow, photo, page 170; Earth Science Curriculum Project, photos, pages 27, 38; John Gerard from the National Audubon Society, photo, page 193; Stuart Glass, courtesy of Manhasset Public Schools, New York, photos, pages 64, 92, 150, 208, 228, 388, 314; Albert Gregory, courtesy of Harvard Project Physics newsletter, photos, pages 104, 110; Harper & Row Publishers from their *Textbook of Geology* by Robert M. Gar-

rels, 1951 (page 57), figure, page 260; Elisa B. Hecker, photos,
pages 22, 130, 133, 146, 191; Richard Lee, courtesy of Queens
College, New York, photo, page 116; Long Beach Public
Schools, New York, photos, pages 30, 51, 58, 68, 74, 120 262,
342; Macdonald & Company Publishers, from their book
The Social Insects by O. W. Richards (page 114, figure 8),
figure, page 196; Manhasset Public Schools, photo, page
96; Soss Melik, courtesy of the Smithsonian Institution,
photo, page 298; National Aeronautics and Space Administration, photos, pages 8, 18, 20, 78, 82, 294, 313; *Newsday*,
Long Island, photo, page 44; Princeton Project, photos,
pages 35, 426; School District of Philadelphia, Pennsylvania,
photos, pages 2, 53, 126, 138, Science Service Incorporated,
photo, page 84; Ed Shalett, courtesy of Port Washington
Public Schools, New York, photos, pages 274, 406; Shell Oil
Company, photo, page 184; Smithsonian Institution, for
painting by Betsy Graves Reyneau, photo, page 41; Eleanor
E. Storrs, in photo, page 84; Cameron Thatcher from the National Audubon Society, photo, page 190; United States Department of Commerce, photos, pages 248, 249, United
States Navy, photos, pages 254, 272; United States Weather
Bureau, Weather Map, page 252; Ward's National Science
Establishment Incorporated, photo, page 243; Ben Werner,
photo, page 124.

CONTENTS

PART I

PHILOSOPHY, PSYCHOLOGY, METHODOLOGY, AND EVALUATION

1

SCIENCE IN SCHOOL
AND COMMUNITY

What community factors influence the kind of science to be taught in our schools? Do these factors affect how much science will be taught? To what degree are teachers and schools responsible for meeting the demands of various pressure groups? How should controversial topics such as sex education and population control be treated in different communities?

A few decades ago, one would boast of our citizens having at least one or more radios in each home. Today, most homes have at least one black-and-white TV set. In the not too distant future it is predicted that most homes will have

Technology Changes

one or more color TV sets. Even today, a few low-income families own color TV sets.

Radio and TV are only two illustrations of applications of science and engineering that brought about tremendous changes in our technology. Man's ability to create new devices and to invent machines that modify his behavior is evident. Thirty or forty years ago people could combine listening to the radio with performing other activities in the home. Today many people are "glued" to the TV set at the expense of other activities. "Spectatoritis" is found not only at the ball field but also in the home.

More than fifty years ago, people had more time to socialize with friends and neighbors, to do basic chores at home, to indulge in hobbies, to do homework and study without interference from environmental factors such as TV, movies, and lengthy telephone conversations. Behavior changed its active emphasis on doing, constructing, reading, collecting, repairing to more passive types such as listening and watching. At the same time more leisure is available today because of scientific applications. Machines to wash and dry laundry, to polish the floors and the walls, to turn the oven on and off automatically, and many other devices provide the individual at home with more time for other activities. Intelligent consumption of time may well become a serious problem within the next two decades. Science and engineering provide gadgets that give us more time; the social and behavioral sciences may provide us with answers on how to use such extra time effectively.

Instruments of communication—from smoke signals and drums to the development of space satellites and laser beams—also brought about changes in our technology. Money and barter were of no concern in lighting a fire to produce a smoke signal. The economics of telephone and telegraph communication made significant changes in our society. Thus, a wide variety of industries came into existence: mines to extract copper for wire; development of plastics, magnets, telephones, and switchboards; research in crystallography; business offices for telephone companies; telephone advertising; and selling by means of the telephone.

In transportation the Pony Express gave way to railroads, buses, autos, ships, airplanes, and perhaps some day to space vehicles. When the horse alone was used for transportation, only the village blacksmith was needed. Today, modern transportation demands accessory industries of gasoline and oil, their production, refinement, transportation, and sales. The manufacture of tires and accessories, among them storage batteries and air conditioners, promoted our economy by providing millions of jobs. Engineers applied scientific principles and designs to develop new inventions. These applications and inventions revolutionized our economy and our society. With continued emphasis on research and development, our technology is constantly changing. Hence, the individual and the community will need to understand how these scientific concepts and technology are to be applied.

The development of computers profoundly increased the output of business, government, education, and even medicine. In a matter of seconds, information can be obtained, such as how many males aged 30–40, and how many females aged 20–30, are contained in the population of the United States. At the same time, the computer can indicate how many people died from heart attacks during a given year. All kinds of information fed into the computer and stored most efficiently as a memory bank can be retrieved in seconds by using the correct code or key.

Computer Technology

The computer extends the senses of man and his reasoning ability. From international and political viewpoints, speech and other intelligence matter can be analyzed and reassembled into the original message from all parts of the world. Because of advances in satellite and laser communication, along with the aid of computers, communication is now a massive network that connects the entire world. One can even raise the question of secrecy among nations of the world and find, perhaps, that the computer can be an asset toward peace.

In education the profound impact of the computer is yet to be felt. A pupil can use a computer that resembles a typewriter; he asks the computer, "What does 2 × 2 equal?" The computer printout suggests that the pupil should try giving the answer. The pupil types the answer "5." Immediately the computer prints back, "Now try again." The pupil types the number "5" again. The computer responds, "You're kidding of course." Finally, the pupil types "4" and the computer prints, "Very good." This computer was programmed so that, if errors are made, the pupil is not discouraged. Instead of reading "how to" books, people can use the computer as an instructor for performing specific jobs.

The effect of computer use outside education is not yet fully realized. Banking, inventories, billing, medical diagnosis and case study, retrieving stored information of all areas, monitoring and analyzing activities of various nations, warning systems, space travel, weather data collecting and forecasting, and system analysis are significant applications of computer technology. Arguments frequently occur concerning whether the computer can perform more efficiently than humans. The output of the machine is not greater than the input. Where information is stored (memorized) and needed for fast retrieval in making decisions, the computer performs an outstanding job. "However, the selection of decision and the formulation of policy, the direction of the humane use of technology, will continue to be the statesman's burden," writes DeCarlo.[1]

A week before the Apollo space vehicles were launched, newspapers described various aspects of the launch, the equipment, and the purposes of the mission. Radio and TV stations would describe much of these space activities several hours before the blast-off. When an accident occurred aboard a spacecraft, mass media provided periodic bulletins and round-the-clock coverage. The first time man landed on the moon, it was difficult to comprehend these applications of science and engineering. The same was also true when the first satellite stayed in orbit for a long period of time.

It is no longer possible for intelligent citizens who receive the impact of mass media to remain indifferent to such achievements. They are curious, for example, to know what keeps a satellite in orbit. Children and adults cannot help but wonder about such phenomena. Hence, teachers will find that mass media (newspapers, periodicals, radio, and TV) serve as the basis for the future content in science textbooks and new syllabi. Yet knowledge of "old" laws such as Newton's law of action and reaction are basic to the explanation of how satellites stay in orbit. One can hardly defend the teaching of scientific laws without their applications, especially if they register such impact via mass media communications.

Newspapers and magazines constantly report on re-

Mass Media Communications

---

[1] Charles R. DeCarlo, "Computer Technology," in *Toward The Year 2018*, ed. Foreign Policy Association (New York: Cowles Education Corp., 1968), p. 113.

THE SEARCH FOR EXTRA TERRESTRIAL LIFE

GEIGER COUNTER

TELEMETRY

ACTIVITY

TIME

RADIOACTIVE GAS

PICKUP STRING

MICROORGANISMS

RADIO ACTIVE NUTRIENT

REPRODUCTION

TELESCOPIC TV

MICROSCOPIC TV

RECOGNITION

SAMPLE PICKUPS

S 62-562

Mass media illustrate research.

search and developments related to science: environmental science (air and water pollution, pesticides, and so on), medicine and drugs to combat disease, space travel, lasers, atomics, and new chemical elements.

Mass Media and Genetic Engineering

The public concern over scientific research in which legislators become involved is illustrated in "Senator John V. Tunney on Genetic Management," *Saturday Review—*

Science (5 August 1972): "When complex problems appear too terrifying or mysterious, some people might seek simple solutions that prove inadequate or improper." Senator Tunney and his legislative assistant, Meldon E. Levine, add on page 23 of the magazine:

> If people become sufficiently frightened—if they feel the need to be rescued from a menace they do not understand—they are more likely to delegate freedoms and less likely to respond with reason. If the polity responds to the scientific community through fear and mistrust, we could witness the erosion of our most precious freedoms. Political alteration—like genetic alteration—might be irreversible. If our personal liberty is ever lost, it might never be recovered.

The teacher might understand Mendel's laws of inheritance, how DNA and RNA operate in transmitting parental traits to the offspring, but he or she must also be prepared to discuss current issues in science such as anxiety about genetic engineering. Philip Abelson writes:

> During the last several years, the public has repeatedly been warned that science is creating additional problems through raising the possibility of test tube babies and "genetic engineering." The response of the public has been negative, with some calling for a halt to research in molecular biology. In truth, the dire predictions of the potentialities of new science have outrun the accomplishments, and the predictors have assumed that society will exercise negatively the options that are provided. Speculation about test tube babies is based on a modest accomplishment—that is, fertilizing a human egg in vitro and keeping it alive for a week or so. . . .
> Talk of the dire social implications of laboratory-related genetic engineering is premature and unrealistic. It disturbs the public unnecessarily and

could lead to harmful restrictions on all scientific research.[2]

Articles in newspapers and magazines will suggest such questions as: What are the desirable traits that should be passed on to future generations? Who is to make such decisions? Is there a concept of "optimum" man and does it suggest a superior type of human? Is there a need for tolerance of the imperfect human being? What are the ethical considerations of genetic therapy? What are the personal rights of the individual in genetically screening the makeup of future individuals? Should the amniotic fluid surrounding the fetus be sampled to detect genetic defects so that a decision might be made for a therapeutic abortion?

Some ethical considerations relate to the use of sperm banks. Newspapers report a new business where a man wishes to deposit his sperm in a bank before undergoing a vasectomy. This assures him of fertilization should he and his wife decide to have children *after* the vasectomy. Some sterile males would like to purchase semen from a bank in which specifications are made in terms of the characteristics of the father or perhaps a "super" individual. What are the ethical factors when IQ and various traits are stipulated for the type of semen to be used in human fertilization? The teaching of elementary concepts in genetics may be taught in grades six through eight if these contemporary and controversial issues are to be discussed and especially if they appear in newspapers and magazines. Before a pupil leaves high school, if not much earlier, he or she should know that the sex of the offspring is determined by the male genes. Hence, it may be possible to kill an old prejudice against the female if the male recognizes it is not the "fault" of the mother if the "right" sex doesn't appear in the newborn baby.

[2] "Anxiety About Genetic Engineering," *Science* 173 (23 July 1971).

Genetic counseling is receiving wide attention. Counselors affiliated with medical groups are now available for consultation to determine if an individual mate is free from certain hereditary diseases or at least if some type of control should be employed. Elementary reading materials can be used to dispel misconceptions and superstitions about heredity.

To read newspapers and periodicals with comprehension requires that readers possess a fundamental understanding of at least elementary concepts in science. Children will read, and therefore learn, about scientific developments in biology and genetics.

Mass media, therefore, may create the need for learning scientific ideas. They are also used, as will be discussed in chapter 8, to teach and to supplement classroom instruction. Citizens in the community may be more sensitive to the mass media's influence on children and apply pressure to include these scientific concepts in the school curriculum.

Industries

Airplane factories, automotive industries, engineering plants, electronics and chemical laboratories, and other science-related industries employ millions of people. Industries would prefer that their employees have at least some knowledge of their roles in terms of scientific production. When a company manufactures a particular part for a space vehicle, it is to be hoped that employees will desire more technical information about the product and its significance.

The primary purpose of teaching science in the elementary school is not to make future scientists of all the children. It is possible, though, that some children may come to enjoy science and consider careers related to science. Meister's doctoral dissertation indicated that third graders can be affected to the point of selecting careers in science as they mature. Industries may influence the teaching of certain science concepts based on the production of their materials. Especially if a parent is employed in a science- or engineering-oriented plant, a child may show considerable interest.

Pupils may bring "show and tell" science materials from the home. Some of the common things brought to class have been magnets, prisms, lenses, transistors, semiconductor materials, seashells, leaves, insects, animals, phosphorescent substances, and rocks and minerals. The teaching of science concepts may be enhanced by local industrial activity, and interest may be generated by field trips or individual visits.

Parents and Their Concerns— Drugs and Sex

Related directly to the teaching of scientific and health information are such topics as dangerous drugs and sex. Parents have always shown concern or anxiety as children show greater interest in these topics. Whether or not these subjects are taught in class frequently depends upon the nature of the community, its parents, the school administration, the teachers, and the children. Although much controversy occurred over the teaching of both of these subjects in some communities, the trend is to favor the inclusion of such instruction in the school curriculum. Usually parental groups work closely with school personnel to avoid conflict and to establish guidelines for this instruction.

Recent evidence exists that many elementary school children in the upper grades and in middle school have become curious and experimental in sampling marijuana or some form of narcotics. This is not confined to a single group of youngsters. Pupils of all backgrounds have experimented with narcotics. Workshops, seminars, and lectures organized for parents and teachers to obtain additional data on this problem soon proved that teaching science concepts or facts did not guarantee a change in pupil behavior. When a youngster became addicted, knowledge alone was insufficient to cause a change in behavior. In subsequent chapters, suggestions will be made for instruction that influences changes in pupil attitudes and behavior. Briefly, the need for organizing instruction in drugs and their dangers is facilitated by using teaching kits, a poster campaign, cooperative sessions between parents and pupils, use of community resources and agencies, pupil motivational devices, and in some instances drastic environmental changes.

Sex education is still being challenged in many communities. Some adults insist it is not within the province of the school to teach sex education. Perhaps the fears and anxieties of parents, and misunderstandings about the nature and meaning of sex education, influence such decisions. Other problems are related to who is best qualified or who should be the one to teach children about sex. Is it the parent, the teacher, the physician, or the clergy?

The formation of attitudes, wholesome and otherwise, about sex occurs in early childhood and continues throughout the beginning school years. Such attitudes affect pupils' behavior as they mature. Boys and girls observe the birth of puppies, kittens, birds, and tropical fish. They observe boy-girl dating and romance activity in the home, in the movies, and on the TV screen. They discuss with one another their observations and interpretations of such behavior. They are keenly aware of their own bodily changes as they grow. Hence, they are forming attitudes about sex regardless of whether such instruction is offered in the school. The teaching procedures for promoting the development of wholesome attitudes and knowledge about sex education will be discussed in a later chapter. It is desirable to enlist the support and cooperation of the community in teaching sex education as well as other topics in the school science and health programs.

Population Explosion and Environmental Pollution

Another concern of parents and youth is the teaching of birth control. This topic is related not only to sex education but also to our environment. Some experts in ecology believe the only solution to environmental pollution problems is population control. They believe that in about thirty-five years the world population will double. Paul Ehrlich writes: "If growth continued at that rate for about 900 years, there would be some 60,000,000,000,000,000 people on the face of the earth. Sixty million billion people. This is about 100 persons for each square yard of the Earth's surface, land and sea."[3] At this rate, predictions[4] were made that the "heat limit" would have been reached. Theoretically this could mean that the great amount of heat radiated by people could not be properly dissipated and would cause substances such as iron to melt.

If these projected estimates are correct, in fewer than 900 years it would be impossible to drive a car. Studies also forecast that the present rate of increase of automobiles will result in an excessive concentration of carbon monoxide and may, under certain conditions, cause asphyxiation. Other pollutants in the air such as sulfur and nitrogen oxides, solids, and organic compounds may become fatal when high levels of concentration are reached because of excessive numbers of gasoline-powered engines and "unclean" smoke stacks from industry and homes.

[3] Paul R. Ehrlich, *The Population Bomb* (New York: Ballantine, 1968).
[4] See J. H. Fremlin, "How Many People Can the World Support?," *New Scientist* (29 October 1964).

Legislation has forced the automobile industry to modify engine and exhaust systems for better emission control; this means that less carbon monoxide and other pollutants will escape from auto engines. Technology is also improving the quality of gasoline for cleaner air.

The contamination of water from the disposal of man's wastes threatens both marine and freshwater life. But this pollution also threatens future and new sources of food, such as seaweed. At present, millions of people are starving throughout the world. The population in underdeveloped countries continues to increase and promotes even greater starvation. If food is to be obtained from the sea to feed a hungry world, an understanding of ecology and all of the environmental sciences is necessary for more intelligent living and ultimate survival.

Agricultural technology may increase the production of cattle and thereby may cause beef to sell at lower prices. In the Sand Hills of Nebraska, ranchers report saving a great deal of manual labor and money when mother cows and their suckling calves are fed a liquid supplement. The liquid feed supplement includes molasses and reduces the risk of urea toxicity. Thus, fewer cattle become sick or die. Chemical food supplements are now widely used. This may also help solve the starvation problem in underdeveloped nations.

The overwhelming concern on the part of the communities throughout the nation with reference to environmental pollution appeared on Earth Day, April 22, 1970. In this first national environmental teach-in, citizens of all ages participated in warning each other of the inherent dangers of environmental pollution. Programs calling for legislation, modification in using materials and machines, a return to more natural ways of living, conservation and population control were discussed in schools, colleges, communities, and on radio and TV. Scientists, economists, sociologists, industrialists, legislators, and all citizens came forth with many helpful ideas.[5]

Population control should be taught in the schools in consultation with the school administration. Other arrangements might be made for pupils whose parents argue that population control, as well as sex education, not be taught to their children. Perhaps these children can study other problems with another teacher during such periods of instruction. Actually, population control is not confined to the teaching of science. Social studies includes problems related to earning a livelihood and obtaining a healthy diet for the family. The economics of a community is affected by population numbers.

Population control in animals, and in insects in particular, presents many problems. Farmers spray their crops with DDT; yet many insects adapt to DDT and other pesticides with the result that higher insect population levels are achieved. Man attempts to control the population of pests such as ants, termites, and rats. Some people claim that if all pests were not controlled by natural enemies or chemicals, the existence of man could be threatened. Imagine how many termites could thrive if each queen termite were to hatch all of her eggs, at the rate of two million eggs per termite, and if all survived. Yet each species has a variety of predators and parasites that can devour an alternate species that may suddenly increase in great numbers. Cole writes: "All this suggests to an ecologist that clean cultivation, routine pesticide application, and other agricultural practices that reduce the diversity of species in the community may be working in exactly the wrong direction. A healthy, diverse biotic community is not easily invaded by exotic forms and has considerable ability to adjust to invaders."[6]

[5] See Garrett De Bell, *The Environmental Handbook* (New York: Ballantine, 1970).
[6] LaMont C. Cole, "The Impending Emergence of Ecological Thought," *Bioscience* (July 1964):32.

It should be noted that DDT as a pesticide will have residues remaining for as long as thirty years. These toxic residues kill aquatic life and cause ecological disruptions. A nonpersistent pesticide, DDVP (trademark VAPONA), which is impregnated on flea collars, appears to be effective in controlling the population of fleas on dogs and cats. To obtain moisture from the pet's eyes, nose, or mouth, the fleas pass by the collar which generates a killing gas. Perhaps biological control is exercised where no flea collars are available. Thus, the flea as a parasite controls canine and feline populations.

Many schools and communities have initiated courses in environmental science. Elementary and middle school teachers have felt community pressures to include problems related to environmental pollution and conservation in the school curriculum. Likewise, pressures were noted in other communities to avoid the teaching of sex education or birth control in the schools. The fact remains that children will learn correct and incorrect information pertaining to sex education from various sources; what may appear to be controversial to teach in one school or community may be most desirable in another. Hence, the school and the teacher must be prepared to teach "controversial" topics in science to children.

Space Science and Research

During the appropriate season, it is common to find many citizens discussing baseball, football, political elections, and catastrophic events as they occur. Recently it has been common to hear people discussing the landing of astronauts on the moon and their return to earth. Such discussions include the speculation of discoveries to be made in space as well as on other planets. Reports of achievements in

A suited test engineer demonstrates the method of embarking on a full-scale all-metal mock-up of the Lunar Excursion Module (LEM).

space science receive prime coverage in newspapers and on TV and radio.

The profound impact of space technology on man's everyday life is much greater and wider in scope than the World Series or other major sports events. The mass media strongly affect people during space launchings. Legislators, industrialists, and all citizens become involved in whether financial support should or should not be given to space agencies. All this activity may create a greater need to understand the scientific principles of space vehicles and their development. C. P. Snow writes: "It would be healthier ... if a far larger proportion of our elected representatives were scientifically informed, and also a far larger portion of our administrators. I don't want to overstate the case. Being scientifically informed is no substitute for wisdom. I would far rather have choices made by wise men who are not scientifically educated than by unwise men who are. But that is not the real alternative. We ought to be producing wise men who are scientifically educated."[7] It becomes increasingly more important for all citizens to be scientifically educated if they are to make intelligent decisions in science and technology.

Space research is only one science that is of vital concern to people of all nations. Other research areas also of concern in varying degrees are atomic energy, eradication of diseases, pollution problems, new developments in communication and transportation, and germ and chemical weapons. McGeorge Bundy, former special assistant to the President for National Security Affairs, writes:

> You don't solve the problem of nuclear weapons and their relation to the world by saying, "here is a nuclear core—that's scientific; here is a nuclear weapon—that's military; here is a treaty—that's political." These things all have to live with each other. There are elements that are indeed military, or technological, or diplomatic, but the process of effective judgment and action comes at a point where you cannot separate them out. ... For interpenetrations of science and government, science and public policy, science and politics, are bound to increase, and the processes of communication from man to man, thick as they are and thickening steadily, are not yet as deep, as thick, as varied—are not, above all, as much taken for granted—as they need to be.[8]

[7] C. P. Snow, "Government, Science, and Public Policy," *Science* 11 (February 1966):651.
[8] McGeorge Bundy, "The Scientist and National Policy," *Science* 139 (1 March 1963):809.

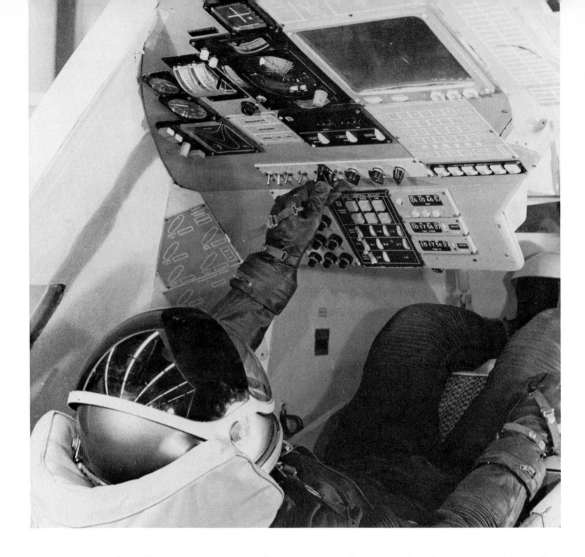

Interior view of Apollo Evaluation #1 showing the test subject adjusting the three-axis attitude ball while in simulated flight.

Students are actively engaged in discussing public policy related to science and government. It is not uncommon to find children in elementary and middle schools writing letters to their congressmen in support of certain legislation. In an editorial in *Science,* one reads: "Any distinction between the man of science and the ordinary man is no longer admissible, any more than a form of segregation based on an inequality of knowledge. Whether we like it or not, the laboratory henceforward opens right onto the street. Science not only affects us at any given moment of our day-to-day existence, it dogs us, it pursues us. . . ."[9] How can we best

[9] "Popularization of Science," *Science* 131 (20 May 1960):1491.

prepare our children with the necessary knowledge, skills, attitudes, and inquiry, to evaluate scientific proposals that affect man in society? Merely to say that authorities make a claim without adequate evidence is insufficient.

A number of years ago citizens had an opportunity to voice their opinions on whether fluorides should be added to drinking water. In some communities people went to the polls. Authorities produced overwhelming evidence that dental caries were minimized when fluoride treatment was administered by dentists. Many people fought for the right to decide when and if they wanted fluoride treatment. They wanted pure water in their reservoirs and the freedom to do as they pleased. Some believed that this was not a matter of protecting people against communicable diseases; hence, the fact that authorities made a claim was insufficient to evoke positive response by individuals. The role of science for intelligent living suggests that we must acquire a knowledge and understanding of current research and developments.

Community Influence and the Nature of Science

As suggested earlier, some communities favor teaching sex education while other communities are opposed. A few citizens in many communities will oppose the teaching of blood transfusions, germ theory, population control, and evolution. They represent several religious groups and consider such concepts to be contrary to their convictions. For example, many years ago the Board of Regents in New York State allowed children to be excused from learning germ theory at the request of their parents. Although provisions are made for the convictions of several minority groups, a need for basic science understandings still exists if we are to have intelligent individual and community action.

Some science-oriented parents, such as engineers, scien-

Curiosity and imagination lead to inquiry.

tists, physicians, may demand that scientific knowledge be taught beyond the comprehension of most children. Some industries may insist that more of "this or that" in science must be taught. Whether the community is urban, suburban, or rural will also influence the nature of science to be taught in schools.

Agricultural problems related to crop production and better fertilization may have greater appeal to children in rural areas. Nevertheless, all children will have common interests in how to grow and care for living things. Perhaps the care of pets—dogs, cats, goldfish—will appeal to both rural and urban children. If a community tends to experience frequent natural disasters, an understanding of weather phenomena and how to protect oneself against them will be most meaningful.

Each community may have a bakery as well as fire and police stations. The scientific use of baking powder or yeast leads to wonderful experimentation, inquiry, and understanding. Fire-fighting equipment depends on chemicals and various principles of physics. The police station is dependent on speedy and effective means of communication. The community is an excellent resource for laboratory study in science, and it augments the educational materials usually available at a museum.

Regardless of the type of community, its people, or special industries, the nature of the science to be taught to children should be carefully examined. All children are curious and imaginative. They want to know what makes day and night, about changes in weather, how things get bigger, what makes toy cars travel, why the sky is blue, what's on Mars, how to care for pets; and they have questions about other natural phenomena and about themselves. These science concepts, common to children in all communities, develop in the daily experiences of children.

Preschool children who have not yet been subjected to formal learning exercises in the classroom will still have developed concepts about the things they see, touch, hear, feel, and smell. "Water is wet," "A tree has leaves," "A frog jumps" are simple concepts formed from mere observation and daily activities. In the attempt to extend the depth and meaning of these concepts, the teacher provides additional learning opportunities by using the immediate environment as a laboratory for enriched experience. The community resources should supplement and reinforce the curiosity and imagination of children in the process of learning science.

Pupils will develop various interests related to science. Some of these interests will be influenced by the type of community and its people: rural children will enjoy cultivating plants; urban children may have a goldfish tank to maintain; suburban youngsters will care for a dog. In addition, most children are interested in seeing photographs of themselves and their surroundings. Hence, photography may have appeal as a science interest in many communities. An ambitious challenge for the teacher is to encourage the children to develop new science interests and extend in depth their currently held interests.

Building a Philosophy of Science Education

Elementary and middle school teachers usually develop a personal philosophy of teaching science to children. Depending on attitudes, background in science, and degree of success in various science courses, teachers will transmit this philosophy. Sometimes much effort is needed to help children acquire a positive viewpoint toward science.

When a teacher displays an unpleasant facial expression on seeing mice, snakes, or other field animals, this feeling is frequently adopted by the pupils. When a parent jumps on a chair to display a fear reaction to a mouse, such behavior may affect the behavioral pattern of the child. A pupil may bring a harmless, lovely snake to class. If the teacher shows displeasure, or fear, or makes inaccurate negative comments such as "that slimy creature," the attitude may become part of the pupil's attitude. Teachers should critically examine the attitudes they transmit by their words and actions.

A positive attitude in which teachers and pupils understand the role played by different living things in their envi-

ronment is helpful in promoting an appreciation and a possible love for science. It is helpful to understand the food chain, explaining how one animal may serve as a source of food for another, for example. To interpret various kinds of natural phenomena such as night or day, rain or sunshine, requires scientific information as well as an *attitude of willingness* to understand such phenomena.

The beauty in observing the food habits and behavior of living things is exemplified in the fascination of watching a squirrel solve a problem of dislodging seed from a bird food station suspended from a thin branch on a tree. Soon the animal discovers he can get the seed if he assumes the upside-down position. The strong drive to get the food is hunger. After a few trial-and-error attempts, the correct approach is learned rapidly. The intelligence and skill that the squirrel displays in learning how to get the seed and the way in which he uses his forelegs to get the food to his mouth constitute a beautiful observation.

Helping children develop positive or wholesome attitudes toward living things and make necessary adjustments to their surroundings should be part of the teacher's daily philosophy. *In teaching science not only are accurate observations essential; they are also the basis for interpretations.* If the teacher makes the children aware of the differences between observations and interpretations, science lessons will take on greater significance. In reading instruments such as thermometers, barometers, and scales, pupils should check each observation by making two or three readings. Class readings or observations may be pooled and a class average value may be assigned. Errors in observation and in measurement should be emphasized wherever possible. Interpretations are based on experiences, readings, hearsay, prejudice, and guessing. If interpretations are to result from scientific explanation, evidence becomes a necessary preliminary.

To teach with the use of the question rather than the exclamation mark will facilitate the development of interpretations and conclusions that are based on evidence. Thought-provoking questions by pupils and teachers can promote scientific thinking, inquiry, or problem-solving abilities. Much creative activity in pupils can be fostered by good questions. It is not always essential to give the quick answer to the question.

An effective approach to good questions is found in the plan and performance of suitable laboratory or other investigative experiences. *Allowing the children to propose both incorrect and correct hypotheses and testing them by proposing appropriate laboratory work whenever possible will promote inquiry on its highest level.* Pupils who reject their own hypothesis following laboratory discoveries will learn more efficiently than pupils who are told that they are wrong. Self-rejection of hypothesis is easier to accept than someone's saying "I told you so."

Science teaching should be based on active participation by learners and teachers. Constructing, testing, interpreting, measuring, investigating, searching, observing, classifying, consulting, counting, mixing, separating, identifying, and performing complement talking, chalking, reading, and listening. They constitute an inquiry, discovery, and problem-solving approach to science. People and objects should be brought into the classroom. Conversely, bringing the pupils to the resource people and places in the community can strengthen the science instructional program. Children actively engaged in learning science will benefit if such opportunities are made available to them.

In developing a philosophy of teaching science to children, it is important to impress on them the idea that *the only constant in science is change.* As new evidence is discovered, old ideas are discarded or modified accordingly. As better and more sensitive scientific instruments are designed,

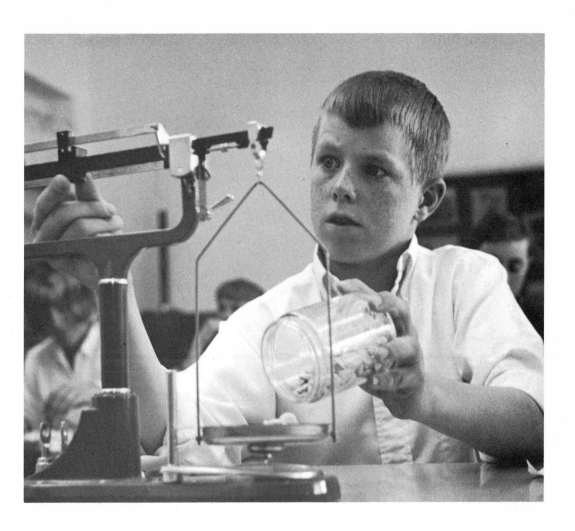

Rechecking your observation makes for accuracy.

new evidence appears and changes previously held ideas. More than one hundred years ago man believed that the atom was indivisible. Later it was thought that atoms were composed only of protons, neutrons, and electrons. Today, over one hundred nuclear particles are postulated, and the number changes as the scientist refines his instruments and his techniques for measurement.

Although children insist on correct answers to all questions, it should be stressed that science does not have the answers to all questions. Perhaps some pupils will discover the answers to some of these questions. Occasionally, teachers should be able to say "I don't know" or "Scientists do not know," in order to further scientific knowledge and attitudes. The hope for further discovery requires that one recognizes that he does not know. Suspended judgment should be taught in cases where there is no evidence on hand to answer a particular question or solve a problem. This vital aspect of scientific thinking is necessary to reduce or eliminate hasty and inaccurate conclusions. It will also make for development of good skills, accurate observations, and ability to distinguish observations from interpretations. Deductive inferences will reflect a more accurate viewpoint when suspended judgment becomes another possible alternative in seeking solutions to problems. Communication with the children on their level should permeate this approach to problem solving and discovery.

Finally, the teacher should reassure the children that they can learn science and achieve in it from day to day. Children, like adults, need to develop confidence in themselves. Because we cannot always have immediate and correct answers to science questions, it becomes essential to help pupils acquire a sense of achievement even though their contributions may be inadequate. If they make mistakes or some of their hypotheses are incorrect, they will need greater reassurance to help them fulfill the ultimate needs for success and enjoyment in learning science.

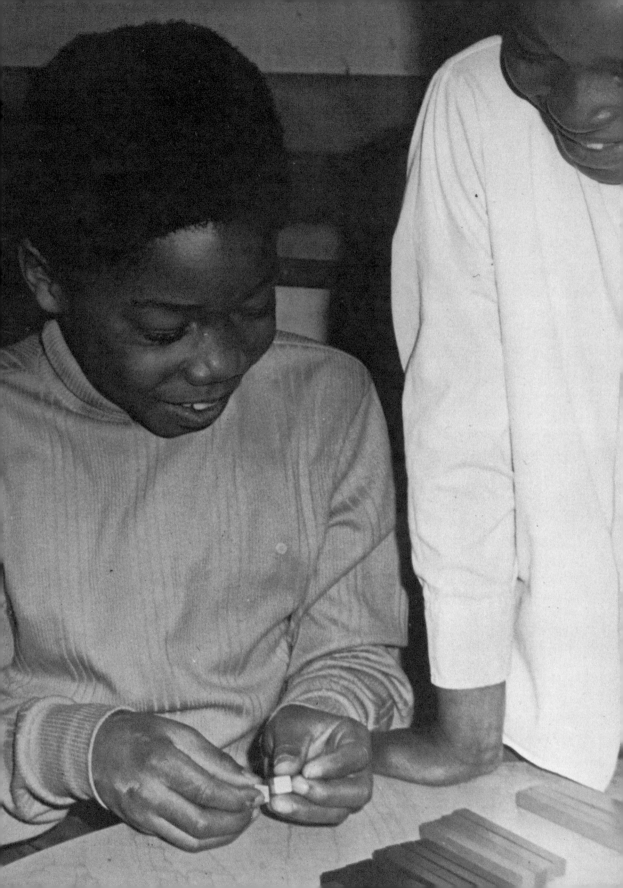

2

OBJECTIVES OF
SCIENCE TEACHING

Why should children learn science? Why should teachers teach science? If the purposes of learning and teaching science were always identical for both learners and teachers, then the teaching-learning process would be relatively simple. Young children learn science primarily because of their curiosity and interest in their surroundings. Older children may also find a *need* to learn science. For example, if scouts go on a camping trip and can eat only if they know how to prepare a campfire, they feel a genuine *need* to learn how to make a fire. If youngsters in the middle school would like to become doctors, engineers, scientists, or nurses, their *need* for learning science is imperative. In such cases, the "adult" or "teacher-made" objectives for teaching science have little impact upon the learners.

Teachers want children to understand and to be able to

**Teacher Versus
Pupil Objectives**

interpret such natural phenomena as what makes the sky blue, what makes rain or snow. They want children to develop scientific thinking and scientific attitudes. The objectives of teaching science from the teacher's viewpoint go far beyond the immediate interests, needs, and curiosity of children. Edward Victor writes:

> Pupil objectives thus also remind us that the children's aims may be quite different from those of the teacher. The teacher may want the children to learn about heat expansion. The children, however, will want to know why cracks are intentionally put into concrete sidewalks. The teacher is interested in electrical circuits; the children want to learn how to connect a dry cell, wires, and a porcelain socket containing a bulb so that the bulb will light up. The teacher is interested in the laws governing vibrating strings; the children want to know what can be done to make the musical note from a violin or guitar higher or lower.[1]

A gap exists between the science objectives viewed by the teacher and those viewed by the pupil. It is possible and desirable to bridge this gap by stating the objectives in relation to functional or behavioral activity. Intelligent pupil behavior still requires the *use* of scientific information.

Behavorial Objectives— Taxonomy

Confusion exists in the way objectives are stated and the degree to which some are emphasized. Some syllabi list the objectives of teaching science in terms of content exactly

---

[1] Edward Victor, "The Unit," in *Readings in Science Education for the Elementary School*, ed. Edward Victor and Marjorie S. Lerner (New York: Macmillan, 1967), p. 119.

as the teacher wishes to develop it. Others state objectives in terms of pupil behavior. The essential difference is the emphasis on content (science information including generalizations, principles, and facts) based on retention and recall.

The behavioral objectives demand content or *use* of scientific knowledge and are primarily related to the active state of pupil learnings. Not all behavioral objectives can be evaluated by pencil-and-paper tests. The science teacher can *observe* if a pupil: (1) *constructs* a terrarium, herbarium, barometer, or engine model; (2) *designs* an experiment to determine where water goes after it enters the roots of plants; (3) *discovers* the effect of the number of turns of wire on an electromagnet; (4) *feeds* and *cares for* selected pets and plants; (5) *conducts experiments* to determine the degree of acidity in common foods and household materials.

Atkin cautions that overemphasis on behavioral objectives may prevent desirable learning activities and goals of instruction. He writes:

> . . . ideas are taught with the richest meaning only when they are emphasized repeatedly in appropriate and varied contexts. Many of these contexts arise in classroom situations that are unplanned, but that have powerful potential. It is deterimental to learning not to capitalize on the opportune moments for effectively teaching one idea or another. Riveting the teacher's attention to a few behavioral goals provides him with blinders that may limit his range.[2]

Critical thinking requires specific skills and these have been stated as behavioral objectives in order to develop the process of inquiry:

[2]J. Myron Atkin, "Behavioral Objectives in Curriculum Design: A Cautionary Note," *Science Teacher* 35 (May 1968):27–30.

observing

classifying

measuring

recognizing space-time relationships and number relationships

communicating

inferring

predicting

formulating hypotheses

making operational definitions

controlling and manipulating variables

experimenting

interpreting data

formulating models[3]

Although a few science educators question the feasibili-
ty of making accurate observations and evaluations of behavioral objectives, many insist that such objectives are essential to teach inquiry procedures. "Science is best taught
as a procedure of enquiry. . . . Science is a fundamental instrument for exploring whatever may be tested by observation and experiment,"[4] write Sears and Kessen. Whether we
measure some of these objectives or not, children will still
make observations on plants and animals, how they obtain
and use food, how they reproduce, how large machines depend on magnets, how simple machines work, how heat affects different things, and many other phenomena. They will
hypothesize, predict, infer, and interpret, as well as experiment in and out of the classroom. Hence, it is wise for
teachers to plan lessons in terms of behavioral objectives
that will require appropriate learning activities.

[3]Arthur H. Livermore, "The Process Approach of the AAAS Commission on Science Education," *Journal of Research in Science
Teaching* 2 (1964):271–82.

[4]Paul B. Sears and William Kessen, "Statement of Purposes and
Objectives of Science Education in School," *Journal of Research in
Science Teaching* 2, no. 1 (1964):3–6.

Principles of measurement are applied by students in the Princeton Secondary School Science Project.

Watson gives four reasons for stating objectives in terms of pupil behavior:

1. The several individuals working on a curriculum need to agree on their targets so that they can work together effectively.

2. During any tryouts of draft materials, explicit objectives in terms of pupil behavior must be used to appraise the effectiveness of the materials. Lacking this, no one knows whether what happened was what was intended to happen.

3. School administrators and parents should be provided with explicit statements of the purposes of the instruction proposed for their children.

4. Teachers need to know what is expected or otherwise they may unintentionally distort the intent of the instruction as initially planned.[5]

If teachers encourage the development of unplanned objectives that arise naturally in the classroom, it is possible to obtain desirable behavioral objectives. If today's lesson suggests the feeding of snakes and a youngster brings in his pet hamster and is prepared to discuss feeding habits of his hamster, such activity has many advantages. In spite of the fact that the teacher planned instruction on the hamster the following day, the basic behavioral objectives such as holding, grooming, feeding, or caring for the animal can be developed most effectively because the initiative and interest in the animal came from the pupil.

Behavioral objectives are essentially pupil objectives. The pupils do, construct, collect, identify, explain, draw, infer, test, classify, and paint. Hence they become actively engaged in learning science. This active involvement increases as more experimentation is encouraged in daily activities. The *construction* of animal cages, electrical circuits, herbaria, or aquariums will demand pupil skill and knowledge in specific scientific topics. The *identification* of rocks, minerals, leaves, different species of frogs and worms, chemical compounds, or series and parallel circuits also bring into play skills of observation, recognition, association, and knowledge of related science topics. During *experimentation* the pupil tests hypotheses, observes, discovers, rejects, modifies, or reinforces ideas or hypotheses. These pupil activities should be considered a vital part of the teacher's evaluation process.

[5]Fletcher G. Watson, "Curriculum Design in Science," *The Science Teacher* 30 (March 1963):13–16.

Without an awareness of the various categories of science-teaching objectives it is possible to teach science to children with emphasis on content only. Other objectives such as scientific attitudes, problem-solving skills, and laboratory skills may be overlooked.

Classifying Science Objectives

Three domains—cognitive, affective, and psychomotor —were listed by Bloom and others. The *cognitive* domain represents the greatest proportion of educational objectives and "includes those objectives which deal with the recall or recognition of knowledge and the development of intellectual abilities and skills. . . . It is the domain in which most of the work in curriculum development has taken place and where the clearest definitions of objectives are to be found phrased as descriptions of student behavior."[6]

How such knowledge is developed by pupil activities or behavior is further explained in part 2 of this text where science concepts are listed. Problem solving demands the retrieval of stored knowledge, which is then translated, interpreted, extrapolated, applied, analyzed, synthesized, and evaluated. Thus pupils use previously held or "stored" concepts or knowledge to modify or extend existing concepts.

When an objective is to understand the concept that *metals expand when heated*, what does the teacher mean by "understand"? To understand means to have knowledge of specific facts and/or experiences such as observing that a heated metal ball no longer goes through a ring because of expansion. The pupil understands the concept by *translating* it into an *interpretation* and *application*. For example, the metal cap on the jelly jar was too tight for a fourth grader to open. He *applies* his concept about heated metals when he places the jar cap under hot water. He *analyzes* this problem and *synthesizes* the information that the metal cap

[6]Benjamin S. Bloom et al., *Taxonomy of Educational Objectives* (New York: David McKay, 1956), p. 7.

The laboratory emphasizes psychomotor objectives

would expand because of the hot water. Previous knowledge about heat and molecules may or may not enter into the synthesis. At any rate, the pupil evaluated the solution to the problem as successful when he opened the metal cap on the jar.

Attitudes, appreciations, emotional biases, interests, and values comprise the *affective* domain of objectives. The manipulative, such as laboratory, skills found in technical and science courses constitute the *psychomotor* group. In teaching children to make an electromagnet, for example, psychomotor skill is necessary for turning the wire neatly around a nail. In using this taxonomy in preparing lessons, the teacher will soon discover that a given objective is not entirely devoid of components from the other two classes.

The psychomotor skill of neatly arranging many turns of wire influences, perhaps directly, the cognitive or knowledge domain of objectives. The pupil discovers that the more turns of wire around the nail, the stronger is the electromagnet in picking up various metallic substances. Likewise, the affective domain may influence the learning process. If the lesson is taught by means of a laboratory or discovery situation, the pupil's *attitude* during various experimental attempts, such as how many turns of wire are needed, will affect the cognitive and psychomotor domains. A student who demands excellent results with only two turns of wire may become discouraged and not achieve the cognitive objective. On the other hand, if he has a persistent experimental or "let's find out" attitude, all three classes of objectives in the taxonomy will be brought into play.

If the teacher is aware of the objectives of scientific attitudes, it is possible to teach for this development. In planning a lesson, the teacher can provide opportunities for children to consider new or additional facts. Are the children open-minded to relate new data to previously held ideas? Is intellectual honesty emphasized? Are pupils taught to suspend judgment in the absence of available facts? These attitudes can be taught if the instruction and the nature of the learning situation demands it.

Significance of Science Objectives

Why teach a particular science lesson or a unit? What is the basis for such plans and organization of learning materials? Unless the teacher has given sufficient thought to specific science objectives for the lesson, the unit, and the entire curriculum, it is likely that major developments may not occur. It is also important to note that a mere listing of beautiful objectives on paper will not fulfill the job.

Objectives of teaching science are most significant in determining the selection of course content and in guiding the science teacher in the development and organization of learning activities. Without them, the elementary school teacher may merely be presenting an array of isolated facts without meaning.

A major objective not only in teaching science but also in other areas is better human relations. Children may gain scientific knowledge and desirable scientific attitudes such as open-mindedness or freedom from prejudice during a classroom experiment but may fail to transfer these attitudes and behaviors outside of class to other people.

The teaching of science alone cannot lead to better human relations. But if other humanities and social science disciplines were to accept better human relations as a vital objective in school instruction, and if a concerted attempt were made to teach for the development of this objective, it might be possible to realize this aim.

Simply to refer to a particular scientist as a Frenchman, German, Russian, Oriental, or Afro-American, or as a Catholic or Jew, is no longer sufficient reason to hope that better human relations will occur. It is necessary to read and discuss how eminent scientists of various nationalities, religious beliefs, and races have related to other humans their achievements. A series of case studies of such scientists might be introduced in the lower grades.

If science is to make its weight felt in promoting better human relations, then case studies, reports, discussions, plays, outside speakers, or individual scientists who represent minority groups should be encouraged. As an illustration, the scientific contributions made by George Washington Carver, an Afro-American, make for fascinating reading and

George Washington Carver

discussion. Carver induced farmers in Alabama to grow pe-
cans, sweet potatoes, and peanuts in place of cotton. From
the production of peanuts and his chemical research, Carver
produced hundreds of products including "instant coffee,"
ink, soap, and salad oil. Carver's humble slave origins and
his highly successful career can be an inspiration to *all*
youth.

    Many scientists came from immigrant or low-income
families; they represent various nations: Einstein, Fermi,

**OBJECTIVES OF TEACHING SCIENCE
RATED BY PUBLIC ELEMENTARY SCHOOLS
ACCORDING TO IMPORTANCE AND RANKED ACCORDING TO
PERCENT OF SCHOOLS BELIEVING
EACH OBJECTIVE VERY IMPORTANT:
UNITED STATES, 1961–62**

	Very important	Some importance	Little or no importance
1. Help children develop their curiosity and ask what, how, and why questions	87.0	12.0	1.0
2. Help children learn (how) to think critically	85.2	14.3	5.0
3. Teach knowledge about typical areas of science study such as weather, electricity, plant, animal life, and others	84.3	14.9	0.8
4. Help children learn concepts and ideas for interpreting their environment	84.2	15.5	0.4
5. Develop appreciations for and attitudes about the environment	82.4	17.1	0.5
6. Help children develop problem-solving skills	73.9	24.2	1.9
7. Develop responsibility for the proper use of science knowledge for the betterment of man	69.3	27.7	3.0
8. Prepare for high school science	42.8	45.2	12.1
9. Develop hobbies and leisure-time activities	40.9	50.4	8.7
10. Develop scientists	17.6	51.8	30.6

Mendel, Pavlov, Lavoisier, Priestly, and Leeuwenhoek. Through a carefully planned series of activities relating to the lives of such scientists, better human relations among minority groups could be taught as a major objective.

Blackwood's[7] table of objectives of teaching science may be found in many school syllabi; it is reprinted on the preceding page.

[7]Paul E. Blackwood, "Science Teaching in the Elementary School: A Survey of Practices," *Journal of Research in Science Teaching* 3, no. 3 (1965):177–97.

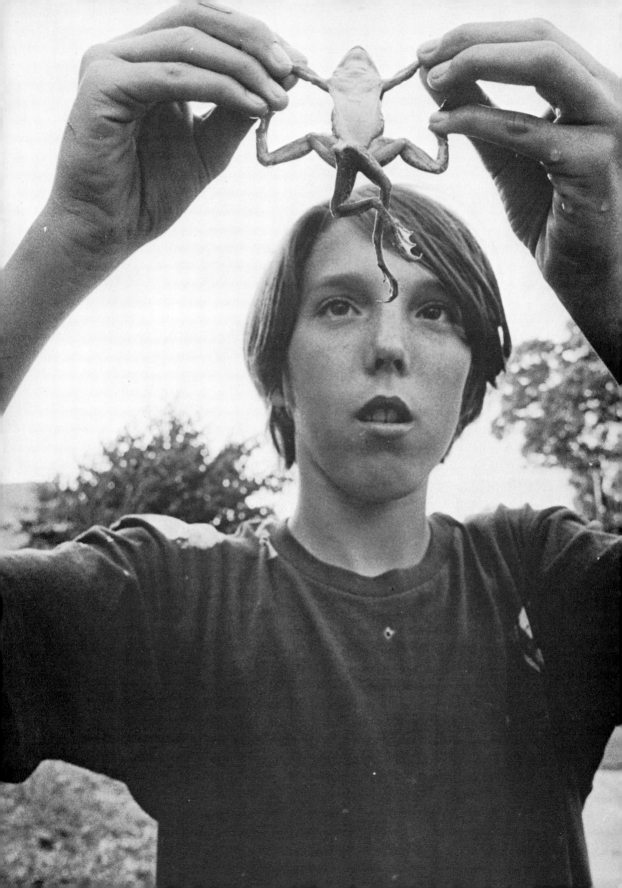

3

PLANNING AND ORGANIZING SCIENCE INSTRUCTION

Imagine that you are suddenly called on to deliver a thirty-minute talk on a topic with which you are unfamiliar. With no time for preparation you would likely be unable to produce a clearly defined talk with succinct objectives. Even if you could recall some of the subject matter you studied in college, you would present only those details you remembered. Such details may not be relevant to given objectives or purposes of the lesson. The need for planning instruction by the teacher soon becomes evident.

It is almost impossible to develop specific objectives related to inquiry or discovery procedures, problem solving, or scientific attitudes without careful planning. Without this planning, behavioral and the complete array of cognitive objectives are frequently omitted during instruction. Also, it is likely that minute and insignificant facts might be over-

Need for Teacher Planning

emphasized at the expense of an important concept or major idea development. Finally, the real test of what is being taught—*evaluation*—demands very careful planning by the teacher.

If only cognitive objectives dealing exclusively with scientific information were taught, then the presentation could be made without much planning, assuming that the teacher knows the subject of science. In such instances, the evaluation consists of measuring recall or retention of facts; but the development of other vital objectives in teaching science is neglected. Hence, in order to realize behavioral objectives, specifically those related to cognitive, affective, and psychomotor domains, it is essential to plan daily lessons and units for more effectiveness. Part 2 of this text provides the basic concepts and learning materials needed for planning instruction.

Daily Lesson Plan— Sample

As a beginning teacher gains experience, he or she will do less formal writing in preparing daily lesson plans. Student teachers and beginning teachers, however, will find the preparation of daily lesson plans invaluable in day-to-day teaching. Soon after, the experienced teacher relies more on resource or teaching units in preparing for instruction.

Whenever possible, the teacher attempts to stimulate the teaching of a new concept by planning exciting questions, describing an unusual observation or experience, providing an interesting demonstration, sharing pupil experiences in the classroom, showing slides or movies, special "action-type" homework assignments, bringing in resource people, and going on a field trip. Such planned stimulants for motivating pupils are part of lesson-plan development.

It does not matter what type of format a teacher uses

for writing the daily lesson plan. Some school supervisors prefer two- or three-column forms or a series of charts in place of a one- or two-page outline. The preparation of the daily lesson plan is based on the thinking required before the actual determination of learning activities is made by the teacher. This enables the teacher to examine the basic ingredients of a daily lesson plan:

TOPIC

Grade Level and Time Allotment

Why teach this topic?	Objectives
What to teach?	Content Outline
How to teach?	Methods and Audiovisual Aids
How do I know I taught?	Evaluation

It is possible that a student teacher or a beginning teacher may revise a daily lesson plan several times before being satisfied with it. The important result of the plan is the teacher's thought, selection, and analysis of learning materials and activities that promote the development of the stated objectives of the lesson.

Sample Daily Lesson Plan (K–3)

Concept

Water evaporates into the air. (Experiment should last from two to five days depending on grade and children.)

Objectives

1. To *interpret* the smaller amounts of water left in a glass for several days.
2. To *observe* changes in the height of water levels in a glass.

3. To *mark* levels of water from day to day.
4. To *experiment* when new ideas are mentioned about heat and evaporation.

(*Note:* These behavioral objectives can be developed in terms of the cognitive, affective, and psychomotor domains as described in chapter 2.)

Content and Methods: Inquiry Approach

Have each child bring a glass with his name on it and a marker to class. Have him fill the glass with tap water and mark the water level on the glass. Each pupil can measure the water level and record the height on a chart for the next five days.

Each day have the children look at their glasses and ask: "What did you observe?" On subsequent days, a youngster might observe that the water is not as high as it was the day before. Ask him what he thinks has happened? Encourage and discuss different responses, such as the possibilities of spilling, pilferage, or evaporation. Free discussion among the children should be encouraged. One youngster might suggest to try it again and repeat the measurement the following day. Daily entries should be made on the chart and daily discussions should take place.

From day to day, discussions of observing water losses in the glasses should lead to several hypotheses. One pupil suggests there was more sun on the glass of water on a particular day. The teacher asks: "What evidence do you have?" The child replies that he is not sure. The teacher asks: "What can you do to find out?" As a result of cross discussion, one child suggests a glass of water be placed in direct sunlight and another glass with the same amount of water be placed in the shady part of the room. Again repeat procedures of observing, measuring, and recording carefully the results.

To develop more discussion and to include the concept of humidity, ask the class, "Do you have other ideas?" One youngster may reply, "A rainy day makes it different." Another may suggest, "Let's find out and set up another glass of water on a rainy day and compare the same amount of water on a sunny day." This series of experiments may last beyond a week. Newspapers and weather forecasts can be introduced at this point. The chart should also be extended to include weather conditions with high humidity such as rain or fog. Perhaps a large class chart could be made:

CLASS CHART

	Water level in inches	Weather	Humidity
Tuesday	4	sunny	52%
Wednesday	3 ½	rain	90%
Thursday	3 ½	rain	92%

Following individual and group experimentation, discussion, and record keeping, pupils should infer the following concepts:

1. Water evaporates into air.
2. Warm air is capable of containing a greater amount of moisture than cold air.
3. Heat from the sun speeds up evaporation of water.

Evaluation

The teacher observes behavior of the children in class and checks their abilities to interpret, observe, mark, experiment, explain, and record data on charts.

Cognitive domain objectives can be evaluated through questions, answers, and discussions. In addition, the following problems or situations can be presented for pupil explanations.

1. In an automobile where all windows are shut on a cool day, the inside of the windows becomes foggy. What makes the fog and where did it come from? (Condensation of water vapor from the air).
2. When water boils in a pot, why is less water found in the pot the longer it boils? (Evaporation.)
3. Morning dew on the grass disappears as the morning gets warmer. Why? (Evaporation.)
4. Introduce questions pertaining to evaporation that children may have experienced, such as why they must add water to, or place a cover on, a tropical fish tank.

**Teaching
and Using
the Lesson Plan**

1. Lesson plans are used as flexible guides for effective instruction. The teacher does not consider them as rigid contracts but rather as means of giving careful thought to developing the most suitable learning situations. The teacher will take advantage of peripheral questions from children that may be related indirectly or directly to the topic. If a better problem, example, or question arises in class than the one planned by the teacher, it may be put to strategic use.
2. The amount of time devoted to the teaching of science to children is influenced largely by the children's span of attention, the nature of the topic and its learning activities, and the grade level. Usually, a given science lesson is taught for about 20–30 min-

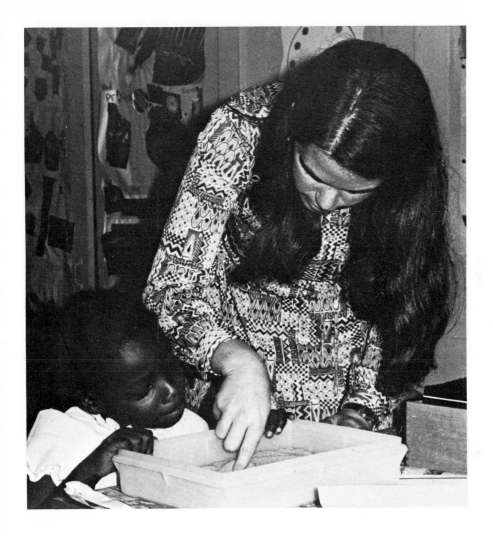

utes in the lower grades, 30–40 minutes in the upper grades, and 40–50 minutes in the middle school. Some laboratory situations such as evaporation will take more than one day unless heat is applied immediately to cause evaporation. Experiments and demonstrations related to growth phenomena in plants and animals will also require longer units of time to develop the objectives in lesson plans. Some experiments may be done at home by children with

Touching and seeing increase attention span.

the results discussed in class. Other types of experiments can be set aside in a special corner of the classroom to enable the pupils to make daily observations and records and to raise questions.

3. When possible, the teacher should attempt to stimulate pupil interest in presenting a new topic. This may be done by any one of different techniques:

    a. The teacher or pupil performs an interesting science demonstration. (Example: for lower grades, have a youngster exhale his moist breath on a chalkboard and observe how quickly the moisture evaporates.)

    b. Ask a challenging question that leads to experimentation and inquiry: "Where did the droplets of water come from that are on the inside of the fish tank glass cover? How? Why?"

    c. Provide an active homework assignment such as discovering how evaporation takes place in kitchen appliances. Pupils may learn that the ice formed in a freezer results from evaporation of water vapor or that escaping steam (evaporation) from an iron is used in pressing clothes.

    d. Have children bring in toys that operate on the principle of evaporation. Many children's toys operate on basic scientific principles involving heat, electricity, magnetism, light, and sound. The introduction of these toys in the classroom as a means of teaching the application of a scientific principle can stimulate a keen interest in learning science.

    e. Pupils perform experiments in the classroom

when materials are given them with the
view of making observations and interpretations. For example, evaporation can be introduced by having them perform the experiment using two milk bottles containing
cold and hot water respectively, topped
with ice cubes.

In this experiment, children can be taught the
need for a control and can relate this to the way a
scientist works. Problem-solving skills, creative
thought, and development of scientific attitudes can
be introduced as an integral part to stimulate the
lesson.

*More than one student should
make readings of
measurement for accuracy.*

4. It should also be noted that not all science topics lend themselves to an exciting means of introduction. Nevertheless, whenever science can be taught *actively* by getting children to *do* science and not only talk science, it will stimulate learning.

5. The lesson plan should also list the filmstrips, slides, movies, and other audiovisual aids that will reinforce the learning of science.

Resource and Teaching Units

The daily lesson plan is usually developed from the outline of instruction, which is either a resource or a teaching unit. A unit of instruction refers to a central topic or theme that may last for one or more weeks of teaching.

A *resource unit* contains far more information, suggested learning activities, and bibliography than a teaching unit. A resource unit may be initiated months ahead of teaching when the teacher and children collect pictures, newspaper clippings, and magazine articles in various labeled folders. The collection of materials on a given topic that could be used for slow, average, and rapid learners serves as a resource for the teacher to develop a teaching unit. If a fourth-grade teacher develops a resource unit, the level of material should contain learning activities that include the equivalent of third- and fifth-, as well as fourth-grade materials. This should provide for the differences in pupil ability so that the teacher can select the appropriate levels for the class. A resource unit contains science concepts to be developed, objectives, content outline, suggested new vocabulary, special classroom equipment and materials, outline of experiments and demonstrations, audiovisual aids, learning activities that include various methods of teaching and reference material.

Following collection of up-to-date resources of instruction, the teacher can readily select the items needed for the actual use of teaching a given class. Hence a *teaching unit* represents the actual use of the selected materials that are organized for effective instructional purposes for a particular class.

A teaching unit should contain the following:

1. an introductory statement that includes the age or grade level of the children, the amount of time needed, and the place of this unit in the overall planning of the course;
2. a statement of behavioral and cognitive objectives, including skills, attitudes, and understandings to be developed by the pupils;
3. an outline of content that relates to concept formation and inquiry procedures;
4. learning activities that are related to the objectives and an approximate listing of time required for the performance of the learning activities;
5. a list of resources such as printed materials, field trips, consultants such as parents in the community, audiovisual aids, and an outline of the procedures needed to facilitate the use of out-of-class resources;
6. an outline of evaluation of student growth and achievement such as questions, discussions, summaries, homework, quizzes, reports, pupil projects, and a check list of observed behaviors and attitudes.

Use of the Unit Plan

As noted above, the daily lesson plan, teaching unit, or science syllabus for a given grade level should not constitute a contract to which the teacher must adhere. He should feel free to use such plans of instruction flexibly and be able to implement or modify them when necessary.

The manner in which a teaching unit is organized will vary from teacher to teacher and from school to school. The units and syllabi will vary in depth of content from one school system to another even though the same topic is listed for a given grade level. Some units of instruction will emphasize questions, the inquiry approach, concept formation, laboratory work, problem-solving activities, or vocabulary and reading skills.

If inquiry or problem-solving activities are to be stressed, the teaching unit should be flexible. The teacher needs to feel free to create new experiments that arise from children's interests and to encourage them to be creative in solving problems. Because of the difficulty in planning some units to coincide with current events, the teacher can permit flexibility in unit and lesson planning where current events in science research and development become an integral part of instruction. Perhaps man will someday land on Mars or on other planets. If this occurs, the teacher should make effective use of all media in current events as a means of teaching science.

Both in daily lesson plans and in planning teaching units, pupil participation should be encouraged and utilized. The potential for learning science is increased with greater pupil participation. Pupil interests are also developed and extended by actively engaging students in planning instruction.

Individual pupil activity should be encouraged for slow, average, and fast learners. In class, audiovisual materials such as tapes and filmstrips should be available so that each child can pursue individual interests in science whether it is electricity, volcanoes, scientists and their lives, or other topics. Outside class activities should encourage individual pupils to visit museums and government and industrial representatives, and to become involved in community projects such as ecology and recycling, antilitter campaigns, and measurement of pollution and conservation problems.

Time

Three to five periods, 20–30 minutes each.

Sample Unit on Magnetism (K–2)

Objectives

1. To *pick up* different things with a magnet.
2. To *observe* some things not picked up by a magnet.
3. To *explain* why some things are picked up by a magnet.
4. To *remove* things made of iron from a mixture.
5. To *inquire* if magnets work through water and cardboard.

(*Note:* These objectives are stated as behavioral objectives so that the teacher can observe pupil behavior during picking up, observing, explaining, removing, and inquiring.)

Content and Methods

This may be separated if desired. The outline of content is listed as concepts to be developed by pupils as a result of the learning activities in class.

An interesting and exciting story to be related in introducing magnetism might be as follows: Imagine in a few years that scientists develop special magnets that repel each other. They are placed on top of railroad tracks and on the wheels of a train. What predictions can you make? How fast will such a train be able to travel? What happens to friction?

Learning concepts on magne-
tism through experimentation.

1. *Concepts on magnetism*
    a. Some things are picked up by magnets.
    b. Things made of iron are picked up by magnets.
    c. A magnet picks up things best at its ends.
    d. A magnet removes iron things from a mixture.
    e. Each magnet has its own strength and is different from other magnets.
    f. Magnets attract things through water, glass, and cardboard.

(*Note:* Concepts are continually being developed, modified, and extended as the learner gains more experience. It should not be assumed that the child is learning any part of a concept for the first time in class, because the environment is constantly furnishing opportunities for the learner to form a concept.)

2. *Learning activities*

   a. Children bring in games and toys that contain magnets, for example, fishing games, dancing dolls on a music box, etc. Magnets in can openers, auto dashboard trays, mathematics boards are also brought into class for discussion.

   b. Pupils should be asked to collect a number of objects including nails, pieces of paper, buttons, wood, paper clips, keys, thumb tacks and to test each item with a magnet. Encourage the inquiry approach by asking pupils to form two columns at their seats— one column to show if a magnet picks up the object, another column to show if it does not pick up the object.

   c. Ask the pupils to prepare a mixture of paper clips, pieces of paper, and shirt buttons. Which of these objects can be removed with a magnet? Invite each pupil to prepare different kinds of mixtures, and note their observations.

   d. Use various types of magnets—horseshoe, bar, small, and large—for pupils to test different parts of the magnet and observe which part picks up an object very quickly.

   e. Pupils should discover which magnet picks up and holds the longest chain of paper clips as they study the various strengths of different kinds of magnets.

   f. Sailboat racing may serve as a game to reinforce several basic concepts and to es-

Fig. 3.1. Making a sailboat.

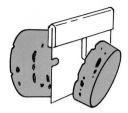

A. Slice a cork $\frac{3}{8}$ of an inch thick.

B. Place a hairpin tightly around cork.

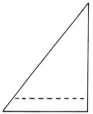

C. Cut a paper triangle $1\frac{1}{2}$ inches high and fold bottom $\frac{1}{4}$ inch up.

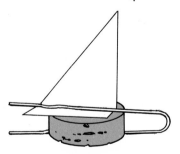

D. Insert paper triangle on fold under top part of hairpin.

tablish a new one: *Magnets attract things through water.* Groups of children may participate in the construction and play of this game.

(1) Prepare four sailboats as illustrated in fig. 3.1.

(2) Place the boats in about 1/2 inch of water in a glass tray.

(3) Two pupils (each one having a magnet in each hand) place magnets on the outside and under the glass tray. Move magnets from one end of tray to another (see fig. 3.2).

g. Display a piece of cardboard, a glass with some water in it, several thumb tacks, and paper clips. Ask questions to encourage pupils to design experiments that will lead to the concept that magnets attract things through water, glass, and cardboard.

h. Fishing games may also be constructed by children to again reinforce the magnetic concept. Instead of fish hooks, use small

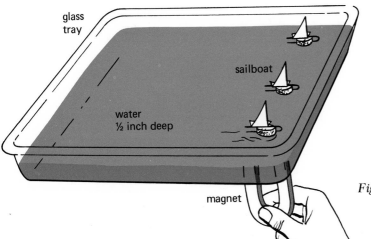

Fig. 3.2. Racing a sailboat.

magnets attached by string to a 12-inch rule. Children can cut out pieces of paper to look like fish and attach a paper clip to the fish. Place several fish in a pot or dish and go fishing.

Resources

1. Outside speakers from the local telephone company, electric company, or construction company where magnets are part of the equipment can be invited to class to discuss the use of magnets. Perhaps they may have visual aids such as telephones to show how magnets are employed.
2. Films and filmstrips on magnets are available from many commercial sources for rental or purchase.
3. Pupil projects and charts can be introduced on the use of magnets in various places in the home: vacuum cleaners, refrigerator doors, buzzers, telephones, and magnetic boards for reminders.

References

1. Bertha Parker. *Magnets.* New York: Harper & Row, 1967.
2. Julius Schwartz. *I Know a Magic House.* New York: McGraw-Hill, 1956.
3. Raymond Yates. *A Boy's Book of Magnetism.* New York: Harper & Row, 1959.

Evaluation

1. Observe children performing psychomotor skills: using magnets to attract and pick up objects, placing magnets under cardboard, glass, and water, and

testing different parts of a magnet for ability to attract objects.

2. Study pupil ability to formulate hypotheses, to test hypotheses by experiment, and to formulate conclusions as they perform tasks such as separating magnetic from nonmagnetic objects in a mixture.

3. Note traits and attitudes such as perseverance and open-mindedness reflected during learning activities. The scientific attitude should be brought to pupil's attention when open-mindedness or flexibility is observed during experiments with magnets.

4. Recognize which children learned the concepts about magnetism as a result of class discussion on "What objects do magnets pick up?"

Summary

Careful planning and organizing of materials promote effective science teaching: daily lesson plans, resource units, and teaching units. The unit should contain:

topic or problem
time required
objectives
concepts to be developed
learning activities (content and methodology)
evaluation
resources (people, audiovisual aids, trips)
references (periodicals, newspapers, and books)

4

WHICH SCIENCE
CURRICULUM?

In recent years many teachers and scientists have been placing greater emphasis on teaching science for developing scientific inquiry (process) rather than stressing the retention of scientific information (product). For many years science was taught primarily for product development, that is, retaining scientific facts and principles. Today it is recognized that scientific attitudes and scientific thinking as part of the scientific process (inquiry or process) are at least equally important as teaching the basic facts or concepts of science.

In planning science instruction as well as selecting the appropriate curriculum, it is interesting to note the kind of questions children ask. Most pupil responses relate to both process and product, although the emphasis by children is on the subject matter (product).

A class of fifth graders was asked, "What is science?"

**Process
and Product**

Science is: something that is discovered; some experimenting about the world around us; experimenting about things that will help us; facts about nature; what a scientist works on; facts about the earth and atmosphere; friction and tests about nature; trying to solve problems; the world's history; nature of the world; discovering new things; about the facts of the world; making things easier around home; chemicals and research. The same class was also asked to state questions in science that they would like to have answered.

The following questions, in addition to pupil interpretations of what science is, might be helpful in developing a new science program: Why does it rain? How do airplanes get into the air and how do they stay there? Why can't people fly? Why do leaves turn color in the fall? How is the hydrogen bomb made? How do doctors make medicine to cure diseases? Will man ever be able to conquer space? What are clouds made of? Why are days twenty-four hours long? Why do doctors kill animals in experiments? Why is the sky blue in the day and black at night? Why does it snow? What is the moon made of? Why do clouds form on some days and not on others? Why does water flow downhill? Where did the air come from? Are the stars as small as they look? Is sand made of small rocks? Why aren't the stars pulled down by gravity? What makes the world turn? What makes ice?

These questions are also an indication of pupil interests that should be considered in a new science program. Interesting insights can also be obtained from additional pupil responses to the question, "What is science?"

The following samples reveal various interpretations and misconceptions of science:

"Science is the never-ending study of life."
"Science tells and asks about people, plants, animals, germs, and a little biography."
"Science is an unknown thing in the world or outer space that men call scientists research."

"Science is something that helps us discover things. It sends rockets to the moon and it has discovered ways to cure many diseases. You could say that science is one of the nicest things that has ever happened. All the conveniences we have we can owe to science. We would not even be in the United States. People say it has to do with citizenship education but if scientists hadn't discovered boats which Columbus went on how could he have discovered the United States? Science is a great thing and we should be appreciative that we have that wonderful science."

Statements of this kind reveal a pupil's attitude, values, and misconceptions, as well as his interests. This should aid the teacher in planning, organizing, revising, or selecting a new program of science instruction. The curriculum alone cannot make for a balance of process and product. The appropriate curriculum, combined with teaching skills from suitable methodology, is needed for the teaching of science process (inquiry) and information (product). Likewise, the social climate of the classroom can affect the total program.

Pupil Needs and Interests

Although children's interests should be determined and used in teaching science, they should not serve as the sole determinant of what science content should be taught. Basic understandings about natural phenomena such as day and night, heat, magnetism, electricity, weather, air, fire, gravity and other scientific laws, food problems of living things, ecology, care of pets and plants, and chemicals for a better life should constitute a significant part of the science curriculum.

These understandings and others are needed for intelligent living regardless of the future occupations or profes-

Relate science to pupil interests.

sions selected by the children. Decisions must be made concerning atomic energy, environmental protection, fluoridation of water, conservation, and use of vaccines. Knowledge and its use are vital for successful living; therefore, this becomes an important study area in the development of a science program that will meet the needs of individual students and society.

Relating Science to Other Subjects

Mathematics, social studies, language arts, music, and art can be employed in the teaching of various science topics. The Minnesota Mathematics and Science Teaching Project (Minnemast), for example, emphasizes processes and concepts through the teaching of numeration, symmetry, and scaling and representation. In teaching the use of a scale or balance, weights and measures are taught in many science curricula. The use of numbers is also taught in reading and interpreting changes in a thermometer while studying weather. Forces are measured by using simple machines.

Science teaching can be used as an aid to language arts and vice versa. Discussions, books, and radio and TV science programs are used for *listening.* Children solve problems in science and give oral reports. Written reports of experiments and other science activities are also encouraged. Reading science publications may stimulate greater interest in science as well as increase reading ability.

Science and social studies are also integrated in teaching various topics such as weather, transportation, communication, and ecology. The social and economic impact of weather on the consumer may stimulate discussion as well as research activity in the community. Children can discover the differences in the price of foods that are shipped from the South to the North. Extreme cases of weather such as drought or frost in orange groves may also affect the consumer.

Although some science topics (such as ecology) lend themselves to integration with social science topics (such as conservation), many topics are taught for scientific literacy. Some teachers are more effective when they can relate scientific applications to areas outside of science. On the other hand, science experiences that emphasize discovery or inquiry may prove equally as stimulating and perhaps more effective.

The place of science for children in the school curriculum should be examined periodically by teachers and curriculum specialists. Although it is important to consider changes in technology and the social impact of science, care should be exercised that hasty changes not be introduced into the school program that may go beyond the learners' capacities. Experiments are needed to determine how complex the science curriculum should be for a given class and a school.

Provisions should be made for the highly interested and capable children in the sciences. On the other hand, it can be dangerous to insist that all bright children be taught to excel in science above other disciplines and experiences. Certainly it is not the function of the schools to make scientists of children. Yet science is occupying a greater role in our daily lives and can be taught for better living.

Organizing a Science Program

In organizing a science program it may be helpful to check the following criteria of a good elementary science program suggested by the National Society for the Study of Education:[1]

1. Is the science program an integral part of a K–12 science program? Is it recognized as an essential part of the total elementary school curriculum?
2. Are *all* children provided for adequately in the elementary science program?
3. Are scientific attitudes being developed in the elementary science program?
4. Is the program well balanced in terms of science content?
5. Are children provided with ample opportunities to participate in a variety of activities such as field trips, experiments, research, group activities, discussions, demonstrations, and construction projects?
6. Are there sufficient materials to enable the pupils to

[1]National Society for the Study of Education, *Rethinking Science Education* (Chicago: University of Chicago Press, 1960), pp. 133–35.

carry on an effective science program? Reading materials, homemade and purchased science equipment? Audiovisual aids?

7. Is expert help (an administrator, curriculum specialist, or other appropriate expert) available to the classroom teacher?

8. Is evaluation of the science curriculum a continuous process?

In selecting and organizing a science program, one criterion emphasized during the last decade was *inquiry*. To what degree does a new science curriculum provide opportunities for pupils to make discoveries? Are problem-solving activities basic to the science curriculum? Yet the development and formation of science concepts are also needed. Actually the teacher and the pupils determine the extent to which inquiry, discovery, or problem-solving activity occurs through the methodology, the nature of the curriculum, and their interaction.

The chart[2] on the following page may be helpful in deciding which program should be considered for adoption in a school science curriculum.

The Alphabet Curricula

Each teacher and school will decide the science curriculum best suited for their needs. If a teacher is not trained to present programs of instruction that require new skills or information, this should be considered in making a final curri-

The "Best" Science Curriculum

[2]From "The Elementary Science Information Unit," Educational Products Information Exchange Institute, 386 Park Avenue South, New York, N.Y. 10016.

GUIDE TO MAJOR CHARACTERISTICS	CONCEPTUALLY ORIENTED PROGRAMS IN ELEMENTARY SCIENCE (COPES)
GRADE LEVEL: Projected grade levels are shown. There is no substantial evidence that the programs work better for one student population than another. Most of the programs were field tested with students of wide-ranging abilities. Analysis suggests the programs are superior to a textbook for slow learners because few reading materials are used and the laboratory approach should interest non-readers.	K-6
SUBJECT AREA: How each program balances the traditional areas of science — physical, biological, etc. — has not been analyzed. Most of the programs cover "general science," but learn toward physical science. Few provide much earth or space science. One program integrates mathematics with science, but all include math to some extent. Most of the programs can be related to other subjects, such as language, music, and art.	General Science
SUGGESTED USE: Some of the programs can be used as supplementary material; others should be used as complete programs. In deciding, weight the advantages of a program tailored to a school's requirements against the advantages of materials designed and tested as a comprehensive program. The recommendations in the chart are based upon three factors discussed elsewhere in the chart: (a) the degree to which goals and outcomes are defined by the developer; (b) the type of unit sequencing; and (c) the degree to which the teaching strategies are prescribed.	Complete program
TEACHER MATERIALS: All programs provide teacher's guides suggesting lesson plans and classroom activities. Some provide additional resource material.	Teacher's guides
STUDENT MATERIALS: All programs require extensive student materials; (all but one provide most of them.) Reading is minimized throughout since the programs are laboratory oriented.	Lab materials specified but not p vided; occasional worksheets
GOALS: A significant trend reflected in all the programs is a shift from teaching the specific facts and theories that are the products of scientific investigation to the investigation itself. These programs emphasize the need for students to learn through experience such general scientific processes as observing, questioning, building and testing hypotheses. They also provide students with concepts that organize an ever-increasing number of facts and changing theories. Although they differ in the emphasis they give to processes and concepts, no program takes the position that one can be taught without the other.	Develop "scientific literacy" throu functional understanding of "ma conceptual schemes"
SAMPLE TOPICS: Although all of the programs intend to teach science processes and concepts, they differ in the content selected as the focus for each unit of activity. The chart lists sample topics from each program.	Structural units of the univers interaction and change, conservati of energy, the statistical view nature
STUDENT EVALUATION: Some developers state lesson or unit objectives as observable student performance; such objectives are called behavioral objectives. Some programs specifying behavioral objectives provide tests and some do not. Other programs do not specify behavioral objectives but do provide enough information to enable the teacher to develop appropriate tests. Some developers object to a heavy emphasis of specific objectives either because they believe current techniques are inadequate or because they believe the teachers and students should be free to set their objectives. These developers place heavy emphasis on teacher observation and judgment for evaluation.	Tests provided, specifying concep to be learned
UNIT SEQUENCING: Some programs are sequenced so that success in one unit depends upon success in a preceding one. Others are designed so that any unit can be used independently. An advantage of sequencing is the "building block" effect; complex skills develop from skills previously mastered. Another advantage is that a prescribed sequence also relieves the teacher of planning the order of lessons. The disadvantages include less freedom for the teacher and the difficulties encountered with late-entering students.	Structured sequence
INSTRUCTIONAL STRATEGY: All programs provide lesson plans and general procedures for handling activities. Some provide an explicit, uniform methodology of instruction. In some cases the methodology is a sequence of specific activities; in other cases, it is a general role or posture the teacher assumes throughout. Where provided, these uniform methodologies should be followed to insure maximum success. None of the procedures are so rigid that they are inflexible; all programs require competent, creative teachers.	No predominant teacher r prescribed. Instructions for ea activity given. Teacher directs tention to concepts.
TEACHER PREREQUISITES: Teacher requirements fall into two categories; (1) amount of science background needed to teach the program; (2) the need for specific training in the style or role to be followed during instruction. Inservice or preservice training is highly desirable where there is an explicit, uniform instructional strategy. Inservice training can be negotiated with some of the publishers. In general, the projects do not provide such training. Some teacher-training can be obtained through universities or summer institutes.	Strong science background neede no special training in method neede
DEVELOPMENTAL AGENCY AND CURRENT PROJECT DIRECTOR: Groups of professionals, rather than individuals, developed most of the programs. Most had Federal support. All programs went through repeated cycles of writing, tryout, or field testing and revision before release.	New York University; Morris Shamos
COST: Costs shown are approximate; they were computed on a base of 30 students per year over a three-year-use cycle and include initial price plus replacement supplies. Teacher training costs are not included. A cost shown as "variable" was not computed because any number of units may be used. Cost can be reduced by use in more than one class per year.	Available from developers
AVAILABILITY: Principal publishng and supply agents are listed with availability of materials. Alternative sources for kit materials are given in the complete information Unit.	One sequence (Conservation Energy) only—COPES: New Yo University

ELEMENTARY SCIENCE STUDY (ESS)	INQUIRY DEVELOPMENT PROGRAM (IDP)	MINNESOTA MATHEMATICS AND SCIENCE TEACHING PROJECT (MINNEMAST)	SCIENCE—A PROCESS APPROACH (S—APA)	SCIENCE CURRICULUM IMPROVEMENT STUDY (SCIS)
K-8	4-9	K-3	K-6	K-6
General Science	Physical Science	General Science and Math	General Science	Physical and Life Science
Supplementary or complete program	Supplementary or complete one-year program	Complete program	Complete program	Complete program
Teacher's guides	Teacher's guides and a background reader	Teacher's guides and a resource handbook	Teacher's guide, and a background reader	Teacher's guides
Lab materials for each student; occasional worksheets; a few supplementary readers	Lab materials for pairs of students; idea books, resource books and response booklet	Lab materials for each student; workbooks	Lab materials for each student	Lab materials for each student; student workbooks
Goals intentionally not specified; materials and activities for a "science experience" that will lead students and teachers to set their own goals are provided.	Develop inquiry skills as the basic process of means of learning in science	Develop "intellectual tools" (concepts) and "operations" (processes) of scientific investigation	Develop skills that lead to mastery of basic scientific processes	Develop "scientific literacy" through functional understanding of basic scientific "concepts"
Seeds, mystery powders, pendulums, bones, batteries and bulbs, mealworms, gases and airs, kitchen physics	Newton's Law of Motion, vectors, friction, centrifugal force, conservation of momentum, gases, changes of state	Numeration, observing properties, symmetrical patterns, investigating systems, scaling and representation, comparing changes, parts and pieces	Observing, measuring, using space-time relationships, predicting, inferring, formulating hypotheses, interpreting data, controlling variables, experimenting	Interaction and systems, organisms, relative position and motion, life cycles, energy sources, populations, ecosystems
No tests; reliance on student and teacher judgment	Some evaluation provided; but heavy reliance on teacher judgment	No tests; behavioral objectives are inferrable	Tests provided; behavioral objectives given	No tests; some procedures suggested or inferrable
Independent units	Independent units	Structured sequence	"Hierarchically" structured sequence	Structured sequence
No sequential procedures; strong emphasis on non-directive approach and student initiated activities and exploration	A sequential pattern: introduce puzzling phenomena; elicit theories; test theories. Teacher provides no "right" answers; students must be free to inquire.	No predominant sequential pattern; no predominant teacher role prescribed	A sequential pattern of activities concluding with testing of performance; no predominant role for teacher	A sequential pattern; encourage exploration of materials; introduce an organizing concept; encourage transfer and application of concept. Teacher role shifts at each phase, distinctive when concept introduced; nondirective elsewhere.
No specialized science training needed; ability to be nondirective highly desirable	Moderate physical science background desirable; ability to follow prescribed "inquiry" approach essential.	No specialized science training needed; no specialized training in methodology needed	No specialized science training needed; training in behavioristic approach of program desirable; an in-service course available	No specialized science training needed; training in specific instructional strategy of program desirable
Education Development Center; Frank Watson	Science Research Associates; Richard Suchman	Minnesota Mathematics and Science Teaching Project; James Werntz	Commission on Science Education of the American Association for the Advancement of Science; John Mayor	Science Curriculum Improvement Study; Robert Karplus
Variable	$6—7 or variable	$6—7 (math & science)	$4—5	$4—5
54 units—McGraw-Hill	All units; Science Research Associates	All units; Minnesota Mathematics & Science Teaching Project; Oregon Museum of Science & Industry; Judy Company	All units; Xerox	Grades 1-3 complete; K and grades 4-6 under development Rand-McNally Publishing Co.

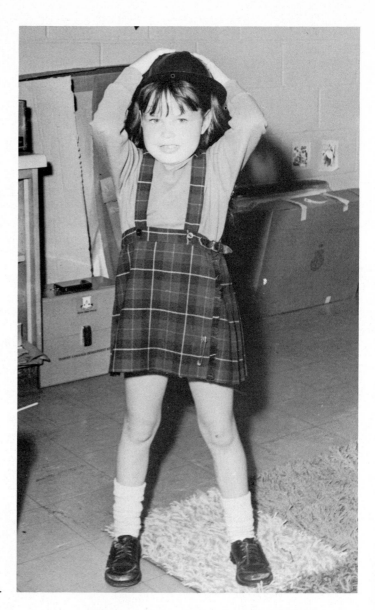

Surprise upon discovery.

culum selection. On the other hand, consultants and supervisors can assist in developing new requirements. Of personal importance is the teachers' enthusiasm for a new program to be adopted. Teachers should be given every opportunity to be as creative as their pupils, so that basic objectives related to inquiry, problem solving, or discovery may be implemented during instruction.

No single science curriculum is best for all schools and all children. Hence each curriculum in science must be adapted or modified to meet the varied needs, interests, and objectives of the local classroom situation. However, common objectives such as ability or skill at scientific inquiry can still be accomplished through the teaching of many kinds of science topics.

No single curriculum is better than the teacher who implements it. The methodology, philosophy, and personality interacting with the children will ultimately accomplish the goals of the selected science program. Perhaps the philosophy, psychology, and methodology of using these science curricula would be more effective if the teacher understood the meaning of inquiry and discovery.

A major approach to inquiry in science is that science is taught more frequently with the question rather than the exclamation mark. It is vital that questions arise from the children and that they propose and screen hypotheses, design experiments, and ultimately make the necessary observations, interpretations, evaluations of data, and conclusions. The teacher as guide in answering pupil questions should lead children to other questions or activities that ultimately lead to solutions.

As an example of this procedure, Suchman reports the following as a result of showing a film, *Ball and Ring:*

A brass ball just fits through a brass ring. The ball is then heated and placed on the opening of the ring which is held in a horizontal position. It does not slip through at once but is held in place by the ring. After some time has passed the ball drops through.

Pupil: Were the ball and ring at room temperature to begin with?
Teacher: Yes.
Pupil: And the ball would go through the ring at first?
Teacher: Yes.
Pupil: After the ball was held over the fire it did *not* go through the ring, right?
Teacher: Yes.
Pupil: If the ring had been heated instead of the ball, would the results have been the same?
Teacher: No.
Pupil: If both had been heated would the ball have gone through then?
Teacher: That all depends.
Pupil: If they had both been heated to the same temperature would the ball have gone through?
Teacher: Yes.
Pupil: Would the ball be the same size after it was heated as it was before?
Teacher: No.
Pupil: Could the same experiment have been done if the ball and ring were made out of some other metal?
Teacher: Yes.[3]

Suchman emphasizes that questions must come from the pupils. The teacher merely answers yes or no and listens to pupil hypotheses. The pupils test these hypotheses through subsequent use of controlled experimentation, observation, interpretation, and evaluation of data. Thus pupils approach science problems in a more systematic and independent manner. The inquiry approach is essentially similar to discovery or problem solving, which is discussed in chapter 6.

In order for the pupil to discover a new idea or skill, he must first be confronted with a problem. He must be baffled with a situation that initiates inquiry. He sees relationships

[3]J. Richard Suchman, "Inquiry Training in the Elementary School," *Science Teacher* 27 (November 1960):42.

of facts and uses previously acquired information on causes and effects. The learner discovers by exploring specific ideas and experiences through observation rather than secondhand experiences if possible.

Inquiry, problem-solving, or discovery procedures can be adapted to almost any type of science curriculum. The curriculum selected and its implementation by the teacher and the pupils will ultimately determine the success of a new or existing program. Current events and social implications of science should be incorporated throughout the science program. In the following chapter, scientific discoveries and the use of current events in science will be examined for classroom use.

5

TEACHING CURRENT
SCIENCE EVENTS

"July 20, 1969—A NEW ERA
STARTS ON A PATCH OF MOON"

"Lunar Dance Has Many Rhythms"
by Kenneth L. Franklin

"Rocks Studied Atom by Atom"
by Robert Jastrow

"One Day Moon May Be a Refueling Stop"
by Paul D. Lowman, Jr.

The above headlines appeared in the *New York Times*
special supplement on 3 August 1969, shortly after man

landed on the moon for the first time. All publications and radio and TV stations concentrated their communications on the first lunar landing. Most people, young and old, suddenly wanted to know more information about the moon. The *Times*, like many other newspapers and magazines, devoted special sections or supplements to man's scientific achievement. People were motivated to learn about the physical makeup, composition, distance, movements, and other features of the moon. This current event in science had stimulated people into learning science concepts and processes or inquiry procedures that led to the act of discovery.

Many science newspaper articles contain far more information on a given topic than is found in a basic elementary textbook. This is especially the case when special supplements appear as current events. For the upper grades and middle school, pupils could be given the *New York Times* special supplement, "The Moon: A New Frontier," 3 August 1969, for reading assignments. The following information is a sample of what appeared in this issue and how such knowledge may be used for instructional purposes.

The Moon—Basic Facts

Diameter: 2,160 miles (about 1/4 that of the earth)
Mass (weight): about 1/81 that of earth
Density: 6/10 that of earth
Largest distance from earth: 257,710 miles
Smallest distance from earth: 221,643 miles
Time for one complete orbit: 27.332 days (for return to same position relative to stars)
Time for one complete orbit: 29.531 days (from one full moon to the next)
Temperature: 250° (sun at zenith); minus 250° (at night).

Visible surface: 41% always visible from earth; 18% sometimes visible; 41% never visible

Who was the first man to draw a map of the moon based on lens sightings and what instrument did he build to make this possible? A discussion of Galileo Galilei based on the brief article, "First the Dream, Then the Deed," will prove most stimulating.

Diagrams that also appeared in the *New York Times* supplement, "The Moon," can be used with demonstration globes and electric bulbs to enable students to perform the types of motions and appearances displayed by the moon.

In the lower grades, children can make up games to demonstrate planetary motion and the motion and change of positions in the moon with respect to the earth and sun. Such instruction is usually planned in advance in accord with a given syllabus. When current events such as the first landing on the moon occurred, natural curiosity facilitated the learning of scientific information needed to understand basic concepts of our solar system (see photo, p. 279).

Using Current Material

It is possible to develop the cognitive domain (retention of information) of objectives in science and the affective domain such as scientific attitudes. Until man landed on the moon, people could merely speculate on the composition of the moon. They were not sure whether or not living things are found there. As a result of the Apollo 11 astronauts' exploration of Tranquility Base and collection of rocks, some mysteries concerning the moon have changed. Theories about lunar dust, volcanoes erupting on the moon, extreme temperature changes, solar winds, the origin of the moon, and its chemical composition were brought into focus from

Landing on the moon. various types of instruments that were placed on the moon by the astronauts.

At various times newspapers and periodicals feature new developments in genetics. For many years scientists accepted the heredity and environment relationship with DNA as the major factor in transmitting traits from one generation to the next. Doctors Roger Williams and Eleanor Storrs Burchfield collected 62 adult female armadillos that produced 61 sets of quadruplets and a litter of quintuplets. Theoretically the "identical" quadruplets should have been alike because each set came from one fertilized egg. But each egg that divided into four parts was asymmetrical. From 2 to 140 differences appeared in these quadruplets. Although each new cell had identical genes, the amount of cytoplasm in each cell varied because of the asymmetry of the cell. It is believed that the varied quantity of cytoplasmic components affects the gene's ability to express the actual traits in the offspring.

A discussion of a newspaper item such as that of the armadillos can encourage children to care for pets and conduct genetic experiments with hamsters or other suitable animals. Not only can elementary principles of heredity be taught from such pupil activity; positive attitudes toward living things may also be developed.

Genetic Experiments

In discussing genetic experiments, pupils should discover that there are many types of factors in heredity. For example, Mendel's laws for predicting specific ratios for offspring in certain species cannot explain other conditions such as cytoplasmic inheritance. The fact that the armadillos displayed great differences in quadruplets arising from the same fertilized egg cell serves to illustrate unpredictable changes from varying amounts of cytoplasm in each cell. Likewide, rare mutations are also unpredictable in many instances.

A mutation or freak can be an asset or a liability. In 1937 at a fur auction in Norway a new mutation of fox—platinum—appeared suddenly with no scientific explanation; two pieces of platinum fur sold for $1,000. Each platinum fox used as a breeding animal was sold at that time for as

Eleanor E. Storrs with baby armadillo.

much as $6,000. The fur breeders thought that Mendel's laws of heredity would apply. They believed that by breeding two pure (homozygous) platinum foxes, all the offspring would be platinum. The breeders, expecting to make a fortune, did not realize that the platinum fox was a mutation from the silver fox and that none of the platinum animals was true-breeding. Platinum genes were dominant. Two heterozygous (mixed pair of chromosomes, one from a platinum parent and one from a silver parent) platinum foxes were mated. According to Mendel's laws, three out of four of the offspring should have been platinum and one silver. Actually, only two were platinum. One was silver, and the fourth embryo died because of a lethal factor caused by a homozygous pair of "platinum" chromosomes. There is no satisfactory explanation for what causes lethal factors in a species. The fur breeders were disappointed financially at losing one-fourth of the expected return on their investment.

A knowledge of heredity is important for health, as in genetic counseling, as well as in economics. In health practices, black children are tested for sickle-cell anemia. In homozygous chromosomes (that is, identical pair, one contributed by each parent) for sickle-cell anemia, the condition is ultimately fatal. This disease is related to genetics and the environment (air pollution): carbon-monoxide concentration is critical for all people, but especially for sickle-cell anemia patients.

Pesticides

It was recently realized that DDT (dichloro-diphenyl-trichloroethane) is absorbed by plants and animals and may be detected as a residue in meat. At certain levels, the amount of DDT can be highly toxic to living organisms, especially since this chemical stays with the organism. The widespread use of DDT (and other pesticides) was publicized in newspapers, and now many localities prohibit its use.

Newspaper clippings on pesticides and the need for their control or elimination can initiate discussions and other learning activities in the study of ecology. Environmental education will play a greater role in our schools and communities during the next few years. It would be desirable to have some pupils collect information showing how we can maintain and upgrade our environment. Children in the upper grades and in middle school can conduct local neighborhood surveys of garbage, incinerators, and pollutants. Reports of such activities can be made in class as well as to the community officials. Earth Day and other days during the year should be dedicated to maintaining a clean environment. Some children might participate in radio and TV programs to illustrate their contribution toward a cleaner and healthier environment.

Newscasts

Newscasts on radio and TV as well as stories in newspapers and periodicals report from time to time new discoveries related to creating living cells from inorganic or organic matter in the laboratory. For example, in November 1970 it was found that the cytoplasm from one amoeba and the nucleus of a different amoeba were placed in a "shell" or cell membrane from a third amoeba to produce a completely different amoeba (fig. 5.1).

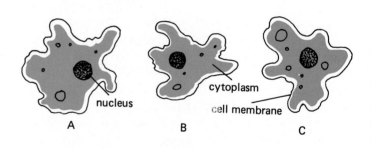

A   B   C

Fig. 5.1. Showing the new one-celled animal (D) created in the laboratory from the 3 parts of the first 3 amoebae.

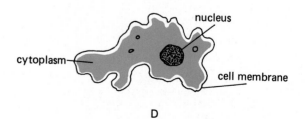

D

Simple microscopes for children in the lower grades as well as student microscopes for children in the upper grades and in middle school can be most helpful in introducing current events of this type. Children are fascinated by viewing microscopic organisms either directly under the microscope or on the screen. Microprojectors and movies can also show various organisms found in a drop of pond water.

Conservation and Pollution

Conservation of such natural resources as water, air, and soil will either be implied or reported directly in mass media communications. Current events pertaining to microscopic organisms can be related to ecology and specifically to purification of water. Pollution of drinking and recreational-use water that affects health should be discussed with children at all levels. Camping trips where pupils depend on drinking water from natural sources can be related to purification processes of water. Boiling, chemical, and physical treatments of drinking water are essential processes to be explored in a functional manner.

There is still much discussion on nuclear vs. "fossil"-powered plants as a source of obtaining electrical energy. The media will continue to report on findings related to smog formed by industrial plants that use oil and coal for electrical energy. At other times, reports will charge that hot water, the result of thermal pollution when nuclear fuels are used, is responsible for killing hundreds of millions of fish.

Additional accurate measurements are needed to determine the amount and kind of damage that is done to various living things, including man, if we are to impress on all citizens the importance of conserving our natural resources for better health. These measurements are needed to determine the standards or criteria for clean air. How much carbon monoxide in the air can a human tolerate before he becomes ill? Some standards were established by law to safeguard the health of a community. The safety levels of other pollutants in our environment need to be determined with a high degree of accuracy. Prompt legislative action may control pollution by industrial processes and preserve a better quality of environment.

The great run of salmon is threatened by the Hanford reactor's discharges (heat) in the Columbia River. Studies there are being conducted to determine the biological effects of heat on the salmon. It is believed that even if the heat does not kill the fish directly, it may cause them to lose the urge to spawn and therefore reduce the fish population. Parasites, disease, and other competitors may appear in the waters as a result of pollution and kill off important living things. "'The south bay of San Francisco,' says Ted Wooster, fishery biologist, California Department of Fish and Game, 'is rapidly approaching the condition of Lake Erie, a dead lake with an oxygen void in which fish can no longer survive.'"[1]

The teaching of current events in science will update the latest research and developments. Children are affected by all mass media in their concept formation, attitudes, and behavior and may need extra guidance to avoid a narrow or incorrect interpretation of science events. Today cloistered laboratory research is made public. Citizens must make decisions on many controversial science topics: pesticides, birth control, ecology for better health or pollution, conquering diseases through better financial research, nuclear reactors vs. fossil fuels, conservation of energy, and radiation problems.

Technology demands continuous research and development. Technological knowledge and its socioeconomic im-

[1]*Science News Yearbook 1969/1970,* comp. and ed. Science Service (New York: Charles Scribner's, 1970), p. 279.

plications need to be taught not only to children but to their elders as well. Hence current events in science should play a vital role in the science curriculum. It may very well be the case that students will see the real need for learning many basic scientific principles because of the impact of science on society. The use or misuse of scientific information is the concern of all people, young and old, scientist and nonscientist.

The dangers of the correct use or misuse of scientific information may be illustrated by the following hypothetical case. A small town, Midville, U.S.A., wishes to purify its water supply. Some citizens complain about a bitter chemical taste, phenylthiocarbamide, or PTC. Other citizens are unable to detect a bitter taste from the same sample. The Board of Health sends an inspector to taste the water in the reservoir to determine if there is a bitter taste.

Use and Misuse of Knowledge

The ability to taste PTC is neither normal nor abnormal. It is determined by heredity. Tasters have either a chromosomal complex (TT) or (Tt) because it is the dominant trait. Nontasters have the recessive chromosomal complex (tt). In the town described above about 70 percent of the population were nontasters and 30 percent were tasters. The inspector, by chance, was a nontaster and he reported to the mayor that there were too many troublemakers in the town. Without a knowledge of heredity and its use, even a referendum would not do justice in understanding or solving this problem. The ultimate solution lies in further study to obtain a chemical that would purify the water so that it would not be offensive to any group.

Another example of how incorrect knowledge can be serious is the problem of the fisherman and the starfish. Normally when one cuts an animal in two parts, the animal dies. Fisherman frequently find starfish enmeshed in their nets. The starfish make holes in the nets, with the result that fish are lost back to the sea. Thus fisherman often cut a starfish into two or three pieces thinking that they are killing it and that starfish will no longer be a nuisance. But starfish reproduce by regeneration, and the fishermen have created a greater problem because each cut has produced another starfish.

The stability of an ecological system can be disturbed by starfish. Small islands in the South Pacific exist because coral reefs protect them from the waves. Coral reefs are formed and maintained by small polyps. Large starfish evert their stomachs and digest these polyps with the result that the reef now resembles a chalklike structure that erodes quickly. Besides threatening the land on the island, the overabundance of starfish feed on clams and oysters and threaten a potential food supply.

Many fisherman have learned not to cut up starfish anymore. Yet the boom in starfish population is staggering on many islands of the South Pacific. What caused this overpopulation of starfish if fisherman are no longer creating the "regeneration" problem? Some theories are: (1) natural predators are collected by skin divers; (2) dredging; and (3) blasting and testing nuclear devices. The answer is unknown at present, and until such scientific information is obtained by accurate means we shall read current science events with keen interest and suspend judgment when necessary.

6

CLASS METHODS OF TEACHING SCIENCE

Although a trend in teaching science to children is to elicit explanations from children whenever possible, there is still a need for teachers to explain. It is not always feasible to encourage children to design experiments when materials needed are not available or if such experimentation may not be directly related to the topic or problem being discussed. But pupil questions may arise spontaneously and other children may not have the knowledge or experience to explain. Thus from time to time a teacher needs to explain a child's question not only because an accurate response is desired but also to ensure the child's confidence in the teacher.

As an illustration, a second-grade pupil noticed several shades of blue and purple in the sky on his way to school. His curiosity made him ask his teacher, "What makes these different colors in the sky?" This was not a planned topic

Explanation and Discussion

for discussion or work of the day. To satisfy his curiosity, the teacher explained that moisture (water vapor or clouds) can act like prisms. The child was told that the other day he had learned how a prism can form a rainbow of beautiful colors from the sunlight. Tiny drops of water in the clouds act like prisms; when the sunlight strikes these prisms in a certain way, a part of the rainbow colors is seen. This type of explanation was a reinforcement of the work done on light last week. If this had not been taught last week, the teacher could have given a quick demonstration of "rainbow formation" if a prism were on hand (see fig. 6.1).

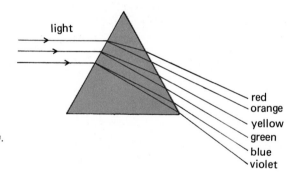

Fig. 6.1. Prism rainbow.

Introducing new science topics where laboratory or demonstration materials are not readily available will require a brief explanation by the teacher. For example, in the upper grades and in the middle school, the teacher may discuss briefly how scientists imagine that an atom looks. One or two models with diagrams that illustrate the position of electrons in the orbits or electron "shells" of two or three light elements such as hydrogen, oxygen, and sodium would be helpful here (see fig. 6.2).

For the lower grades, most explanations will be brief, seldom more than five minutes. In the upper grades, the in-

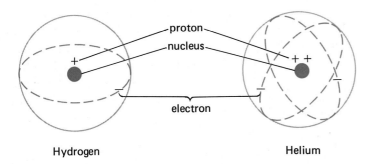

Fig. 6.2. Model of atom.

troductory talk by the teacher may last from five to ten minutes followed by a class discussion. After the teacher presents an atomic model or diagram, children will ask, "How do scientists know what the inside of an atom looks like?" This can lead to a lively discussion when carefully directed by the teacher. A series of questions by the teacher and the pupils can serve as discussion stimulants. For example, a child will ask, "If you can't see one atom even with a microscope, how is it possible for scientists to make these drawings?"

This pupil question can be used by the teacher to explain how scientists and all people make *deductive inferences.* The "black" or "surprise" box can be introduced. This box (perhaps a painted cigar box containing three ball bearings) is displayed and the teacher asks, "How can you find out what might be inside this box without opening it?" The teacher invites hypotheses from the children. The teacher holds the box at a slight incline and the children hear something rolling. The children guess or speculate that whatever is inside must be round like marbles. Some children may say there are a few marbles inside the box. Others may think there are steel balls inside the box. The teacher suggests, "Can we test if these objects are made from steel or metal?" One pupil proposes that a strong magnet placed

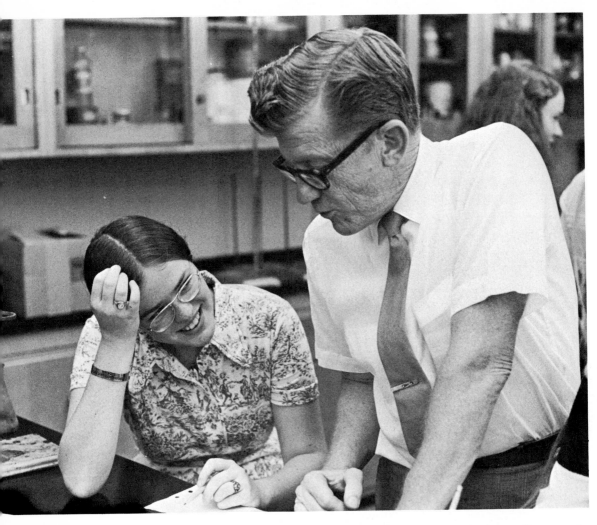

Teacher-pupil interaction promote hypotheses.

on the outside and at the bottom of the box will move the balls on the inside of the box if they are steel balls or ball bearings like those found in roller skates.

After discussion, the box is opened and the children note whether their deductive inferences are correct. This technique of investigating and discovering that scientific information can be obtained indirectly and may be reasonably correct is transferred to the problem of what is inside the atom. Similar to the magnet that was used to determine if the round objects inside the box were made of glass or metal, scientific instruments were used to make deductions about the inside of an atom.

X rays and special equipment to penetrate and photograph the atom help the scientist determine atomic weight. When the needle on a scale moves to the right to a higher number, we say that an object is heavier. By the same reasoning, scientists observed that the X rays formed different lines farther to the right on the photograph when a heavier element (atom) was used. This deductive reasoning is used not only by scientists but also by detectives and burglars. A burglar, for example, deduces that no one is home when he: (1) telephones the home from a drugstore and no one answers; (2) rings the doorbell and pretends to be a salesman when no one comes to the door; or (3) throws a heavy rock that breaks a window and there is no sign of activity such as calling police, opening the door, or putting on the lights. Helping children make deductive inferences is an important part of scientific reasoning and of inquiry, discovery, or problem solving. Whenever explanations (teacher and pupil) and discussions result in deductive inferences, greater potential exists for developing scientific attitudes in children.

Recitation and Art of Questioning

The three-and-one-half-year study resulting in the Carnegie Corporation report describes how docility is practiced over creativity. "Because adults take the schools so much for granted, they fail to appreciate what grim, joyless places most American schools are, how oppressive and petty are the rules by which they are governed, how intellectually sterile and esthetically barren the atmosphere, what an appalling lack of civility obtains on the part of teachers and principals, what contempt they unconsciously display for children as children."[1] Hence it is recommended that we help people more when they know *how to learn* rather than the mastery of a given skill. Although how to learn is essential if we are to survive in a changing world, certain skills in science or other areas should not be neglected.

Perhaps the recommendations of the report may influence the methodology of teaching. Specifically, in the recitation method the traditional science teacher would ask a factual-type question such as, "What is the speed of light?" The pupil would reply, "186,000 miles per second." The teacher would continue asking a battery of such questions that would be answered by the pupils. In the traditional recitation approach, few thought-provoking questions arise because such questions would lead into a discussion rather than a recitation. The nature of the questions formulated by the teacher emphasizes retention of scientific information.

Most of the science curricula described in chapter 4 suggest the use of an inquiry or process approach where emphasis is placed on *how to learn* as well as the development of affective and psychomotor objectives. Thus the art of questioning plays a significant role. The teacher now asks primarily thought-provoking questions that might resemble a recitation (question-and-answer) method; but in reality a discussion may follow.

For example, in the SCIS program, a first- or second-grade teacher displays a system of two pulleys beside another system of two pulleys of unequal size. The teacher asks the children, "What do you see?" The following replies were given by several children: "The pulleys are red and there is a cord around them." "In the first set both pulleys are the same size." "In the second set one pulley is bigger than the other."

The teacher then asks the children, "What is the interaction in the second set?" One of the pupils says, "When

[1] Charles Silberman, *Crisis in the Classroom* (New York: Random House, 1970), p. 172.

you turn the big pulley by the handle, the little pulley makes more turns than the big one." Such thought-provoking questions based on demonstrations or experiments can promote the children to make deductive inferences.

In chapter 4, reference was made to Suchman's approach to teaching science via inquiry. The questions were formulated by the pupils rather than by the teacher. The teacher merely acknowledged them, primarily with a "yes" or "no," in order to stimulate further questions by the children. In either case it is possible to develop scientific inquiry by carefully directed questions and replies by the teacher.

Taxonomy of Pupil Questions

It is difficult to determine what, other than curiosity, motivates children to ask scientific questions. Some children will ask questions to gain attention. Others will need clarification when an idea is not understood. Regardless of the purpose behind the question, it may prove helpful for the teacher to recognize the hierarchy to which a question may be assigned.

A system of classifying pupil questions can help the teacher decide whether the type of question can lead to creative thinking or problem solving or whether a quick response of factual information is needed. Following a high-level question, the teacher can guide the pupil into problem-solving activity rather than answer the question for the pupil. The teacher needs to make a prompt decision on hearing the pupil's question. Does the teacher: (1) give an answer to the pupil's question; (2) refer the question back to the pupil and ask him to suggest an answer; (3) refer the question to another pupil who volunteers the reply; or (4) suggest to the pupil a specific activity that leads to the solution of the problem or an answer to the question?

The chart below can be used as a reference.

TAXONOMY OF PUPIL QUESTIONS

Classification of question	Description	Examples
1. Factual questions	Low-level type answered by text or reference	What travels faster, sound or light?
2. Questions related to scientific principles or laws	Stating principle or law answers the question	Does everything come down that goes up?
3. Questions related to transfer or applications	Transfer or apply knowledge	Why should there be less air in a bicycle tire on a hot day compared with a cold day when I take a long and fast bike ride?
4. Spontaneous questions, curiosity	Curious, instantaneous need to find out	Would a needle float in water?
5. Problem-solving questions	Applying knowledge from previous experience or current experimentation to solve problems	How can I keep my cup of soup hot on the table without using any more heating?

Source: Nathan S. Washton, "Teaching Science Creatively: A Taxonomy of Pupil Questions," *Science Education* 51 (December 1967): 428–31.

Teacher-made Questions

In almost all methods of teaching science there is a need for the teacher to ask questions based on a talk, discussion, or observation. Many questions of the factual type are short answers that can be given by a brief statement or word. For example, in the question, "What is the speed of sound in air?" little reasoning or thinking is involved. Instead the emphasis is placed on scientific information (facts, principles, or concepts) and these are referred to as *convergent* questions. In convergent questions, pupils depend on recall and retention of scientific information to a greater degree than in divergent questions.

In *divergent* or open-ended questions, pupils go beyond the information they already possess and evaluate data obtained as evidence. They frequently propose hypotheses and test them to arrive at a solution to the problem or answer the question. Divergent questions usually require an explanation rather than a statement of a fact or a phrase. They are thought-provoking questions. A few rules for developing good questions are:

1. Avoid unnecessary preambles such as "do you suppose that" or "how many of you can tell me" in phrasing your questions.

    State questions directly and succinctly such as, "How does evaporation take place?" "How do plants make their food?" "What predictions do you make when metals are heated for a very long time?"

2. Science questions are sometimes answered by describing what and how various phenomena occur. Therefore begin science questions with "how" or "what." Although many teachers and pupils state their questions with "why," they really explain by describing *what* and/or *how*. For example, a child asks, "Why is the sky blue?" An answer usually given describes the droplets of water in the sky as prisms. The prisms break up sunlight into the rainbow colors. The explanation may continue explaining how and what. If, after the answer about prisms, refraction, and reflections is given, the pupil can still ask "why," the teacher will find it necessary to say that scientists answer the questions of what and how rather than why. They may begin their experimentation with a "why" but in reality "what" and "how" are answered.

3. When emphasizing inquiry or problem solving, begin many questions with:

   "What is the problem?"
   "Suggest other possibilities or ideas."
   "Design an experiment to test the idea."
   "What do you observe?"
   "What interpretations do you make for this observation?"
   "What are the conclusions?"

4. In stating a question orally before the class, think of the question and state it clearly. Pause for a few seconds in order to give students a chance to think of an answer. For example, "What materials in the soil do green plants need to make their food?" A poorly formed question or series of partial questions can confuse the pupils. For example, a question that is not carefully formulated and stated might be: "What gases are involved in green plants that ... no—can you tell me in making food what do green plants ... how do green plants make their food?" Note the three approaches to the question. In lesson planning, it would be wise to list a few key questions to develop basic concepts.

5. In general, state the question before a pupil's name is mentioned to answer the question. In this way, most of the children can feel involved and that they may be called on to respond. Good attention is maintained in most cases.

6. When a pupil reply to a question contains a correct or partially correct response, try to use the correct material and give the child recognition for getting it at least partly right. Be positive in encouraging youngsters to seek the correct response. If an incorrect answer is given, indicate to the pupil that he

can try again another time; such indication should be done in a sympathetic, friendly manner.

7.   If a particular youngster raises his hands for almost every question, talk with the child privately after class and explain that all children must be given a chance to participate in class. Again, this approach should be gentle and friendly. If necessary, consult either the assistant principal or guidance counselor to determine a pupil's need for continuous attention.

8.   In developing inquiry or discovery procedures, make open-ended comments such as, "What other possibilities ... ?" "Is this the only way ... ?" "Any other ideas ... ?"

9.   Make students feel comfortable about asking questions about anything that may be unclear. Indicate to the pupil that to admit that he does not know is knowing something. At least he knows that he does not know, which is better than the person who *thinks* he knows but really doesn't.

10. Encourage a free atmosphere in the classroom during question-and-reply activities. Do not feel compelled to comment beyond a recognition word such as "good," "fine," "splendid," or "okay" as several pupils make a response to a given question.

Problem Solving

Torrance and others consider problem solving as similar to creativity. Torrance defines creativity as "the process of becoming sensitive to problems, deficiencies, gaps in knowledge, missing elements, disharmonies, and so on; identifying the difficulty; searching for solutions, making guesses, or formulating hypotheses about the deficiences; testing and

Testing hypotheses in problem solving.

retesting these hypotheses and possibly modifying and re-testing them; and finally communicating the results."[2] Problem solving as a method of teaching science requires all of

[2] E. Paul Torrance, "Scientific Views of Creativity and Factors Affecting Its Growth," *Daedalus* 94 (Summer 1965):663–64.

the elements of inquiry practiced by scientists. Not all topics lend themselves to the problem-solving approach. However, if problem-solving activities are given periodically to children in elementary and intermediate schools, they should be able to develop affective objectives such as scientific attitudes and the psychomotor skills in and out of the laboratory.

Anecdotes, actual situations, or demonstrations can provide pupils with the opportunity to identify and formulate the problem. Teachers can encourage children to state the problem rather than have the teachers pose it as a question. If creativity is to be fostered, children should be given the chance to recognize, identify, and state the problem. Frequently this initial phase in problem solving is neglected because so few children are experiencing the skill in identifying and stating the problem.

Van Deventer describes problem solving as follows:

> An individual is confronted with a new situation, or with a modification of an existing situation, such that a problem or challenge is presented. The nature of the situation demands that the problem be either solved or avoided. Possibly if it can be avoided there is no problem, or at least the solving of it can be indefinitely deferred. Probably most of us avoid such problem situations when we can. However, if the problem must be met, it must. The individual, if he is proceeding in a practical way, surveys the situation as well as he can. He draws on his own past experience and the experience of others for whatever may bear upon the problem. Then he sets up one or more tentative solutions to the problem and tries these out, one at a time. If the first attempt succeeds, he goes on his way, the problem solved. If it does not succeed he adds the results of the unsuccessful attempt to his experience. On this basis he builds a new or modified solution, or tries another of his first possibilities. He repeats this procedure again

and again, until he either finds a workable solution or comes to the conclusion that a workable solution cannot be worked out, in which case he "tables" the problem as unsolved and perhaps unsolvable, and lives around it as best he can. . . . Once a solution is reached it is used again and again, whenever the same or similar problem arises. Affinities between related types of problems are recognized, and established solutions are used and modified as necessary.[3]

Trial-and-error activity should be encouraged as a major step in problem solving. Students will propose incorrect hypotheses or designs of experiments. After testing and determining that they are incorrect, the pupils will reject them as incorrect. Thus, problem solving is suggested by the teacher as a "let's find out" approach.

The table[4] on the following page lists the sequence of activities for problem solving:

To illustrate the problem-solving method, a teacher in the upper grades or in middle school wishes to teach the concept of *kindling temperature*, the lowest temperature at which a given substance will undergo combustion (burning). The teacher knows the concept (refer to table above, item 3, under "Teacher"). He displays (item 2) a paper container that he made by folding a sheet of paper $8\frac{1}{2}'' \times 11''$ and fastening with four paper clips. Beside the paper container he also has a very large fresh leaf from a plant that implies to pupils it can be folded into a container. The third display item is a large piece of bark from a tree, which has a part "scooped out" and resembles a ladle. To launch the problem-solving lesson, the teacher now writes an anecdote on

[3]William C. Van Deventer, "A Simplified Approach to the Problem of Scientific Methodology," *School Science and Mathematics* 58 (February 1958):99.
[4]Adapted from Nathan S. Washton, *Teaching Science Creatively* (Philadelphia: W. B. Saunders, 1967), p. 229.

Pupils	Teacher
1. Identify, formulate, and state the problem.	1. Describes anecdote or situation or performs demonstration that leads to the statement of the problem by pupils.
2. Propose and screen hypotheses.	
3. Design and perform experiments to verify hypotheses.	2. Displays a variety of laboratory equipment that indirectly suggests to pupils the forming and testing of hypotheses.
4. Evaluate observations, data, and deductive inferences from the experiments performed.	3. Knows the concept to be developed and the conclusion to be formulated by pupils as a result of problem-solving activity.
5. Formulate a conclusion based on experimental evidence to solve the problem or suspend judgment.	

the board or distributes a printed sheet containing the anecdote as follows:

> Susan went on a camping trip with other Girl Scouts. They were all sitting around a campfire near a brook. It was cold and Susan wanted a hot chocolate. No cooking utensils were there. Susan had powdered chocolate.

For nonreaders, the teacher would read the anecdote aloud two or three times. Referring to the anecdote, the teacher says to the class, "What is Susan's problem?" If the first and second pupil response is not fully correct, the teacher refers to a section of the anecdote that serves as a clue. For example, at the outset a pupil says, "Susan doesn't have water; where is she going to get water?" The teacher says, "Let's read the second sentence." "Oh, yes," yells one pupil, "Susan is near a brook so she has water there." Within three to five pupil responses, the teacher usually obtains the statement of the problem: "How can Susan heat water to make hot chocolate without cooking utensils?" This statement might be given in two or three parts. Nevertheless, the teacher guides the pupil response by referring to various parts of the anecdote. The teachers writes Susan's problem on the board or states it for the younger children.

The next step for the pupils is to propose hypotheses. The teacher asks, "What ideas (or hypotheses) do you suggest for Susan to heat the water?" One youngster says, "Let's try heating the water in the piece of scooped out bark." The teacher tries it over a candle light, Turner, or Bunsen burner. The bottom of bark is dried and soon catches fire. The teacher asks, "What do you suggest?" The same youngster rejects his hypothesis and another youngster thinks that the leaf could hold the water until he discovers otherwise. Finally, another youngster proposes that the water could perhaps be heated in the paper container (see fig. 6.3).

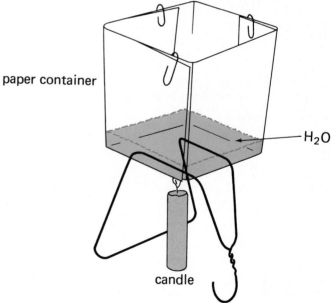

Fig. 6.3.   *Heating water in a paper container.*

In making the paper container, be certain that the corners are tucked inside so that the water doesn't drip out. The candle flame should touch the bottom side of the paper container but the flame should not envelop the sides of the container. A metal clothes hanger can be bent into a tripod to support the container. From a glass, pour a ¼-inch layer of water into the paper container. In about three to five minutes invite two or three children to feel the warm water. Ask them to feel the water before you heat the container. Why?

Older pupils can assist or perform the actual experiments that they propose as a result of the hypotheses they suggested. The pupils are now asked to make their observations. The important question is, "Why didn't the paper catch fire?" The teacher moves the candle to the top portion of the paper container and asks the pupils to observe very carefully. The water inside the container covered and made contact with only ¼-inch at the bottom. Pupils observed that the top of the paper container (2–3 inches tall) was dry because the water did not make contact with it. Hence they observed the upper, dry part of the container catch fire.

With a somewhat exciting and amazing reaction, the pupils concluded that as long as a piece of paper is wet, it will not catch fire. In upper grades, the teacher will introduce the concept that the kindling point not reached was the reason for the paper's not burning. Also, in the upper grades, the teacher can explain the three conditions required for something to burn: (1) fuel such as paper; (2) air or oxygen; and (3) kindling temperature (the lowest temperature to begin burning). If one of the three conditions is removed, burning will not occur.

Another way to introduce the same type of problem-solving lesson will have the teacher perform the demonstration and the pupils supply questions and answers. The

Demonstrations illustrate science concepts.

teacher directs the discussion that *emphasizes inquiry by asking at strategic places,* "What is the problem?" "What is your explanation for this idea?" "What prediction can you make . . . ?" "Let's try and find out if . . . ," "What are your observations?" and "What are your interpretations?" Older children might perform the demonstration under the close supervision of the teacher.

Science Demonstrations

In addition to the skillful use of a demonstration to introduce a problem-solving lesson, the demonstration serves to reinforce the development of science concepts. The demonstration is frequently used to illustrate, clarify, and amplify a scientific concept or principle. Demonstrations should provide opportunities for pupils to make careful observations in order that they can make deductive references.

The important factor is for the teacher to elicit from the pupils their ideas and arguments that are based on observations and analysis of the demonstration. Careful questioning is necessary to provoke pupil thinking. The teacher should avoid as much as possible giving too much information in a demonstration that stresses several elements of scientific thinking and problem solving.

Actually, the demonstration method, like any other method of teaching science, is combined with other methods of teaching such as discussion or recitation. There is artistry in teaching when the teacher can successfully blend one or more methods of teaching science with another, wholly or partially, in such a way that students can progress toward the goals or aims of instruction. The teacher should therefore always be cognizant of the objectives of teaching science, as discussed in chapter 2, and of how each method can contribute most effectively toward the development of those objectives.

The following outline of the demonstration method was employed successfully in teaching a sixth-grade general science class. It is a typical illustration of how a science teacher combines several methods (such as discussion, demonstration, and problem solving) to make a teaching situation more interesting and effective.

Sound—Demonstration

1. Hold a ruler over the edge of the table or desk.
2. Vibrate the extended part over the edge of the table by striking it.

3. Repeat this procedure by moving the ruler so that different lengths of the ruler extend over the edge of the table or desk.
4. Compare differences in audible sounds with variations in length of ruler.

Another useful demonstration can be performed by a pupil who plays the violin. Have him bow when the strings are very loose; note the difference when strings are tightened. A discussion may follow on how dogs are able to hear sounds that the human cannot hear.

Before a pupil performs a demonstration, the teacher should first try it out. This will ensure the procurement of the necessary equipment in advance and will enable the teacher to be better prepared to give guidance in the classroom for a successful demonstration.

Something going wrong while the teacher or pupil performs the demonstration might provide an excellent opportunity for pupils to infer deductions and analyze a given problem. For example, a stopper popping up as a gas generator is being heated can stimulate discussions before the answer to this problem is found. Perhaps in this particular demonstration carbon particles solidified in the delivery tube from the generator and prevented a free flow of carbon dioxide; in the continuing process a buildup of CO_2 in the generator continues to force the stopper out as long as the delivery tube is filled with carbon.

Other criteria to be used in planning good demonstrations are: Is the purpose of the demonstration clear to the science teacher and to the pupils at the beginning and during the demonstration? Can everyone in the classroom easily observe all parts of the demonstration? Is the equipment simple so that it does not obscure the function of the demonstration? Are the demonstrations and their related methods such as discussion pertinent to the objectives of the lesson?

Another important consideration of the demonstration is whether it should be performed by a student or by the teacher. If the purpose of the demonstration is to show, verify, or illustrate a clear-cut scientific principle, the teacher should perform the demonstration. This is especially important if the experiment might be dangerous or injurious to children. At times the teacher will wish to perform accurate procedures and demonstrate skills so that students may learn how to perform these and related skills in the laboratory.

On the other hand, science objectives such as the encouragement of scientific thinking, scientific attitudes, and problem solving will lead the teacher to use the demonstration as a means of eliciting active and verbal responses on the part of the pupils. It may be desirable to have some demonstrations performed by the pupils to encourage interest and to stimulate further learning in science through experimentation and additional study. Having pupils perform a demonstration may allow the teacher to concentrate on discussing pupil observations while the demonstration is in progress.

For over forty years many investigators have tried to determine whether the demonstration method is superior to the laboratory method in teaching science. There is no longer competition between these two methods of teaching science. Many laboratory skills, manipulative (psychomotor) as well as investigative (problem-solving) skills, cannot be developed as well with the demonstration as they can by means of a laboratory experience. The demonstration, on the other hand, can be a very effective and economical method of developing concepts (cognitive). In general, the more active pupils are in thinking and doing, the more likely that concept formation will occur on a higher level. Smith writes:

Concept development requires the active participation of students. The emphasis is on involvement: students must experiment, generalize, react, discriminate, compare, select, reject, and verbalize. The contribution of a rich background of classroom experience is obvious. The experience background which the student brings to the classroom also becomes monumentally important when viewed against the perspective of concept development; it is a resource to be mined and exploited.[5]

Discussion, recitation, questioning, problem solving, and demonstrations are class methods of teaching to groups of children. Although creativity and inquiry can be fostered to a certain extent through the use of class methods, individualized activity by pupils, when properly guided, can promote creativity on a higher level. In the next chapter, the open-ended laboratory, field trips, projects, research, science fairs, and case study are examined as means of emphasizing individual and independent learning activity.

[5]Herbert A. Smith, "The Teaching of a Concept," *The Science Teacher* 33 (March 1966):112.

7

METHODS FOR
INDIVIDUAL ACTIVITY

Creative Science

Although the inquiry approach to teaching science that was discussed in chapter 6 is desirable for developing creativity, individual pupil activity is needed for effective science learning. The laboratory method, field trips, projects, research, science fairs, and case study methods provide for individual pupil activity. Each has unique objectives to be developed.

Laboratory Method

Children enjoy learning basic skills, among them picking up different things with magnets, connecting batteries to several bulbs and making them light, growing plants from seeds, and using simple machines to make work easier. Conventional laboratory procedures where pupils learn to follow directions carefully can be effective in mastering several basic skills. In such situations the teacher shows and tells the pupils what and how to perform, but little opportunity is given for creativity. The conventional laboratory exercise stresses the psychomotor skills, and the pupils verify concepts rather than discover them.

One illustration might show a teacher giving specific instructions on how to make an electromagnet. He tells the pupils to make twelve turns of wire around a large nail and to connect both ends of the wire to a dry cell (see fig. 7.1). He then tells the children to prepare another electromagnet with only four turns of wire around the nail.

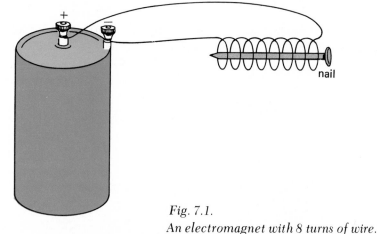

nail

Fig. 7.1.
An electromagnet with 8 turns of wire.

The teacher actually showed how these two electromagnets should be constructed and at the same time demonstrated how the neatly arranged twelve-turn electromagnet was much stronger than the four-turn electromagnet. The children observed the greater strength in the twelve-turn wire coil by how many extra thumbtacks were picked up compared with those picked up by the four-turn coil. The children followed directions and merely imitated the teacher's activity to verify the concept of a stronger electromagnet. Learning can be made more meaningful by the manipulation of objects in the laboratory.

Today, greater emphasis is placed on pupil discovery through the use of individual laboratory activity. Children discover concepts or ideas and meanings and learn skills through the open-ended type of laboratory. In this situation the teacher merely provides the children with materials such as wire, dry cells, nails, and thumbtacks and with little direction attempts to induce the children to learn by trial and error. This open-ended laboratory is more time-consuming, but it emphasizes other objectives—inquiry or discovery, scientific attitudes, persistence, manipulative skills, and so forth—in addition to the cognitive objective where the concept of electromagnetism is reinforced. The amount of direction given by the teacher varies from class to class and from pupil to pupil.

Open-ended Laboratory and Concept Development

In performing open-ended laboratory experiments, precise answers usually cannot be obtained from a book. Each child must perform his own experiment. Some pupils will make or try out fifteen or twenty turns of wire instead of four or twelve. Such individual variations are to be encouraged. Under these conditions children think and reason. Some pupils drive themselves to be creative in designing their own experiments to test, not to verify, self-made hypotheses. Children will learn that neatness in making the turns of wire close together will improve the strength of the magnetic field. They will soon learn how to connect a sim-

Connecting a series circuit in the laboratory.

ple series circuit. The discovery or inquiry approach is thus developed from an open-ended laboratory situation.

Concept formation is also reinforced through open-ended laboratory experiences when children are exposed to guided, planned sequences of learning. Scientific information becomes important to the learner when facts and theories are related to a science concept. "... the child's science concepts are simply rules and principles that he has devised to help him understand nature. The basic science concepts, i.e., length, time, and mass, are relative in nature. Their meanings are derived by performing a set of corresponding operations on two systems and determining the degree of congruity between the relevant properties of each system."[1]

The teacher guides an open-ended laboratory experience for pupil concept development by asking questions orally or on paper to accompany the laboratory activity. If the pupils are making electromagnets, as discussed earlier, the planned sequence of activity should include asking the pupils to determine the relationship between the number of turns of wire around the nail and the strength of the electromagnet. The pupils may suggest that they would first make only four turns of wire to see if the electromagnet can pick up eight thumbtacks at once. Then, eight turns of wire to be followed by twelve turns would be used to test the same number of thumbtacks.

The teacher asks another question such as, "What if you wanted to pick up twelve thumbtacks all at once? How would you find out what to do?" These questions serve as a guide to pupils in developing the concept that *the greater the number of turns of wire around the nail, the stronger the electromagnet.* Thus, well-planned and guided open-ended laboratory experiences can reinforce concept formation.

The following five ideas were listed as trends in studies on concept formation by Johnson:

1. Learning that is meaningful is more effective than learning that lacks significance.
2. Learning takes place somewhat in proportion to the involvement of the learner in learning activities.
3. The role of the teacher as a guide or participant in pupil-teaching planning stimulates learning.

[1]Ronald Raven and Herbert Strubing, "The Effect of Visual Perception Units on Achievement in a Science Unit: Aptitudinal and Substantive Transfer in Second Grade Children" *American Educational Research Journal* 5 (May 1968):333.

4. Manipulation and sensory learning continue to demonstrate superiority over verbal learning.

5. The goal acceptance by the learner appears to be involved in the learning situation.[2]

Field Trips

Our environment may be considered a laboratory. The planned use of the environment in the form of suitable field trips may be construed as a special form of laboratory experience. The use of scientific apparatus such as test tubes and flasks is only one limited use of laboratory work. Today, with active interest and participation in pollution control by pupils and other citizens, it is not difficult to find field trips to survey means of minimizing the pollution content of our surroundings.

On field trips students actively engage in collecting, observing, identifying, labeling, classifying, evaluating, and manipulating various objects such as leaves, trees, shrubs, rocks, minerals, and insects.

On other trips children have opportunities to gain specific information from visits to industrial plants. An engineering plant, a bake shop, a fire station, a museum, a park, and a construction site which temporarily houses a crane constitute points of interest for stimulating scientific learning.

In planning field trips such as visits to industrial plants and museums, the science teacher should discuss and plan with the class what to look for and how to obtain the information desired. Unless pupil-teacher planning is done before the visit, some pupils may merely "go along" and fail to ac-

[2]Donovan A. Johnson, "Implications of Research in the Psychology of Learning for Science and Mathematics Teaching," *Review of Educational Research* 27 (October 1957):402.

complish the objectives of the field trip. It is also important for the teacher to contact the appropriate official at the industrial site or museum to make arrangements and to agree on how the objectives of the field trip can best be developed.

The day following the field trip, it is good to discuss with the class what they learned from the visit. The teacher should evaluate whether the purposes or the objectives of the trip were accomplished. A discussion of this type becomes more meaningful if all the students in the class have observed the same things and places. It is thus desirable to keep the class together if possible rather than to separate them into smaller groups.

In teaching life sciences and ecology in particular, a study of a local pond can teach many concepts: plants and animals depend on each other for food; some living things serve as food materials for other living things; green plants are eaten by living organisms such as fish in the pond; animals give off carbon dioxide that is used by green plants to make their food; animals such as frogs can live in water and on land.

Before actually going on the trip, the teacher should ask the pupils to bring materials needed for an ecological study: various sizes of collecting bottles, plastic bags, camera, thermometers, nets for collecting insects or aquatic specimens, magnifying lenses, field glasses, note-taking materials, and a first-aid kit. The use of a traveling library (a handbook or manual) should be encouraged to permit identification of some specimens. Some teachers may prefer to do this at school, but many report effective results as students learn to identify and study various species on the spot. Special assignments or tasks can be delegated to interested students and to those who have developed a liking for outdoor education.

With proper pupil-teacher planning for a field trip in

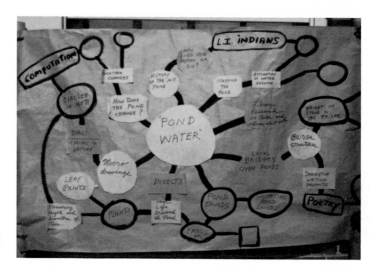

Studying ecology in a pond.

studying ecology, it is possible that some students who never cared for science may suddenly become highly motivated. Outdoor education may have a popular appeal for those students who may not be fond of the typical indoor laboratory. The skill with which the teacher makes pupil assignments may determine the nature of motivation in pupils.

Some children will make plaster-of-paris imprints of leaves. Others will make spatter prints and/or preserve actual leaves representing local trees. A collection of such leaves can be preseved by coating the upper and under surfaces with white shellac. Such projects may evolve from field trips and should be encouraged for all children regardless of age or grade level.

Projects and Research

Science corners, science fairs, science assembly programs, and science hall exhibits provide pupils with opportunity to display their individual projects or research activities. Projects selected by pupils usually stimulate further interests in science. The preparation of charts, models, demonstrations, and displays should not be required of all students, but recognition should be given to those students who participate in such projects.

Some projects may be research oriented. The type of research project may be related to an actual problem. For example, a pupil's tropical aquarium at home contains some fish that are attacked by fungi. One pupil learns that potassium permanganate is the chemical that kills the fungi. The pupil soon discovers that both the fungi and the fish are killed by the chemical. He is now faced with a problem that is essentially a research project. What concentration of potassium permanganate is needed to kill the fungus without killing the fish in the 10-gallon tank?

Projects conceived and carried through to their final solution by the students are excellent learning situations. The teacher can also guide pupils into creating ideas for projects. Some students are given aid from teachers in helping them decide in selecting specific projects. Teacher enthusiasm toward pupil projects can be contagious where many pupils become enthusiastic in developing their projects.

The following suggestions for science projects were made by Dr. Francis St. Lawrence:

1. The teacher must invite continual, genuine interest in the student's undertaking. Boys and girls frequently need assistance and assurance in overcoming the many obstacles which are certain to be encountered all along the way.
2. Most projects require many, many hours of freedom from other distractions for concentrated attack on the science problem. Good working climate, including space, light, equipment, and the like are essential. Often money is an important limiting factor. Hence, it is sometimes necessary to confer with

Weather projects.

parents. Parental approval and understanding should be obtained.

3. The superior student needs frequent opportunities to share with his fellow classmates unusual problems arising from his own peculiar method of approach. These problems are submitted to the class orally. In the free give and take of these buzz sessions, criticisms flow freely. Not only the student himself benefits, but his peers profit also.

4. It is advisable to establish a working calendar for the project construction. Ordinarily, each student proceeds at his own rate of speed, conditioned

by the amount of time he has available. A progress report is required about the first of November. This may be submitted to the teacher in written form if the work is proceeding smoothly. If not, it may be presented orally to the class for the reasons noted earlier. A second report, including sketches and plans, is due about the first of December. These are later arranged in the school display cases. It is hoped in this way to kindle the interest of the entire student body in the activities of the science students. A third report consists of the project itself. This takes place the first week of January. Each student is provided with an opportunity to demonstrate his handicraft to the class. Suggestions are made at this time for final improvement.[3]

As children work on projects, the teacher can observe their overt behavior attitudes and skills. It is important to observe that children modify their opinions when new evidence appears. Individual learning activities such as open-ended laboratory experiences, field trips, excursions, projects, and research will enhance the inquiry or problem-solving approach to understanding science.

Strategic Use of Methodology

There is insufficient evidence to support any one method of teaching science as the best method of teaching for all pupils or for all teachers. A given method such as open-ended laboratory or discussion may be appropriate for some science topics and not for others. A psychomotor objective such as the skill in picking up a snake or a mouse, or in middle school the use of a microscope, is taught more effectively through demonstration and laboratory when students

[3]Francis St. Lawrence, *Science Projects for Superior Students* (Washington, D.C.: National Science Teachers Association, 1958). Gold Medallion Winner, STAR Program, 1958.

are participating in such activities. Recitations and discussions may be helpful for imparting information. Likewise, methods of teaching may have to be modified in different classes even though the same objective is to be taught.

Just as artists mix colors to develop different tones and hues, teachers use several teaching methods to develop cognitive, affective, and psychomotor objectives. The artistry of teaching science is dependent on how skillfully the teacher blends several methods into a unified teaching lesson. The nature of the lesson, the personality and goals of the teacher, the climate of the class, and the interests and needs of the pupils will determine the ultimate selection and utilization of appropriate teaching methods in science.

A Guide for Effective Methodology

1. Is the particular teaching method(s) most suitable for developing the given objective?
2. Are concrete, meaningful materials introduced into new teaching situations?
3. Are pupil's past experiences used to stimulate new ideas for discovery and problem-solving activity?
4. Are contemporary issues and science problems examined in and out of class?
5. Are pupil interests and hobbies related to science concepts whenever possible?
6. Are positive attitudes toward school and science being developed in group work and in individual activity?
7. Are firsthand experiences or experiments provided for pupils whenever they are most appropriate?
8. Are pupils given confidence by the teacher to promote achievement of scientific knowledge, attitudes, and skills?

8

AUDIOVISUAL AIDS: REINFORCING SCIENCE CONCEPTS

Preschool children, like most people, are curious about their surroundings. The first time a child under the age of two touches water, sand, and pebbles, he feels materials with a new kind of experience. Wetness, dryness, softness, hardness, and variations in size, shape, and form are new, important observations and experiences. Even when mother places the gelatin, berries, bananas, and other foods on the table, the very young child squeezes these foods to satisfy a feeling of curiosity. Lacking any knowledge of gravitation, he is also amazed at his first experience of seeing something fall to the floor. Such environmental experiences provide the first means of learning science.

Toys that have gears, wheels, lights, batteries, magnets, and other playthings also introduce the preschool child to a world of wonders. The addition of colorful picture books in

Environmental Materials and Experiences

a child's room and reading to the child will influence his educational development in science. Providing youngsters with the opportunity to play in gardens or in a backyard where seeds are planted is a natural introduction to life science. In apartment buildings, children water bulbs and seeds and observe the growth of plants. Whether children observe or care for tropical fish, the cat, canary, or dog, this type of experience teaches many basic concepts in science.

Reading Materials

Picture books, textbooks, supplementary reading books, magazines, and newspaper clippings contain much scientific information. Science concepts are continually expanded as children are exposed to new reading materials. The learning and formation of science concepts are reinforced through the use of reading materials. Children in the lower grades make worthy achievements in science from hearing stories that are referred to in picture books.

Picture books and stories about the moon, sun, stars, desert, forest, sea, minerals, trees, flowers, size, weather, machines, rockets and jets, energy, and other related subjects are available for all grade levels and abilities (see appendix C). Classroom libraries containing such publications are most helpful and augment main library collections. If children are encouraged to include science books in their own libraries at home, they will reinforce many science concepts and interests. Teachers in the lower grades may invite children to tell their ideas about the pictures they see in books. A discussion follows, perhaps about a magnet. The teacher directs the experiment with the magnet and helps children discover which things a magnet can pick up.

The trend in using science textbooks and supplementary readings integrates laboratory experiences with readings.

Sensing is learning.

Science concepts are thus evolved and reinforced with better meaning. Some texts will emphasize the process or inquiry approach. A few books will deliberately raise questions to be answered only by investigation (reading, consulting, or experimenting). Whether or not a teacher adopts a single science text for all pupils, it is desirable to have several different science textbooks in each classroom to facilitate further investigation and reading in science. A few science textbooks are accompanied by laboratory kits to encourage individual pupil experimentation. Individual laboratory work such as reading will reinforce the understanding of science concepts.

Pictures

Frequently children find science pictures and clippings from newspapers and magazines. Current events in science such as the space activities and new discoveries can enhance the classroom bulletin board as well as serve as a library file for future reference. A picture of a new type of aircraft can become the focus of a stimulating science discussion. Problems of how aircraft stay aloft, how they take off and land, and how radio and radar help them are a few of the vital topics to be discussed. Children should be encouraged to bring toy models of aircraft to school for extended "show and tell" sessions.

Overhead Projector

One of the most useful visual aids in teaching science is the overhead projector. Not only is it used when there is a shortage of chalkboard space, but also for detailed science drawings, charts, graphs, and demonstrations that have been prepared in advance. The teacher can prepare his own transparencies and proceed at whatever rate he finds most suitable for his students. Commercial transparencies in black and white and in color are available for many science topics.

Many interesting demonstrations such as showing the magnetic lines of force can be shown on the screen with the aid of an overhead projector. Petri dishes are used to show formation of precipitates and how some of them are dissolved. Alyea writes:

> Overhead projection of chemical experiments . . . the teacher uses drops; the student sees them live, in color, as huge as baseballs in test tubes six feet tall and two feet wide. Invisible macro-reactions become clearly visible 100 ft. away . . . First, we propose to project all of beginning chemistry demonstrations, not just a few special ones. Second,

only 28 devices will be required to carry out at least 1,000 different experiments.[1]

Overlay transparencies are used to portray difficult concepts as well as to emphasize various parts of a concept. For example, an acetate sheet will show only the male structures of a flower. Another transparency will show the female structures in a flower; when superimposed both sexual structures will be seen on the screen. A third transparency will be superimposed to make up the overlay tranparencies, and the petals and sepals will be shown so that a complete flower with all of its parts can be studied.

There is a wealth of science materials in color and black-and-white filmstrips, slides, and movies (see appendix E). If the school budget does not permit the purchase of the materials for the school district, most of these materials may be rented at reasonable cost. A filmstrip or a slide is usually available for almost all science concepts.

Filmstrips, Slides, and Movies

Single-loop movie films (8 mm. or super-8 mm.) are excellent for grades four to nine. Each film loop may last from three to five minutes and emphasize one particular concept such as a series circuit or a parallel circuit in electricity, or making solutions. These loops are inexpensive and projectors are very easy to operate. Four or more of these projectors can be used at the same time in a given class, permitting simultaneous levels of group work. Each projector has a built-in screen resembling a TV set; pupils can be taught to insert the loop or cartridge and turn the operating switch on. Each group can view a different set of science loops at its own

[1] Hubert N. Alyea, "*Tops* in General Chemistry: Tested Overhead Projection Series," *Journal of Chemical Education* 39 (January 1962): 12.

pace. One group could view four or five loops on volcanoes while another group views loops or cartridges on electricity. These projectors can also be used to individualize science instruction.

Color slides and filmstrips can stimulate and reinforce learning in science. On vacations many families take color slides of beaches, mountains, animals, deserts, national parks, waterfalls, and others scenes of scientific import. Children enjoy bringing such material to show to the class. Commercial sources have also developed series of filmstrips and slides. For example, a set of six filmstrips in color on *Aerospace* (Coronet) with or without phonograph records teaches the basic principles of how airplanes fly, how rockets are launched, how satellites stay in orbit, and how satellites are monitored from the ground. These instructional aids become effective when followed by a discussion.

Colorful movie films such as those dealing with ocean life are available for children in kindergarten through grade three. Such films usually depict underwater life around coral reefs, living things on the ocean floor, adaptations for feeding and protection, and the interrelationships among plants and animals in the sea.

Concepts such as the need for air, light, and food are developed in these films. Curiosity about the unknown on the ocean floor is brought to the screen with striking interest when children view how the porcupine fish, the hermit crab, and the jellyfish protect themselves.

In selecting appropriate movie films, filmstrips, or slides, the teacher determines what the film does more effectively that cannot be duplicated by the teacher without the use of the visual aid. Ocean life, for example, cannot be made available in the classroom without the film. Therefore the vivid concepts and experiences portrayed by the film—which cannot be duplicated by words alone—are the basis for selecting the film. Some filmstrips may consist of only a series of diagrams that can be duplicated by the teacher on the board. Here it may not be desirable to purchase such an aid under strict budgetary considerations. On the other hand, the film, filmstrip, or slides can be used to stress the concepts being developed (refer to Anderson's study).[2]

Assuming that a stimulating or exciting filmstrip or movie is selected, the teacher should indicate before showing the film that a discussion will follow. This will increase attention while viewing the film. In certain films several science concepts are demonstrated; the teacher may wish to suggest what to look for in order to initiate a good discussion afterward.

Using Visual Aids Effectively

To reinforce learning or retention of science concepts, a healthy discussion should follow the viewing of the audio-visual aid. Where possible children should be encouraged to relate their own experiences with those observed in the film. Assume that the first- or second-grade class saw a film on ocean life. The discussion could then be directed by the teacher to include children's seashore experiences during the summer. If the children witnessed beach sand, seashells, fish, starfish, or jellyfish during the summer, these activities of play can reinforce comprehension of many science concepts. To talk about the tiny hard spicules or "bony" structures on the surface of the starfish presents a feeling that cannot be learned from viewing the film alone. In addition to developing feelings and attitudes about starfish, various science concepts can be written on the board after discussing the film.

[2] Kenneth E. Anderson et al., "An Evaluation of the Introductory Chemistry Course on Film," *Science Education* 45 (April 1961):254-69.

Projects are displayed in halls as well as in the auditorium and gymnasium for the Science Fair.

Children frequently collect specimens such as rocks, seashells, insects, leaves, and many other items that range from a simple "show and tell" in the lower grades to a very sophisticated collector's hobby. Specimens and models made by children should be introduced in class discussions as well as in a school museum. Well-constructed picture books are available on almost all subjects pertaining to the science collector's hobby. At strategic intervals a temporary display of a collection of specimens, coupled with selected picture books, will enhance the interest in and knowledge of science concepts. Some children may enjoy the responsibility for arranging such exhibits and thus learn much science information on an informal basis.

Most movie films, filmstrips, slides, and educational television programs are accompanied by teacher guides. Frequently thought-provoking questions and suggested readings for pupils and for teachers accompany suggested learning activities. The teacher's guide can be used with the film or filmstrip to direct discussion and inquiry. This may lead to experimentation or other types of investigative activity by pupils. For example, questions for class discussion based on *We Explore Ocean Life* (Coronet Instructional Films) Teacher's Guide include:

1. Why are aquatic plants placed in home aquariums?
2. Some ocean animals use camouflage to protect themselves. Can you name some land animals that also use camouflage?
3. What body parts of sea animals are used to capture food?
4. What are some of the ways in which sea animals protect themselves?
5. How do some animals in the sea move without fins?

The teacher's guide may also suggest class activities that are related to the film such as:

1. Bring specimens or pictures of coral, seashells, seaweed, or other objects from the ocean to class.
2. Write to your State Conservation Department and ask about the fish and animal life laws that protect life in the sea or in other bodies of water.
3. Visit a civic or private aquarium. Where can fish for a small aquarium be obtained in your area?
4. Take a trip to the ocean, the shore of a lake, or a small pond. What kind of life do you find in the water?

In using visual aids such as films or filmstrips, the teacher should preview such materials and read the teacher's guide before classroom showings. Correlated readings in science books are also suggested in most of these guides. Availability in the classroom and library of related books, pictures, and magazines encourages further reading. Children who have some of these books or pictures at home are invited to bring them to class for discussion.

Children may ask the following questions that are not answered in the film on ocean life:

Do all sharks eat people?
Are whales fish?
Do whales eat people?
What is the biggest fish?
Where does the salt in ocean water come from?

These questions suggest further reading and investigation; pupils should be encouraged to seek answers.

Teacher Check List in Using Visual Aids

1. Preview the film or filmstrip and study the teacher's guide.
2. Select the film for class showing because it can be used for excellent stimulation and/or learning of scientific concepts.
3. Raise questions that encourage further investigation.
4. Bring in books, pictures, magazines, and specimens related to film and display them.
5. Assign projects and other learning activities (e.g., field trips) that arise from class questions and discussions of the film.
6. Display projects in a class or school exhibit or museum.
7. Have pupils give oral and written reports based on related activities of the film or filmstrip.

Radio and TV programs frequently deal with contemporary science problems. Space travel, rockets, moon explorations, undersea experiments with radar and animal life, ecology, lasers, and health and disease problems can be taped and played back in school and at home. Phonographs and tape recorders can be used to enrich and reinforce learning science.

The audiotutorial approach to learning science can be very effective. Science concepts are developed as pupils play records and tapes at a leisurely pace either in class or at home. Individualized learning can be achieved efficiently.

Many phonograph records and cassettes have been developed in conjunction with filmstrips or slides. Individualized projectors with sound are available to permit pupils to view science concepts. The film-loop type of projector also is used for individualized learning. Here the pupil can view the concept film as many times as necessary. Such equipment makes it possible for pupils to do different things in and out of class.

Programmed instruction is also used in the audiotutorial approach. Frames of information (concepts) are followed by multiple-choice questions. This program permits flexibility, errors, and "I don't know" responses. Electronic teaching machines are used in the Auto-Tutor where programmed instruction promotes individualized learning.

Using slides in sequence can be a striking technique in developing a science concept. For example, on a trip along a stream, slides were taken to show meandering, stream curvature, the end of the curve, and the formation of a new curve. A series of slides that show: (1) a portion of straight stream; (2) a dead, fallen tree across one-half the width of a stream; (3) moving water against the fallen tree causing a new directional current; (4) a new bend or curve formed along the stream. Pupils may be asked to arrange the correct sequence of such slides to show what meandering is; thus

Phonograph Records, Tape Recorders, and Audiotutorial Devices

the concept is developed by involving the pupils with visual aids.

Many phonograph records and tape recordings deal with specific science topics such as magnetism, electricity, energy, and nature study. Those with lyrics that were made for singing and bouncy, rhythmic tunes can serve as an excellent stimulant to the introduction of a new topic such as energy. With younger children singing and dancing to these science recordings reinforces the learning of science concepts. For creative children volunteer assignments can be fun when they write lyrics for simple science concepts.

Play and Toys

Dolls, trains, dump trucks, cranes, steam shovels, fishing games, quiz games, musical instruments, and toy radios usually contain equipment that relates to science concepts on sound, magnetism, light, work, machines, and electricity. To introduce a lesson on any of these topics, many children might be encouraged to bring these toys to class. How a drum, violin, piano, or trumpet makes sounds stimulates learning experiences. The pitch or number of vibrations per second in a given musical note is taught through exciting musical play. The concept of a vibrating column of air and the production of musical sounds are developed through pupils' play and inquiry by their questions and their discovery of replies to these questions. To encourage creativity and reinforcement of science concepts, pupils make their own musical instruments as laboratory experiences for understanding the nature of sound. Cigar boxes with different sizes and thicknesses of rubber bands can be used to make a violin. A large straw with holes in it to resemble a flute can be used. The musical scale can be demonstrated by using eight glasses each containing a different volume of water.

The varying volumes of air in each glass will demonstrate, on striking each glass, the different musical notes or sounds produced.

Summary

In summary, to reinforce science concepts through use of audiovisual aids, teachers can:

1. Provide exposure to play activities involving water, sand, toys, gardening, and caring for pets. Playing in sandboxes, making mud pies, playing with the magnetic, dancing ballerinas, and motor toys re n-force science concepts.
2. Use picture books to have children tell stories about pictures that are related to science phenomena such as weather, sun, moon, airplanes, and ma-chines. Ask children to show pictures that show what makes rain and snow, what makes night and day, and how airplanes fly.
3. Collect pictures of scientific interest from maga-zines and newspapers and post them on a bulletin board for periodic class discussions. Space travel pictures, newspaper clippings about scientific and medical discoveries, how pollutants poison our environment, and food additives that harm our bodies reinforce science concepts.
4. Distribute science books and periodicals for individ-ual and class reading activities. For example, a re-cent paperback series included booklets on oceans, deserts, grasslands, forests, farms, cities, suburbs, fresh water, and others that emphasize many science concepts.
5. Develop a classroom library of current science

books to supplement the class museum. Many children receive science books as gifts that can be loaned to a classroom science library where pupils can exchange books.

6. Use effective filmstrips, slides, and movies that are related to the science concepts to be developed (see teacher check list mentioned above). Audiovisual aids should be used for individualized learning as well as class instruction.

7. Construct exhibits and museums of audiovisual aids including specimens brought to class. Pupils can display models of flowers, or digestion in a frog, or show microscopic organisms such as a paramecium, a working model of circulation of blood in a mammal's heart, a model of an oxygen and a hydrogen atom, a display of simple machines, a collection of leaves, insects, and rocks.

8. Play phonograph records and tapes of important science ideas and developments including current events. Pupils can bring in tape recordings of science programs from radio and TV, especially important events about astronauts, eclipses, atomic energy, and other current events.

9. Integrate toys related to science concepts with instruction in science. For example, models of heads that grow grass by watering the planted seeds will stimulate concept formation.

10. Display, refer to, and talk about particular audiovisual aids more than once at strategic and appropriate times during science instruction. Simply to show a chart of the parts of a flower at the beginning of instruction is not enough. At strategic points in the lesson, pupils should become involved and point or refer to the chart or whatever aid to instruction is being used.

9

EVALUATION OF
SCIENCE INSTRUCTION

If teaching were like selling and if learning were like buying, it would be easy to evaluate how much a teacher had sold. The salesman can produce a given number of dollars for the merchandise bought. He knows he made a sale when he rings it up on his cash register. Unfortunately the teacher may never know how much or how little he has sold to his pupils at the end of the day, week, month, or year. Frequently the teacher must be content with knowing how much or how little a pupil knows about scientific information by comparing one pupil with another. By administering tests that emphasize the cognitive domain or the subject matter of science, judgments are made by the teacher in terms of determining the relative standing of a pupil's knowledge in a group.

The evaluation of instruction involves a great deal more

**Philosophy
of Evaluation**

than the teacher's preparing tests and the children's answering them. Wittrock writes, "I maintain that to evaluate instruction, one must first measure at least three parts of instruction: (1) the environment of learning, (2) the intellectual and social processes of learners, and (3) the learning. Second, the relationships among these three parts of instruction must then be quantitatively estimated."[1] Wittrock suggests that, by using multivariable statistics, we should be able to measure cause-and-effect relationships that exist among the instructional environment, the individual learners, and learning. He describes in detail an approach that can be used by teachers and administrators to make decisions about curriculum as well as judgments based on values.

The Environment and Evaluation

Are there sufficient books, magazines, and other reading materials in and near the classroom? Do students have to travel a long distance for library materials? Are laboratory materials and facilities readily available for pupils to experiment? Does the school per-pupil budget provide adequately for these learning materials in the environment? Does the teacher have sufficient college credits in the sciences to teach science with comfort and ease? These are environmental factors and a careful examination of their relationships is needed to study the impact on the behavior of the learner.

The Learner and Evaluation

How little or how much science does a pupil know at the beginning of the school year? What changes occur in the behavior of pupils during and at the conclusion of the

[1] M. C. Wittrock, "The Evaluation of Instruction: Cause and Effect Relations in Naturalistic Data," UCLA *Evaluation Comment* 1 (May 1969): 2.

school year? Most tests, teacher-made and standardized, enable the teacher to discriminate differences in individual pupils. They do not necessarily reflect the evaluation of an educational program or of instruction. At best, an attempt is made to discriminate differences existing among a class of individuals. A more thorough analysis is needed in studying the learner's interests, aptitudes, and achievements at the beginning, during, and at the end of an instructional program. Careful measurement of the scientific knowledge a pupil possesses is needed when he first enters a given program of instruction. The salient features of the environment also need to be related to the learner.

Learning and Evaluation

Many tests are constructed with the view that most of the pupils will receive an average grade such as *C*. Hence the test items really enable the teacher to measure differences among pupils rather than the amount of individual learning. Teachers are trained to assume that test results should provide as many *D* and *F* grades and *A* and *B* grades. This provides no indication of how much learning occurs within a given student. As Wittrock writes, "Our prevalent habits of discarding valid but non-discriminating items to find some ways, perhaps irrelevant, in which individuals differ in achievement skirts the main issue: What instruction is best for each individual to help him learn?"[2] The type of standardized and other tests in science generally used make for less individualized instruction.

One of the major concerns in evaluating learning is the change in pupil behavior. It is necessary to define and state clearly the objectives of pupil behavior as part of instruction. It is also necessary that pretests and posttests be used to evaluate these behavioral changes. For example, one objec-

[2] Ibid., p. 5.

Evaluating learning through pupil activity.

tive in teaching science to children is to care for plants and animals or pets at home. Although a pencil-and-paper test does not measure one's ability to care for a plant or animal, observations of pupil behavior in the care of living organisms will determine the success or failure of developing such pupil behavior. Specifically for plants, do the children know how to water plants or provide them with proper amount of light, chemical food, or natural fertilizer? Do they know how to transplant when necessary?

The teacher is aware of this behavioral objective before instruction begins. On a pretest (pencil-and-paper), the teacher can determine if the children know how to care for a plant, a salamander, a frog, tropical fish, a cat, or a dog. If some children do not know what to do as shown by the test items, such items are not declared invalid and unreliable. The basic principle is that instruction should be changed, not the test items based on behavioral objectives. The teacher directs the instruction to the development of this objective and evaluates on a posttest by observation and/or pencil-and-paper tests.

Greater concern is shown for the learner as an individual in his own behavioral changes that show growth rather than comparing him with others. Later in this chapter a discussion of the cognitive and affective domains of objectives of teaching science and their effect on the behavioral objectives will be given. The fact that a youngster knows how to care for an animal or a plant is no assurance that he will care for it at home. The attitude of liking or disliking the tasks involved in caring for a pet will be influenced by many environmental factors: the teacher, the subject, and the interrelationships of the teacher and pupil, friends, and others.

Instruction and Evaluation

The interaction of the environment, the learner, and learning determine the degree of success of instruction. Perhaps the most important question the teacher may ask is, "What is the purpose of evaluation?" If the object is to evaluate a typical instructional science program where all children receive the same instruction simultaneously, then sampling should be made of the class and not individual youngsters. In other words, it is not necessary to test all pupils in the class. Merely a sample is needed. Also, it is not necessary to give identical test items to the sample pupils if the science program in the class is to be evaluated.

If computer-assisted instruction is used or if other individualized methods of teaching are employed as discussed in previous chapters, the method is primarily tutorial and the sample unit is the individual pupil and not the class. Likewise, provisions for different systems of evaluation are needed for varied tutorial procedures. Changes in behavior are measured within a given pupil rather than comparing him with others. The reader is referred to Wiley's[3] chapter, "Design and Analysis of Evaluation Studies," for a more detailed explanation on how to quantify data in evaluating instruction based on the cause-effect relationships of the environment, the learner, and learning.

Experimentation is needed to determine the cause and effect of each of the above factors. The science teacher teaches a pupil to like or dislike science in addition to the presentation of scientific information. The pupil's motivation to learn is determined by environmental and personal problems. Previous experiences with parents, peers, teachers, materials, and living organisms in the environment likewise affect instruction. For example, a pupil sees his mother jump on a chair when a mouse appears in the kitchen. An attitude of dislike or fear for mice is developed. The teacher would find it very difficult to teach about mice to this pupil. Pupils who possess no fear of mice can assist teaching such positive attitudes (see chapter-opening photo). Likewise, if a teacher showed a distasteful facial expression on seeing a garter snake brought to class, such behavior transmits negative attitudes in children. It becomes the basis for developing fears.

Many attitudes and behaviors that display a dislike for a given animal originate in the home. A fearful or anxious parent who continually uses insecticides to kill insects in or around the house often creates similar fears in the children. On the other hand, the adult who picks up a caterpillar and

[3] M. C. Wittrock and David E. Wiley, *The Evaluation of Instruction* (New York: Holt, Rinehart & Winston, 1970), chap. 8.

shows enjoyment in holding it frequently influences wholesome attitudes toward living animals. An important criterion for evaluating such attitudes is: to what degree do I kill (or care for and love) insects, other animals, and plants?

The affective domain of objectives in teaching science to children is very important. Feelings, attitudes, and interests of children will greatly influence the degree of success in the cognitive domain. If children enjoy learning and show interest in mice, caterpillars, hamsters, frogs, seeds and plants, and other natural phenomena, the potential for understanding and retaining factual information is reinforced. Likewise, overt behavior (fear) such as jumping on the chair because of the appearance of an animal will hinder the development of cognitive objectives.

Evaluating the Objectives

Although affective domain and behavioral objectives (constructing, interpreting, identifying, collecting, and explaining) influence the degree to which children retain scientific information (cognitive), psychomotor objectives are also important. It should be noted that all psychomotor objectives are behavioral, but not all behavioral objectives are in the psychomotor domain. Illustrations of psychomotor objectives are bringing the microscope into high power to view a one-celled animal, constructing a herbarium, heating a chemical in a test tube, and making a series circuit using four flashlight bulbs. These psychomotor skills all involve neuromuscular activity. They can be observed by the teacher without pencil-and-paper tests and are also considered behavioral objectives.

The psychomotor objectives develop many basic skills such as constructing a thermometer, a barometer, a weathervane, a cage for an animal, an electromagnet, and many other "doing" activities. If a youngster had little information or knowledge (cognitive) about electromagnets, for example, he might become curious and motivated to learn more about them *as a result of his success in constructing an electromagnet quickly and effectively*. Hence, the psychomotor objectives influence the mastery of knowledge as well as affect attitudes toward what is being learned. Some teachers believe that knowledge is needed before the psychomotor objectives can be developed. No evidence indicates which came first as a universal practice. In either case, concept formation will occur as a result of the learning activities suggested in the following chapters.

An *accidental* or *incidental discovery* in science leads the investigator to explain the act. For example, the accidental discovery of penicillin led to the use of a new regime in medication—antibiotics. The investigators, Florey, Chain, and Fleming, had no intention of discovering antibiotics and cures for many ailments. Fleming, by accident, washed a bacteriological culture plate that had picked up some mold and he observed a significant change. The staphylococci that cause disease were no longer present in the culture. Knowledge of antibiotics and penicillin production came much later after Alexander Fleming's accidental observation in his laboratory. Perhaps this is a case in favor of why laboratory or psychomotor objectives should be used at the beginning to promote retention of knowledge.

On the other hand, Robert H. Goddard, the rocket pioneer, was interested in means of speedier travel. He made an *intentional discovery* of liquid fuel for rockets. Applications of his physics knowledge led to laboratory success.

The science teacher is alert to children's comments, questions, and behavior in assessing or evaluating instruction. A pupil's question can lead to one or more experiments, as will be noted in the chapters that follow. The strategy of knowing when to give a verbal answer to a pupil's question and when to guide the pupil into discovery or inquiry is an art that varies with different children, classes, topics, and teachers. The decision is made by the teacher in terms of the objectives being sought and whether there is available time for balancing the menu of many learning requirements.

Observation in Evaluation

The teacher needs to observe children in preschool and in the lower grades to evaluate pupil achievement in science. To see how a child reacts to picking up a paper clip with a magnet for the first time, or how he can heat water in a paper dish without burning the paper container, can give the teacher a feeling of a successful experience. More important, the child has a feeling of achievement or accomplishment. Teacher observation of pupil activity in the class is a vital process in evaluating pupil achievement. The teacher observes pupil success, satisfaction, a genuine interest and a desire to learn more.

Nonreaders will look at and play with picture books, puzzles, toys, games, and living things including home pets. Teachers will elicit comments and discussion involving play activities from the children. Questions raised by children will also suggest to the teacher how much learning occurs. Some questions are analytical; others will cause children to conduct research for the answers.

Self-evaluation by the learner is most important. Children should experience success in handling, constructing, and manipulating materials that suggest scientific concepts or understandings. They will observe other children perform learning activities and will learn from classmates. The self-evaluation of experiencing success in being able to make a noise from using a buzzer is a significant process in observation and evaluation. Simply asking children to relate what they learned from an experience will reveal much about pupil concept development.

Interpretation and Evaluation

Children enjoy interpreting natural phenomena. Questions such as, "Where does snow go in the winter?" "What is a cloud?" "Why is the sky blue?" "What makes rain?" will provoke various interpretations in the explanations given by other children. Both the questions and the interpretations serve as an intelligent basis for evaluation of instruction by the teacher.

Pupil-made and teacher-made demonstrations can provide a wide spectrum of interpretation. First, the children should recognize the difference between an observation and an interpretation. Second, the children should provide the interpretation for the observed phenomenon. For example, an object resembles an ice cube and it floats in a glass of liquid. Some of the pupils will immediately proceed to give explanations (interpretations) without making careful observations. Some will say the object is an ice cube because it looks like one. Others will say the liquid is water because it looks like water. A few students will detect an odor from the liquid and will say kerosene. One youngster will say it is alcohol. Another will notice that what looked like an ice cube is not melting. The pupils can suggest different combinations of testing the proposed hypotheses. Try it in oil, water, kerosene, or alcohol. The inquiry or problem-solving approach is also used for evaluation as well as instruction.

Evaluation— Integral Part of Instruction

The most significant methods of teaching science may be the techniques used by the teacher during evaluation. The instructional procedures call for determining at frequent intervals the degree of retention or understanding on the pupil's part. Evaluation becomes a continuous process throughout the lesson with pupil-teacher questions and answers. The teacher observes pupil behavior in the classroom as part of the evaluation process. Pupils in the upper grades and in middle school write on the board or in notebooks at their seats. They are given pencil-and-paper tests; homework is discussed. These procedures all constitute the total evaluation process without necessarily considering the improvement of instruction.

What progress do children show they have made at any given stage of development? Do brighter students show their ability and readiness for advanced work? Do slow learners demonstrate their difficulties? For example, in the lower grades, have the children understood the addition and subtraction of numbers before being able to read the changing temperature on a thermometer? The teacher may have to determine if the pupils can subtract before it can be noted that they can read thermometers. This determination of progress toward the development of objectives is a continuous evaluation procedure. The teacher learns how much diagnostic or remedial instruction is needed by the slow learners. It also helps the teacher plan the new and advanced work for average and bright students.

Assuming other factors are the same, is one of the methods of teaching (discussion, laboratory, problem solving) more effective toward developing the objectives? Perhaps the laboratory method is better than a demonstration method for teaching children how to make a thermometer or a barometer. A laboratory test based on performance of skills and production of the instrument (thermometer or barometer) would serve as a better means of evaluation of this objective. If certain objectives such as skills have not been obtained by the use of a specific method of teaching, either a different method should be employed or the basic objectives reexamined. Can provisions be made for individualized instruction? Evaluation, therefore, is a continuous and integral part of instruction that enables the teacher to validate the objectives, content, and methods of teaching. Evaluation as defined by Wiley "consists of the collection and use of information concerning changes in pupil behavior to make decisions about an educational program."[4] This demands more than the use of most of the conventional tests being used.

Teacher-made tests   Good pencil-and-paper tests can provide good learning situations. Evaluation of instruction can be improved by making tests good learning situations. In some instances, these tests may resemble play-type or game situations. It should be fun to experience tests that instruct rather than threaten children. For example, the display of different types of leaves, insects, and situations where pupils are asked to identify on paper as they move around the classroom could become an enriching experience.

Teacher-made Tests—Samples   Do your tests:

1.   actually measure what they are supposed to measure? This is validity. It is invalid to give sample items on a test to pupils where no such instruction was given. On the other hand, if the teacher is testing for applications or problem solving, then this type of question is on a higher level and provisions for including lower-level questions should be made.

[4] Ibid., p. 261.

For example, in the seventh grade a teacher taught that on a hot day when you ride the bicycle rapidly, the volume of air in the tire increases. The teacher taught the pupils Charles's law that states that the volume of air is directly proportional to the temperature provided that the pressure remains unchanged. No instruction was given on how to solve a problem involving a mathematical application of Charles's law. It would be valid to ask the pupils to state Charles's law and to test their comprehension by asking them to give an illustration such as the bicycle tire.

In a valid test a good sampling of content is included with respect to the various parts of the subject covered. The understanding of a law or a concept as found in part 2 is more complex than the mere retention of isolated facts. In the section following these nine criteria, specific examples will be given of test items that vary with the objectives and give greater meaning "to understand the concept."

Finally, a *valid* test should be made for appropriate levels of difficulty. It is difficult to imagine the same test items being suitable for children in elementary school, high school, and college. The test maker is concerned with test items to account for different abilities of pupils within the same class. The slow, average, and fast learners may be able to state Charles's law. The comprehension test items may be appropriate for most pupils. The fast learners may be able to solve mathematical problems where they apply Charles's law, while slow and average learners may experience difficulty.

2. show consistent results in other similar classroom situations, using the same tests?

Tests merely serve to sample pupils' knowledge. If another test of equal level of difficulty is administered to the same pupils, will they receive similar grades or ratings on both tests? If yes, then the test is considered reliable.

For example, do tests administered at different times have equal numbers of items reflecting the sampling of knowledge, comprehension, translation, interpretation, extrapolation, application, analysis, synthesis, and ability to judge? If the first test concentrates on knowledge where specific facts, categories, definitions and generalizations are given, the same pupil may obtain a very different score from a second test that emphasizes applications, analysis, and synthesis.

3. become scheduled frequently so that no one test assumes too much importance?

Pupils can become easily discouraged if they learn that the final grade for a marking period is the average of all tests, especially if they obtain an extremely low score on one test. Are pupils encouraged to make up tests without penalty?

4. enable pupils to measure their own progress by comparing the same pupil's change at different stages?

Pretests and posttests on a given unit of instruction will show the degree of achievement. Otherwise, the pupil may have acquired the knowledge in a previous class, and the teacher may assume that he learned everything in the current class.

5. promote a zest for learning?

Test items should be interesting learning experiences. Pupil success based on good ratings obtained on tests will promote learning. Pupils enjoy maintaining success if they are encouraged to achieve good results. The teacher should review test results with the pupils to promote a zest for learning.

6. allow students to understand the purpose of these tests?

Students should be aware that good tests are learning devices and are not limited merely to obtaining a grade. Some tests will perhaps be used to reinforce a skill. This type of objective should be made clear to the pupils. For example, the ability to interpret graphs and the ability to construct a pictorial graph are different types of abilities. Pupils should be informed of the reasons for giving a specific test.

7. set levels of achievement that are reasonable?

Unfortunately an occasional teacher maintains that he raises his standards of instruction by giving difficult tests to cause most of his pupils to fail. Pupil success should be based on reasonable criteria of achievement.

8. promote additional learning?

No one test could really be final in the sense that there is no additional learning. Questions that arise from good test items after they are scored should be discussed and will usually promote further learning.

9. show pupil weaknesses as well as achievements?

Good test items will help both pupils and teacher to identify weaknesses such as lack of knowledge such as definitions, or whether pupils lack other abilities such as applications or analysis.

1. *Knowledge of specific facts*

Examples of Test Items of Various Categories

Number of annual rings at *base of the trunk* of an old tree	(a) is greater than (b) is less than (c) is same as	number of annual rings at point *halfway up the trunk* of the same tree.

SOURCE: Benjamin S. Bloom et al., *Taxonomy of Educational Objectives, Handbook I: Cognitive Domain* (New York: David McKay, 1956), pt. 2.

2. *Knowledge of conventions*

   Magnetic poles are usually named:
   1. plus and minus
   2. red and blue
   3. east and west
   4. north and south
   5. anode and cathode

3. *Knowledge of classification and categories*

   The stages in the life history of the housefly are, in order:
   1. larva, egg, pupa, adult
   2. pupa, larva, egg, adult
   3. pupa, egg, larva, adult
   4. egg, larva, adult, pupa
   5. egg, larva, pupa, adult

4. *Knowledge of methodology*

   When the scientist is confronted with a problem, his first step toward solving it should usually be to:
   1. construct or purchase equipment
   2. perform an experiment
   3. draw conclusions
   4. urge other scientists to cooperate with him in working it out
   5. gather all available information on the subject

5. *Comprehension*—translation from one level of abstraction to another

   When a current is induced by the relative motion of a conductor and a magnetic field, the direction of the induced current is such as to establish a magnetic field that opposes the motion. This principle is illustrated by:
   a. a magnet attracting a nail
   b. an electric generator or dynamo
   c. the motion of a compass needle

d. an electric doorbell

6. *Application*

BEHAVIOR. This adaptation of a Progressive Education Association item requires the student to select the appropriate principles and extrapolate beyond the situation given. The principle must be drawn from memory in this essay-type item.

SITUATION. The situation, while probably not within the direct experience of all, is at least within their vicarious experience. It could be considered as a new slant on a fairly common phenomenon.

John prepared an aquarium as follows: He carefully cleaned a 10-gallon glass tank with salt solution and added a few inches of fine washed sand. He rooted several stalks of weed (*elodea*) taken from a pool and then filled the aquarium with tap water. After waiting a week he stocked the aquarium with ten 1-inch goldfish and three snails. The aquarium was then left in a corner of the room. After a month the water had not become foul and the plants and animals were in good condition. Without moving the aquarium he sealed a glass top on it.

What prediction, if any, can be made concerning the condition of the aquarium after a period of several months? If you believe a definite prediction can be made, make it and then give your reasons. If you are unable to make a prediction for *any* reason, indicate why you are unable to make a prediction (give your reasons).°

7. *Analysis* (based on reading a passage in the test booklet)

Which of the following is an assumption, specific to this

° Adapted from Test 1.3B, "Application of Principles in Science," Progressive Education Association, Evaluation in the Eight-Year Study (Chicago: University of Chicago Press, 1940).

experiment, that was made in the determination of the charge?

1. The force of gravity is the same whether the drops are charged or not.
2. Opposite charges attract each other.
3. Only a single charge is present on a drop.
4. The mass of a drop is equal to its density times its volume.
5. None of these.

8. *Synthesis*—derivation of a set of abstract relations

The formulation of reasonable hypotheses.° A housing concern has made some experiments on methods of heating houses. A room was constructed with walls that could be heated or refrigerated at the same time that air of any temperature was being circulated through the room. Several individuals were asked to record their sensations as the conditions were varied as follows:

Trial	Wall Temperature	Air Temperature	Sensations
1	85° F.	85° F.	Uncomfortably hot
2	85	50	Uncomfortably hot
3	70	85	Comfortable
4	70	70	Comfortable
5	70	50	Comfortable
6	50	50	Very cold
7	50	70	Uncomfortably cold
8	50	85	Cold

How can you explain the sensation of coldness by a person in a room where the air temperature is 85° and

°Adapted from *The Measurement of Understanding*, Forty-fifth Yearbook of the National Society for the Study of Education, Part I (Chicago: University of Chicago Press, 1946.), p. 118.

the wall temperature is 50°? Consider the following questions and organize your thinking under the outline given below.

(a) Make all the suggestions you can which you believe will explain why a person is cold in a room where the air temperature is 85° and the wall temperature is 50°. Give your reasons as to why you believe each of these suggestions will explain the phenomenon.

(b) What kinds of evidence would you want to collect which would enable you to decide among your suggested hypotheses?

(c) Now go over the suggestions which you have made above and select the one which you believe to be the "best" explanation and give your reasons for your selection.

9. *Evaluation*

Jane is faced with the problem of selecting material for a school dress. The dress will receive lots of wear and will be laundered frequently. Which of the fabrics would be her best choice? (The test should include examples of fabrics, including some rayons. This would allow more reasons to be given below.) Check the qualities the fabric you choose possesses which make it superior for Jane's purpose.

The teacher may be interested in acquiring pupil opinions in terms of which the following items are "most helpful," "helpful," or "of little help":

Pupil Opinionnaire of Learning Situations

1. If I ask questions in class.
2. If I recite in class.
3. If the teacher asks the questions.

4. If other pupils recite.
5. If the teacher performs a demonstration.
6. If the teacher conducts an experiment.
7. If I write the demonstration in my notebook.
8. If the teacher explains ideas and asks questions.
9. If the class visits a museum or other place of scientific interest.
10. If the teacher shows a good science film.
11. If I make a science project.
12. If I keep a good science notebook.
13. If I do a science demonstration in class.
14. If I do experiments in class.
15. If I read a science book in class.
16. If I read a science book at home.
17. If the teacher asks my ideas about scientific experiments.
18. If my teacher asks me ways of how to solve a problem.
19. If I am asked to bring in science things for "show and tell."
20. If I am asked to bring in newspaper and magazine pictures about science.

Evaluation Through Observation

The teacher observes children at play and at work. Playing with science materials can show a varying degree of interest and enjoyment as children react to materials in the environment. For example, younger children may reflect their eagerness to play with water and sand. Ideas about density, floating objects, properties of dryness and wetness become important concepts to preschool children. A teacher can observe the coordination of pupils as they pour water into bottles or other containers, close and open boxes, or fit objects in scientific play toys into their appropriate spaces.

As children mature they still want to have a feeling of accomplishment or achievement, whether a good grade on the test or the satisfaction of mastering a skill such as making a buzzer ring or an electric bulb glow. As children are encouraged by success, greater interest usually develops. This continued feeling of achievement can encourage children to develop greater interests in science. A constructive form of evaluation by pupil and teacher will nourish further learning of science—especially when based on pupil success.

PART **II**

SCIENCE
CONCEPTS
AND
LEARNING
ACTIVITIES

10

LIVING PLANTS

Grades K–2

Concepts

1. Some plants are big and others are small.
2. Plants have leaves, stems, roots, and sometimes flowers.
3. Plants need many things from the soil.
4. Each part of a plant has a specific job to do.
5. Seeds need water in order to grow.
6. In the fall, many plants lose their leaves.
7. New leaves and flowers grow in the spring.
8. Fruits, berries, and nuts ripen during the summer.
9. Plants are used for food, clothing, and shelter.
10. Plants grow in different places.

Grades 3–5

11. Green plants make their own food.

12. To make food, plants use carbon dioxide and water with the help of light.
13. Flowers produce seeds.
14. A seed contains a baby plant.
15. Roots grow downward in soil and leaves grow upward toward the sun.
16. Liquids travel to all parts of a plant.

Grades 6–8

17. Photosynthesis changes carbon dioxide and water into sugar and oxygen in the presence of light.
18. Photosynthesis is a food-making process in green (chlorophyl-bearing) plants.
19. In leaves, glucose may be changed to starch.
20. Special structures in higher plants absorb and transport water and other liquids throughout the plants.
21. Green plants respire twenty-four hours a day.
22. Using simple inorganic substances, many plants can produce carbohydrates, fats, and proteins.
23. Auxins are hormones that promote plant growth.
24. Plants respond to light, chemicals, gravity, temperature, and water.

Concept Formation and the Spiral Curriculum

For the above three levels: (1) K–2, (2) 3–5, (3) 6–8, note the extension of concept formation. For each of the three levels there are concepts related to specialized structures in plants. Each type of structure performs a given task. This type of differentiation or specialization of cells and tissues becomes more evident as pupils examine and study the various parts of a plant: root, stem, leaf, flower, bud, root hairs. The more advanced the plant becomes, the more specialized structures are found. By examining some pond algae (such as the green, hairlike plant called spirogyra), pupils can determine if roots and stems are found in such simple pond-dwelling plants.

Examine the concepts dealing with plant structures:

2. Plants have leaves, stems, roots, and sometimes flowers.
4. Each part of a plant has a specific job to do.

(*Note:* The above concepts may appear in many science syllabi. Children may develop these concepts from environmental experiences in and out of school. They observe the external parts of a plant. Not all children may have had an opportunity to observe algae, mosses, ferns, fungi, and seed plants. In the next section under learning activities, including experiments, children should be given opportunities to observe, experiment, relate, and discuss their findings which will help them formulate the concepts 2, 4, 16, and 20.)

For the upper grades and middle school level, the following concepts on specialization of structures were stated:

16. Liquids travel to all parts of a plant.
20. Special structures in higher plants absorb and transport water and other liquids throughout the plants.

Although the generalization such as differentiation or specialization of tissues to perform specific tasks may seem to be repeated from one grade level to another, the teaching of the topic is entended in depth for many meanings. Therefore the learning process is not mere duplication but a reinforcement of the idea based on greater experiences through experimentation, discovery, observation, and discussion. This approach is used in most of the spiral curricula. From kindergarten through the ninth grade, it is possible that the same topic may appear on three or four different grades.

The nature of the content and the pupil experiences become more complex as the pupil progresses from one grade level to another. Hence the spiral curriculum reinforces with extended meanings based on greater experiences.

Examine the following concepts:

3. Plants need many things from the soil.
11. Green plants make their own food.
12. To make food, plants use carbon dioxide and water with the help of light.
17. Photosynthesis changes carbon dioxide and water into sugar and oxygen in the presence of light.
18. Photosynthesis is a food-making process in green (chlorophyl-bearing) plants.
19. In leaves, glucose may be changed to starch.
22. Using simple inorganic substances, many plants can produce carbohydrates, fats, and proteins.

Demonstrations —Experiments   Depending on the nature of the experiences to which pupils are exposed, the above concepts can arbitrarily be placed on other grade levels. The type of demonstration or experiment that is performed in class or at home will influence the formation of concepts. The above concepts on photosynthesis may be inferred by some children on a given grade level. Other children may formulate several concepts while others state one or two from a given experience.

Some teachers find it helpful to encourage children to state what they know about how plants obtain their food. This can be a useful technique in planning instruction more effectively by including learning activities that will produce newer, or extended concepts. This approach can also assist the teacher in correcting misconceptions held by the children. Even if pupils formulate incorrect hypotheses, the teacher can say, "Let's find out," or, "We shall soon discover if that's right."

Photosynthesis

Some responses to the problem of how plants obtain their food were given by children of different ages:

"A man feeds plants."

"A farmer gives them fertilizer."

"They make their own food."

"Leaves make starch."

"Roots absorb minerals from the soil."

"Plants don't eat."

"Plants get fed through the soil."

Any or several of the concepts can be used as the initial phase for introducing a series of demonstrations and/or experiments.

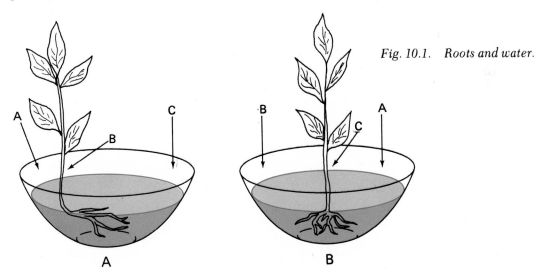

Fig. 10.1. Roots and water.

In fig. 10.1, A and B, twenty drops of water were given to each of the young seedlings for ten days. Both roots are

Learning Activities

growing in the soil. According to these illustrations, what observation do you make about the growing of the roots?

At what point, A or B or C in these diagrams, was the daily water added?

Water was added at point C, suggesting that roots grow toward the water.

What would happen to both plants if from the eleventh to the twentieth day water drops were poured daily on point A? If you examine the roots after the twentieth day, you will find the roots growing toward point A below in the soil.

Discussion

One pupil asks if water is necessary for these plants to survive. After twenty days, no water is given to one of the plants and within one week he observed that the leaves were wilting. The plant died shortly afterward.

Another pupil asked what would happen if the roots were cut off from one of the plants. He planted the stem with the top five leaves in the same dish. In class discussion some students proposed the following hypotheses:

1. The stem will not develop roots.
2. The stem will develop roots in this dish.
3. The stem will not develop roots unless placed in a suitable mixture such as vermiculite (which may be purchased in a nursery or a variety store).
4. The stem will grow roots if placed in a glass of water for one or two weeks.

After testing all the hypotheses, the following concepts were developed:

1. The top part of a plant (four or five leaves and a piece of stem) can form roots in water or vermiculite and grow into a new plant.
2. Plants are living things that require water.

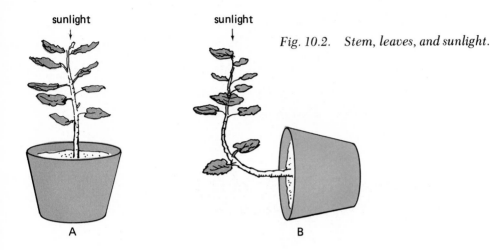

Fig. 10.2. *Stem, leaves, and sunlight.*

3. New plants can be made from old ones by making a
    cutting (stem and a few leaves).
4. Roots grow toward the water.

In fig. 10.2, *A* and *B*, the sun is shining on both plants
from the top. Originally both plants (geranium or coleus)
looked like fig. 10.2*A*, when both plants were in an upright
position. Then the plant in fig. 10.2*B* was placed on its side for
one week. The plant in fig. 10.2B was placed in an upright
position only when it was given water for a few minutes on
three occasions during the week.

Problem   **Problem Solving**

Examine both plants in fig. 10.2, *A* and *B*. What is the
problem?

One pupil says, "I wonder what made this plant grow a
crooked stem and leaves?"

Hypotheses suggested by different pupils included:
"One plant fell on its side and that caused it to grow like it's bent."
"The plant with five leaves is heavier than the one with four leaves so it couldn't grow straight."
"This plant grows toward the sunlight."

Experiment

After discussing several experiments, most of the pupils decided to try this one. A large shoebox with only one open slit permitting sunlight to enter was used for growing the small, "bent" geranium plant (see fig. 10.3).

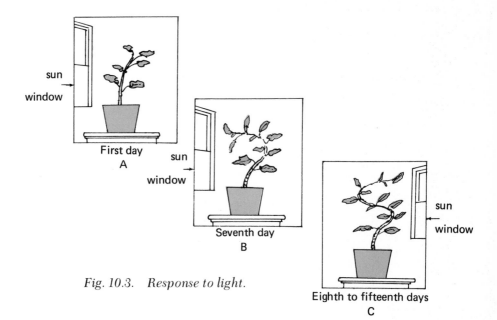

Fig. 10.3. *Response to light.*

Discussion

Study the experiment in fig. 10.3, *A*, *B*, and *C*.

How long was the sunny window on the left side of the shoebox? During this time, what happened to the shape of the stem and growth of the leaves?

At the end of the seventh day, the sunny window on the left side of the shoebox is sealed. A new sunny window is made on the right side of the box and a little higher than the first one. Be sure that the sun is able to enter the sunny window.

One pupil suggested that the plant should be watered every other day for just a minute and the box should be sealed with the exception of the sunny window.

The following concepts were soon developed:

1. The geranium and other green plants grow toward the sunlight.
2. In order to grow toward the sunlight, some green plants, like the geranium, will twist and turn their stems.
3. Plants grow in different places.
4. Roots grow downward in soil and leaves grow upward toward the sun.
5. Plants respond to light.

In the discussion, one pupil asked why it is important for a green plant to have sunlight. One pupil suggested that light is needed for a green plant to make its food. Another pupil said it is important to have light for a green plant to grow. A third pupil said we should find out. The proposed experiment would need a small geranium plant.

Inquiry

Ask the pupils to list the conditions needed (or design the experiment) to find out if green plants need light to grow: same water, temperature, soil, size, heredity. Discuss the importance of having a control. One pupil suggests placing one plant in a dark closet for two weeks. Another proposes that the second plant be placed in direct sunlight. A third pupil might propose a third plant should be away from all sunlight but under a light bulb. Several children design and execute the experiment, and in two or three weeks enough evidence is accumulated to solve the problem.

Perhaps a youngster may suggest that he knows of a potato growing in a dark kitchen drawer; he reports seeing many leaves. Questions pertaining to how long this plant will continue to grow in the dark and the source of food supply in the potato compared with a plant that could make its own food would be suitable for discussion.

Background Information

I. Angiosperms or flowering plants
    A. Develop seeds that are enclosed within the ovary.
    B. Are broad-leaved shrubs and trees, including weeds, grasses, and cereal grains.
    C. Contain roots, leaves, and stems.
        1. *Roots* anchor plant in soil and absorb minerals and water.
        2. *Leaves* are flat and thin and are needed for photosynthesis.
        3. *Stems* support the leaves and flowers and permit liquids to travel up and down the plant.
        4. A *shoot* contains both stem and leaves together.
    D. *Annual* plants live only for a single year.
    E. *Biennial* plants live for two years.
    F. *Perennial* plants live three or more years.
    G. Specialized tissues such as *xylem* and *phloem* conduct the liquids through various parts of plants.
    H. *Stomates* are openings surrounded by *guard cells*

found in leaves and they control the amount of water loss (evaporation) and the exchange of carbon dioxide and oxygen in the plant.

I. The particle size of soil (from smooth or small to rough or larger) such as clay, silt, sand, and gravel will influence the mineral and water content available to plants for nutrition.

    1. *Mineral soil* contains more than 80% (by weight) of solid mineral particles.

    2. *Organic soil* contains more than 20% organic matter.

    3. *Humus* permits a better exchange of water and minerals between plant cells and the soil.

J. Vegetative reproduction (without sexual processes) occurs in most flowering plants by using leaves, stems, and roots.

    1. Most frequently the stem is used to propogate plants.

        a. The tip of a stem with a few leaves, a *cutting*, when placed in water, vermiculite, or moist soil for a few weeks will usually develop roots.

        b. Stems called *runners* creep along the ground and develop roots, as seen in cultivated strawberries.

        c. A twig (*scion*) of one plant, when transferred to a stem of another plant (*stock*) develops into a new plant; this is called *grafting*.

    2. Modified stems or underground stems develop into new plants.

        a. An underground stem that creeps (*rhizome*) may develop roots at the nodes along the length of the rhizome. Iris or sod-forming grasses reproduce by these rhizomes.

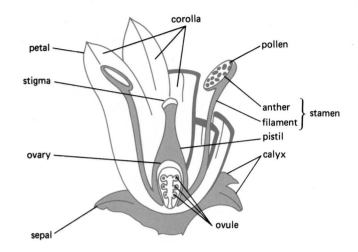

Fig. 10.4. Flower and its parts.

    b. *Tubers* are thickened portions of a rhizome and develop into new plants. Potatoes are examples of tubers.

    c. A stout, very short underground stem is called a *corm* and usually stores enough food to develop into new plants such as crocus or gladiolus.

    d. Corms also include *bulbs*.

K. Flowers and sexual reproduction.

    1. Flowers contain the sexual reproductive structures.

        a. The *pistil* (female part) consists of three externally visible parts: ovary, style, and stigma.

        b. The *stamens* (male organs) consist of a slender filament, anther, and pollen sacs.

        c. The pollen is either blown by wind or carried by an insect from the anther to the stigma of the flower.

d. A pollen grain on the stigma germinates into a tube that grows down through the style and fertilizes the ovules inside the ovary.

e. The fertilized ovules develop into seeds that later are used to germinate into new plants (refer to fig 10.4).

11

ANIMALS AND THEIR SURROUNDINGS

Grades K–2   **Concepts**

1. Animals, like plants, are living things that need air, water, and food.
2. Animals depend on plants and other animals for their food.
3. Various kinds of animals live in different environments.
4. Animals obtain their food in different ways.
5. Animals produce young that usually resemble the parents.

Grades 3–5

6. Animals that survive are able to compete for food in their environment.

7. Animals are classified according to similarities in structure and function.
8. Animals behave and adjust to different conditions.

Grades 6–8

9. Simple-type animals reproduce by asexual means.
10. Sexual reproduction occurs in animals when a sperm cell fertilizes an egg cell.
11. Animals maintain their kind through several reproductive processes.
12. The development of locomotion varies in different types of animals.
13. In order for animals to inhabit land they require a good supply of water.
14. Specialized cells enable animals to respond to various changes that occur in the environment.

Concept Formation

In the concepts numbered 1, 2, 6, and 13 the emphasis is placed on various requirements of living animals: air, water, food, and a satisfactory environment. In the lower grades, children will verbalize their observations about pets at home. They know that their dog, cat, fish, bird, or turtle needs food in order to survive. Picture books and magazine and newspaper articles read by the teacher in class, along with experiences in playing with and caring for animals, will contribute to the formation of these concepts.

By the time children are in the upper grades and in junior high school, they will have had extensive experience in either caring for pets, observing animals in their natural habitats, or playing with some animals belonging to a friend. Soon children will discover that in the natural habitat animals compete for food. Ecological considerations are introduced along with structural adaptations. If an animal is structurally suited to escape from a predator, its survival rate is much higher. How fast can a bird fly away from its natural enemy and still obtain food? How many ants develop from their eggs? Would there be enough food for all ants if all eggs were hatched? How would all of the insects affect us in our homes, in the garden, and on the farm?

The concepts numbered 3, 8, and 12 relate to ecology, plant-animal, and animal-animal interrelationships and their ability to adjust to different environmental conditions. In the upper grades, a study is made of specialized structures for locomotion where animals are able to change their location for survival. Learning experiences through the employment of pictures, movies, slides, and field trips to museums and zoos will provide understanding of animals that live in the desert, in the ocean, in fresh water, under the soil, on land, and in the air. Within a forest one can compare the types of animals that live on the ground with those that live high in the trees.

The concepts numbered 4, 7, and 14 are formed as one gains an awareness of specialized structures and organs such as teeth, bills, claws, webbed feet, wings, body shape, and other characteristics. The specialized structures for procuring food from different environments frequently upset the balance of living organisms in a community. For example, plant life grows in a pond. Insects thrive in a pond as they eat green plants. Frogs eat insects in the pond and the population of insects diminishes. Along comes a water snake and eats frogs. Temporarily, the population of insects increases due to the smaller number of frogs eaten by the snakes. Yet, if some of the snakes are found on the bank of the pond, the hawk can swoop down on the snakes and change the population in the pond. With fewer snakes, more frogs will appear and fewer insects will be noticed. Changes in popu-

A killer whale has very sharp teeth to catch and eat large animals such as porpoises, seals, and penguins.

lation of different species in a given community occur constantly. The structures or organs of food acquisition, locomotion, and protection of animals in a particular habitat may affect the balance of nature. This type of discussion can be encouraged in the classroom by displaying a picture such as that of the osprey on page 190. The other illustrations can provide stimulation to find out what eagles, whales, and roadrunners eat. What special organs do they have to capture animals that they use for food? What changes occur in the types of living things that are found in a given community?

The concepts numbered 5, 9, 10, and 11 pertain to asexual and sexual reproduction as well as an introduction to heredity. From storytelling, picture observation, and experi-

A roadrunner has a very strong beak and powerful legs for chasing down animals such as lizards and snakes for food.

ences with pets at home, children in the lower grades can be introduced to these concepts pertaining to the perpetuation of species. Children may observe the mating of dogs, tropical fish, and other living things. Some will have observed the hatching of birds' eggs and how the mother bird feeds her young. Common observations in some homes are the birth of puppies. The beginning of life can serve as a beautiful introduction to sex education.

In the upper grades, children may have white mice, hamsters, gerbils, or other animals as pets at home. These pupils will soon discover the number of days of pregnancy in a female, how many offspring in a litter, the frequency with which litters are produced, and the characteristics that are passed on from parents to offspring. The excitement of caring for these animals at home and in the classroom may well serve as a very strong source of stimulating the learning of science. Not only are cognitive objectives developed but also important attitudes and skills are formed.

Display Pictures

Display pictures of various animals showing:
1. Animals have special parts of the body—wings for flying, legs for walking or crawling, fins and webbed toes for swimming.
2. Animals have structures to capture and eat food such as the claws in an eagle, the strong beak of a bird, and the powerful legs and teeth of a lion.
3. Animals eat different parts of a plant: squirrels eat nuts, rabbits eat carrots (roots), birds eat seeds, some worms eat tomatoes, cows eat grass.
4. Animals are suited to live best in certain places:

An osprey or fish hawk has a powerful beak and strong claws to catch fish from a pond.

moles and earthworms under ground, birds in the air above ground, lizards and snakes in the desert, fish in the water, and deer in a forest.

Things to Collect and Observe

Pupils and teachers collect pictures of various animals and encourage "show and tell" sessions. Magazines can be used for appropriate pictures for storytelling. Displays and collections of photographs that show specific concepts related to food gathering, locomotion, adaptation to different environments, and resemblance of young animals to their parents should be varied from time to time.

Children who do not have a pet at home can relate stories such as, "If I had a parakeet at home, I would take care of him by . . ." In place of a parakeet, other children may prefer a parrot, a dog, a cat, or fish. Children who do

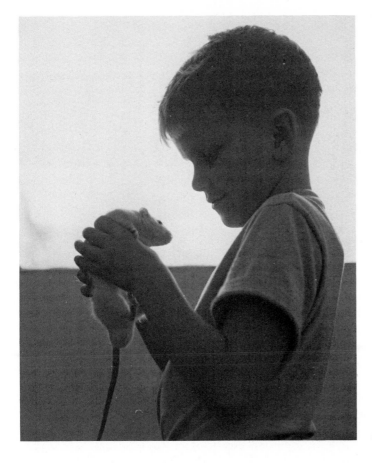

Observing animal behavior.

have pets at home can relate many experiences pertaining to the development of concepts on their care and feeding.

Field trips or visits to local pet shops, zoo, aquarium, and museum will stimulate much curiosity about the habitats of various animals and their problems of survival. Picture postcards, picture books, and pamphlets about animals in these places are usually available for purchase. Some children may wish to purchase one or more picture cards of their favorite animals. After the visits, a discussion such as why seals get so many fish to eat in the zoo may lead to other interesting observations and explanations.

Children have favorite photographs at home of places

and animals. Some may also have toy animal models or dolls. These materials foster inquiry when brought to class.

At appropriate times during the year children may bring certain pets such as white mice, guinea pigs, and hamsters to school, and a temporary zoo may be established when teaching these concepts about animals. Pupils can educate other pupils on feeding habits, behavior, and other interesting facts about their favorite pets. A few children may collect grasshoppers, earthworms, tadpoles, frogs, caterpillars, and bugs. These can be placed in special containers or moist fish tanks where children can observe and study their development. They may wish to experiment with different kinds of food requirements and effects on their growth and health.

Learning Activities
(Grades 3–5)

For the concept, *animals that survive are able to compete for food in their environment,* the following activities are suggested. Locate an anthill or a beehive, or purchase one of these colonies from a science supply house. Over a period of several weeks, pupils can observe the queens and their tremendous body size before the eggs are hatched. After the eggs are hatched, observation of competition for food will reveal interesting behavior of these insects. Discuss what happens in the woods when an ant gets lost and approaches a spider web. Is there enough food in the ant colony or bee colony to feed all the offspring?

Another example of competition for food exists between different animals. For example, the vole or meadow mouse is found on farm land and on ranches. Each female vole may have up to seventeen litters per year with four to nine offspring per litter. At this rate, one might expect the farm or ranch to be overwhelmed by these creatures. Although

The vole.

the voles have enough food in the forms of grass and other plants, competition for survival exists. Before voles are a year old, many are eaten by foxes, skunks, weasels, wolves, snakes, hawks, owls, bears, and other animals. From these discussions and observations of various types of animals including the bees and ants, pupils will formulate many concepts related to behavior, adjustment, and reproduction of animals.

Environmental conditions such as temperature, moisture, plant life, and light and their effects on caterpillars may be studied experimentally by children in the classroom. Each child may have one or more caterpillars to observe. The children decide which plants are to be grown in very large jars. A caterpillar is placed into each jar. A record of moisture, temperature, light, and the availability of food (leaves) is kept for each caterpillar and its variable (conditions such as moisture and so on). The design of this experiment and the hypotheses formulated by the children constitute important steps in the inquiry approach. This procedure will enable children to continue to use the problem-solving or inquiry approach in more advanced courses in the secondary school.

Another simple animal of interest to children is the common earthworm. Several experiments by children can be encouraged that show how an earthworm adjusts and behaves in different environmental conditions. After a heavy rainfall, earthworms will usually come near or to the surface of the soil, because worms need air as well as moisture. By placing a worm on a flat dish with about 1/16 inch of water, observe the movement and direction of the worm. What happens if the soil is too acidic? How do earthworms behave? Place a drop of lemon juice or vinegar in the water at the end of the dish, and observe if the worm goes to or away from this acidic substance. If a drop of vinegar is placed immediately in front of the worm's head region, note its behavior. Pupils may suggest other stimuli to study the worm's behavior. Perhaps salt, sugar, some spice, or other proposals can be made by the children. A discussion of the hypotheses and design of the experiment can be made first, or an evaluation can be made after the experiment is performed. For inquiry or "process approach" teaching, the pupils should identify the problem, propose hypotheses, test them by experiment, and evaluate the observations before a conclusion is made.

Learning Activities
(Grades 6–8)

The concepts listed for this grade level suggest more sophisticated experiments and a greater degree of open-ended laboratory work. For example, the planarian worm can be used to demonstrate regeneration by asexual means. One of the basic questions pupils will ask is how much of a piece of planarian is needed for it to grow back into a full worm. The same question may be asked of the starfish.

Recall the story of how starfish upset the fishermen's nets. As the starfish clung to and tore the nets, when the fishermen brought the nets to the surface, the fishermen would cut each starfish in two or three pieces and would throw them back into the water. The following season had many more starfish in the ocean because of regeneration; a half starfish can develop into a new starfish.

Open-ended laboratory that emphasizes inquiry should occur as a result of pupil questions. Such questions usually relate to how much of a piece of worm will regenerate into a whole worm. Does a piece of the head region need to be part of the worm for regeneration to occur? Is the same true for a starfish? As a result of laboratory experimentation both in and out of school, pupils will discover the answers to these questions. At the same time, they will have been given an opportunity to formulate several hypotheses about how much and what part or parts of the animal are needed for regeneration. They will also have designed several experiments to test their proposed hypotheses. This inquiry or process approach represents the open-ended laboratory procedure as opposed to the conventional "cookbook recipe" approach.

Field Trips

Field trips enable pupils to study the social insects such as bees and ants, where concepts relating to reproduction, specialization, and organism-environment interaction occur. In urban communities, the teacher can order a bee or ant colony from biological supply houses. Pupils can see the problems of individual insects in obtaining food and water. They will observe the hatching of eggs and how the young are cared for by special individuals within the colony.

In the case of a bee colony, little dishes of sugar and water at varied distances from the hive will attract bees. The bee that discovers the outside dish of sugary water will return to the hive and communicate the information about the sugary water and its location to other bees. The language of communication is by means of a tail-wagging dance. If the hive has glass walls, the bee dances can be observed as in commercial beehives. The tail-wagging dance consists of a figure-8 with two joining loops. Experiments showed that if the food such as sugary water was further away from the hive, the dance was performed more slowly.

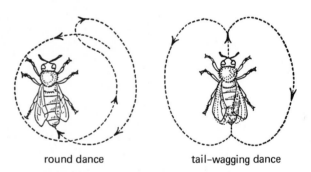

round dance   tail–wagging dance

Fig. 11.1.   The bee dance.

The need for water by a land animal is demonstrated by the behavior of millipedes. In dry weather, they migrate and increase their population in wet depressions where they feed on decaying leaves and other organic matter. Millipedes need moisture and thrive best in poorly drained forests. They have higher reproduction when the seasons are wet.

Place a few drops of water in a corner of a glass plate. Place an earthworm or a millipede in the center of the plate. Repeat this procedure at least ten times with several other earthworms or millipedes. Observe the direction in which the animals move. Using other earthworms or millipedes place each one on a glass plate without any drops of water. Ask the pupils why this procedure is used and why it should be repeated. As a result of this discussion, pupils should understand the need for a control in any experiment.

The need for moisture or water, changes in locomotion and structural adaptation, and reproduction can be demonstrated by cultivating frogs from eggs. In early spring, children may be able to locate a jellylike mass (colorless with large black specks) in a freshwater pond. Otherwise, it is possible to order fertilized frogs' eggs from a supply company and watch their development in a fish tank partially filled with water. Changes in transition from the tadpoles with gills for respiration to the development of frogs with lungs can be observed with much interest. Pupils may wish to keep a day-by-day record of changes in tail length of a tadpole and the development of legs. Contrary to popular opinion, the tails of tadpoles do not fall off; they are absorbed into the body and used for nutrition.

The need for moisture in the adult frog still persists, and it is difficult for a frog to be away from a pond for twenty-four hours or more. Respiration takes place through the skin in a frog as well as in the lungs. The skin needs to be moist to permit exchange of gases during respiration.

Advanced students in the upper grades and in the intermediate school may wish to develop experiments to speed up the development from tadpole to frog. By placing various minute amounts of thyroxin in the tadpole tanks, they can study the change in time needed for the development of a frog. Interesting discussions can develop in which a hormone (e.g., thyroxin) significantly speeds up physical development.

Concept formation pertaining to structural adaptation —from tail to legs (swim to hop) in water to land and from gills to lungs in water to land—becomes evident. In addition, sexual reproduction in a frog can be understood by having pupils dissect preserved frogs. Female and male frogs should be procured for these purposes so that the pupils can identify the reproductive systems in each sex.

The same frog may also be used to study nutrition, circulation, responses, excretion, and anatomical features such as the skeleton and muscles. It is interesting to discuss how a frog catches flying insects with its forked tongue. Also discuss the decrease in mosquitoes and other pests in the area where frogs are found.

Background Information

I. Classification—Animal kingdom

Biologists interpret similar structures in animals and the evidence concerning their kinship as a means of belonging together in a major division. Such evidence arises from studies in embryology, physiology, genetics, and morphology. When new evidence appears, the classification of a particular division or group of animals is modified. Thus it is possible as one examines different textbooks in biology to observe slight modifications in the taxonomy of the animal kingdom. Not all biologists agree on the taxonomy of living organisms because of various interpretations of phylogenetic evidence.

A common expression is "animals with backbones" are vertebrates and "animals without backbones" are invertebrates. This important structural difference is responsible for Subphylum Vertebrata or Invertebrata. Children will play with many invertebrates such as insects, the six-legged animals (grasshoppers, butterflies, moths, ants, and so on). They will also enjoy collecting caterpillars and observing how they spin cocoons to become moths or butterflies.

As an illustration, the following classification would be made for man:

Kingdom Animalia
  Subkingdom Metazoa
    Superphylum Deuterostomia
      Phylum Chordata
        Subphylum Vertebrata
          Class Mammalia
            Subclass Eutheria
              Order Primates
                Genus *Homo*
                  Species *sapiens*

Among the vertebrates commonly found in the woods near ponds are frogs, salamanders, turtles, snakes, field mice, small mammals, and birds. Stimulating learning activities may arise from collecting some of these animals and from providing suitable housing for them in the classroom. Feeding and caring for these living organisms will give children a sense of responsibility as well as teach them the habits and behavior patterns.

II. Classification and structure
    A. Protozoans: one-celled, acellular, or colonial organisms; amoeba, paramecium (microscopic)
    B. Sponges
        1. Sessile (do not move about, attached to rock or stick)
        2. Body with many pores or holes—openings that lead to canals that make up the gastrovascular cavity
    C. Coelenterates: jellyfish, hydra, corals
        1. Radially symmetrical body
        2. Nematocysts or stinging cells in body
        3. Only one opening into gastrovascular cavity

through which food enters and undigested food exits

D. Flatworms: planaria, tapeworms, flukes
   1. Appearance of an excretory system called flame cells
   2. Single opening in digestive tract
E. Roundworms: ascarides, hookworms
   1. Mostly parasitic in man
   2. Two openings from digestive tract: mouth and anus
F. Segmented worms: earthworms, sandworms, leeches
   1. Ringlike segments
   2. A true body cavity (coelom) between the digestive tract and the body wall
   3. Setae or bristles, which are hairlike projections for locomotion, on most segments
G. Arthropods: insects, spiders, crustaceans
   1. Segmented body and appendages
   2. Exoskeleton (hard, crusty skeleton on outside of body)
H. Mollusca: clams, snails, squids
   1. Unsegmented bodies
   2. Ventral part of body for locomotion—foot
I. Echinoderms: starfish, sea urchins, sea cucumbers
   1. Water-vascular system and tube feet
   2. Radial symmetry
J. Chordates: man and other vertebrates
   1. Notochord
   2. Dorsal hollow nerve cord
   3. Bilateral symmetry

III. Major biological concepts
   A. Life comes only from living things.
      1. Previously held theories that worms, flies,

rats, and so on would appear by spontaneous generation were disproved.

 2. Although some scientists still argue whether viruses should be considered living, the reproduction of viruses needs preexisting viruses.

B. Living things are made up of cells and cell products.

C. Molecules of DNA (deoxyribonucleic acid) or genes constitute the physicochemical basis for transmitting traits from one generation to the next.

D. Living things have descended gradually from previously existing organisms.

 1. Darwin presented much evidence in his book, *The Origin of Species.*

 2. Darwin's theory of natural selection states:

  a. More offspring are produced by most species than can survive.

  b. As a result of great numbers born in a given population, there is great competition for food.

  c. A struggle for existence goes on.

  d. "Survival of the fittest."

  e. More advantageous characteristics are transmitted to surviving individuals.

E. Enzymes, hormones, and vitamins affect the growth and development of organisms.

F. Plants and animals are interdependent in given communities and the balance of nature can be upset by man's use of the environment or the introduction of a new species or environmental condition.

IV. Understanding the structures and functions of common animals

A. Jellyfish

   1. Mostly transparent, open-umbrella-shaped animals that live in seawater
   2. Mouth located on the underside of the body, surrounded by tentacles
   3. Stinging cells found in tentacles
   4. Size: very small to as wide as seven feet
   5. Movement by floating or swimming (waving its body)
   6. Lives on sea animals, mostly small fish that swim into its tentacles

B. Common earthworm

   1. Body is divided into segments that look like rings.
   2. Digestive system consists of a tube beginning with the mouth and ending with the anus. A crop and gizzard are slight swellings of the digestive tube that perform several of the functions of a stomach and teeth in higher animals.
   3. Blood is pumped by pulsations of a large, dorsal blood vessel and five pairs of loops ("hearts") that connect with the ventral blood vessel. Hemoglobin, the oxygen-carrying red substance, is found in the blood.
   4. In almost every segment is a pair of nephridia (coiled tubules) that opens to the outside of the segment and removes waste products.
   5. The nervous system consists of a "primitive brain" or cerebral ganglion connected to other ganglia, passing around the pharynx and hooking up with two parallel nerve cords running the length of the body. Specialized nerve cells or ganglia are found in each of the segments.

6. Sperm and eggs are found in the same earthworm (hermaphrodite). Two earthworms are needed to fertilize the eggs, which are then deposited in the soil, hatch, and develop into young earthworms.

7. Respiration occurs through the moist skin (moisture is essential) as oxygen is absorbed and carbon dioxide given off.

8. Movement is achieved by two sets of muscles (one set makes the worm long and thin; the other makes it short and thick) and bristles or setae sticking out from the sides and undersides of all body segments except the first and last.

9. Earthworms help farmers by keeping soil loose and porous and permitting air and water to enter plant roots.

C. Starfish

1. Star-shaped, it usually has five arms that come together at center of its body.

2. It is not a fish and it does not have a head.

3. It lives in the ocean.

4. Many tiny spinelike structures cover the body and arms.

5. On the underside, in the center of the body, is the mouth that leads into the stomach.

6. Tube feet (hundreds of little tubes) are found on the undersurface of each arm.

7. With suction-cup-like action, the starfish pushes the tube feet strongly on both sides of shell of a clam. The starfish crawls on top of the clam and pulls on it till the clam tires, opens its shell, and falls prey to the starfish.

8. After digestion, the starfish ejects the wastes from its stomach through the mouth.

9. A starfish is either male or female; the female may deposit more than one million eggs in a season.

10. Fertilization occurs in the water where both eggs and sperm are discharged.

11. In addition to sexual reproduction, starfish reproduce by regeneration when a piece of arm and center of its body remain intact.

D. Snail

1. Two tentacles protrude from head.

2. Tentacles are withdrawn upon touching.

3. In some snails an eye is found on tip of each tentacle.

4. It crawls on a large foot.

5. Some snails have lungs in place of gills.

6. A "tongue" picks off food in aquaria by eating algae, bacteria, and dead or decaying matter.

E. Grasshopper

1. Mouth parts include jaws that move from side to side as they chew plants, especially grain crops.

2. Two sets of wings; the back pair, folded lengthwise, resemble a fan.

3. Large pair of rear legs enable it to jump easily.

4. Rubbing of rear legs against wing veins causes sounds.

5. Incomplete metamorphosis means the grasshopper develops from an egg that is hatched to become a nymph (looks like a young adult without wings) and then becomes an adult grasshopper.

F. Moth and butterfly

1. Moth

a. Abdomen usually fat

        b.   Usually has feathery antennae

        c.   Usually flies at night

        d.   At rest, wings horizontal

   2.   Butterfly

        a.   Abdomen usually thin

        b.   Knobs at end of antennae

        c.   Flies during daytime

        d.   At rest, wings vertical

G. Fish

   1.   Fish, along with frogs, snakes, birds, and mammals, are *vertebrates*, animals with backbones.

   2.   Many fish are located in oceans and are called saltwater fish; others live in fresh water such as ponds, lakes, rivers, and brooks.

   3.   The fins on a fish are used to help in swimming, steering, and balancing.

   4.   Because the temperature inside the body of a fish is the same as the water outside its body, it is known as a *cold-blooded* animal.

   5.   Fish have gills for respiration: The water containing dissolved oxygen passes over the gills and the oxygen enters through the thin walls of the blood vessels. The carbon dioxide leaves the blood vessels and goes into the water.

   6.   As gases enter or leave the air bladder, fish can rise or sink.

   7.   Reproduction in fish is accomplished first by *spawning*—laying of eggs in the water. Shortly thereafter, a male fish swims over the eggs and sprays *milt*, a liquid containing sperm cells.

   8.   Tropical fish in fresh water, like guppies or swordtails, undergo internal fertilization.

The male deposits sperm cells inside the female's body; the young fish develop internally and are born alive.

H. Reptiles: turtles, lizards, snakes, alligators, crocodiles
   1. Vertebrates with thick, dry, skin covered with scales
   2. Breathe through lungs
   3. Internal fertilization (sperm fertilizes eggs inside body of female)
   4. Cold-blooded animals
   5. Chameleon—a common lizard
      a. Two inches in length with a tail about 3 inches long
      b. Frequently changes color

I. Birds
   1. Vertebrates whose bodies are covered by feathers
   2. Wings for flying and a pair of legs for hopping or walking
   3. Horny beak with no teeth
   4. Internal fertilization
   5. Warm-blooded animals—internal temperature the same regardless of temperature outside the body
   6. Different birds in various types of environments: ponds, marshes, grasslands, tropics, deserts, cities, trees

J. Mammals: dog, cat, rat, cow, horse, man
   1. Hair is found on body.
   2. Mammary glands nurse the young by providing milk.
   3. Some mammals eat only plants and are called *herbivorous*—cow and horse; some eat only animals and are called *carnivorous*—lion and

tiger; others eat both plants and animals and are known as *omnivorous*—man and bear.

K.   Conservation and ecology

1.   Pesticides or insecticides such as DDT kill off not only certain insects but also valuable birds, and over a period of years many small animals.

2.   Over two or three years, the insect becomes immune to the pesticide and survives, but the pesticide may poison the soil for up to thirty years or more.

3.   Some pesticides find their way into our food and bodies. The complete effect of these poisons on humans is still being studied, but it is thought, over a long period of time, much damage is done.

4.   Pesticides as well as garbage disposal wastes and industrial wastes also appear in our streams, rivers, and lakes. The safety of drinking water and the well-being of fish are being threatened. Some fish have already been poisoned in the waters by mercury and other chemicals. Laws are being passed to control the safety of water and clean air.

5.   People must not litter if our environment is to remain safe, healthy, and clean. Recycling and proper garbage disposal are essential.

6.   Air pollution should be controlled by cutting down automobile exhaust and improving the quality and burning of fossil fuels such as coal and oil.

12

THE HUMAN BODY AND GOOD HEALTH

Grades K–2

1. The human body is made up of skin, bone, blood, and organs.
2. Food is needed for energy, work, and growth.
3. Proper care of teeth is essential for good health.
4. A good diet, play, rest, and cleanliness make for good health.

Grades 3–5

5. Good health is a condition that exists when all these systems are working together very well: muscular, skeletal, digestive, circulatory, respiratory, excretory, and nervous systems.
6. A wise selection of foods promotes better health.

7. Digestion of food is the breaking down of large molecules to smaller, simpler ones.
8. Blood circulation and breathing speed up or slow down according to physical activity.
9. Sense organs such as the eyes, ears, and nose require special care to avoid damage.

Grades 6–8

10. A balance of nutritional requirements such as proteins, fats, and carbohydrates promote good health.
11. Nutrients are absorbed in the bloodstream, and waste materials are eliminated from the body.
12. Appropriate tests can be made for the presence of various nutrients in foods.
13. The alimentary canal is a long tube with specialized parts to enable nutrition to take place.
14. The heart pumps blood throughout the body for proper circulation and nutrition.
15. Reproduction provides for the continuation of the human species.
16. Heredity and environment determine the kind of people we become.

Concept Formation

In the concepts numbered 1, 9, 14, and 15, emphasis is placed on structures with lesser emphasis on the functions of structures in the human body. In the lower grades, children are aware of how big, tall, skinny, fat, strong, or weak other children might appear. They ask questions as a result of their observations. Specifically, they wish to know why Johnny is fat and why David can run much faster than the other children. Some children might make fun of others because of physical appearance. Pupil observations and experiences can be directed toward constructive understanding of the anatomy of the human body and the care required for good health. Pictures, picture books, talks by physicians, charts, and models can be used very effectively for the development of these concepts.

In the upper grades, suitable movies and film loops pertaining to the human body are available. Outside activities such as visits to local hospitals and health agencies will also reinforce concepts of anatomy, physiology, and good health. Models of the body may be purchased at scientific supply companies so that pupils may remove and examine various organs such as the heart, liver, and stomach to extend the meaning of these anatomical concepts, teach pupils to locate each organ and its adjacent parts. Older pupils in the intermediate school may dissect a heart or a kidney from a sheep, cow, or pig. Diagrams, ditto sheets, and colorful charts can reinforce formation and understanding of the concepts pertaining to human body structure.

Concepts related to nutrition (numbered 2, 6, 7, 10, 11, 12, and 13) include systems such as digestion, circulation, excretion, and respiration. These concepts are evolved through daily activities and should therefore play a vital role in their teaching. For example, all children are eager to tell which are their favorite foods. Which of these foods have greater food value and which do not help in promoting dental caries might provoke a very stimulating discussion. Informal surveys of friends and relatives with regard to diet and tooth decay might be encouraged as a laboratory activity. Many health and dental charts are available and can be introduced to the class. Dentists may be invited to show the proper care and cleaning of teeth.

Breakfast meals usually create problems at home. An inventory of foods eaten at breakfast by each of the children on a daily and weekly basis might reveal some interesting dietary behavior patterns. How do these foods and nutrition as a whole affect the functioning of the pupil during the course of a day's activity both in and out of school?

In the intermediate school, pupils may list all foods eaten for each meal during a week. An analysis of these foods in terms of what they offer and what the body demands for energy, growth, and repair could be a stimulating activity. Menus may be written on the board or mimeographed (without writing pupils' names). Suggestions for improving nutrition for better health can be offered in class by other pupils under teacher guidance without offending pupils. Pupils will become familiar with foods rich in protein, carbohydrates, and fats. They will recognize that some of these foods offer greater numbers of calories than others. Vitamins and their importance for good health can also be introduced.

Problem Solving

In developing a concept such as *certain chemicals in the mouth help to change starch to sugar,* the teacher may find the problem-solving approach helpful. The teacher relates the following anecdote: John wanted to eat sweet cake with his milk, but there was no cake in the house. John's mother said, "Chew the unsweetened crackers we have, and as you continue to chew slowly, they will become sweet." John questioned this statement. To his surprise, after a while the crackers did taste sweet.

The following equipment is then displayed: sugar-free soda crackers, Lugol's solution, Benedict's solution, test-tube clamp, Bunsen burner, and gas outlet. (Earlier in the course, the pupils had been taught the tests for starch and sugar.) The problem is then formulated by the pupils and several hypotheses are proposed.

The children stated the problem as, "What makes the cracker taste sweet when you chew it?" The hypotheses proposed were:

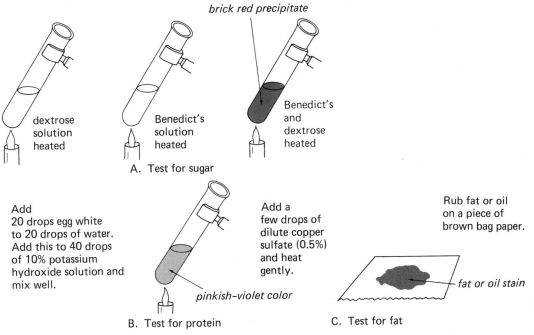

Fig. 12.1. Tests for proteins, carbohydrates, and fats.

1. "John had an upset stomach so the cracker didn't taste sweet right away."
2. "All things taste sweet after you chew them."
3. "Crackers contain starch and change to sugar when you chew them."
4. "Chemicals in the mouth change starch to sugar."

The teacher invites the students into chewing several crackers (in the front of the mouth). Because they already learned how to test for starch and sugar, samples of the chewed crackers are tested. After a discussion in which evaluations are made of these experiments, the pupils conclude, "Digestive juices in the mouth help to change starch to sugar." Students in grades six, seven, or eight will have learned how to test for the basic nutrients: carbohydrates (starch and sugar), proteins, and fats (see fig. 12.1).

Food and Calories

A careful analysis of menus will reveal the amounts of nutrients found in each food. The quantity of food and the nutrients will determine the available number of calories. A young adult man requires about 1,600 calories per day if he remains in bed without eating or moving. This is basal metabolism, the minimum number of calories required to keep alive. At higher temperatures, chemical reactions occur more rapidly in the body. Thus a person with fever usually loses weight. Early adolescents concerned with their appearance, body weight, and figure can apply knowledge gained from a satisfying study of nutrition. From the chart of calories, pupils may determine the number of calories consumed in the course of a day.

Food	Calories
Orange juice (½ cup)	85
Soft-boiled egg (or poached)	75
Dry cereal	100
with cream and sugar and	140
½ banana	50
2 Griddle cakes	200
with syrup and	50
butter (1 tbsp.)	100
2 Sausages	350
Black coffee or tea	0
Toast	75
with butter (tbsp.) and	100
jelly	100
Grapefruit (½)	70
Hard roll	95
Butter (1 tsp. or half a pat)	30
Pineapple juice (4-oz. glass)	55
Cup of cream of tomato or potato soup	250
3 Saltine crackers	45
Fruit cocktail	90

Baked potato	90
Ham and cheese sandwich	350
2 Celery stalks	15
filled with mayonnaise	100
1 Pork or veal chop	235
Duck (4 oz.)	350
Macaroni and cheese (1 cup)	300
1 Lamb chop	130
Beef tongue (3 thin slices)	160
Slice of chicken	100
Eggplant (4 slices)	50
Bouillon or consomme (1 cup)	25
Broccoli (1 large stalk)	40
Carrots ($\frac{1}{2}$ cup)	25
Pineapple slice	50
Green peas ($\frac{1}{2}$ cup)	55
Apple	75
1 Cookie	75
Skim milk (8-oz. glass)	90
Asparagus (6–7 stalks)	20
Summer squash ($\frac{1}{2}$ cup)	15
Canned peaches (2 halves)	100
Clear tomato soup ($\frac{3}{4}$ cup)	75
Green beans (1 cup)	30
Sweetened applesauce ($\frac{1}{2}$ cup)	100
Ice cream sundae or	
lemon meringue pie	335
Milk (8-oz. glass)	170
Chocolate layer cake	400
Cantaloupe ($\frac{1}{2}$)	50
Tea with lemon	0

Discussions of common foods eaten every day in school and at home will illustrate several deficiencies. Vitamins, minerals, and the proper balance of nutrients may be determined.

Experiments and Demonstrations

Nutritional experiments on rats, mice, or hamsters will stimulate much learning. Pupils are interested in devising laboratory experiments showing the importance of the presence or absence of a given vitamin. In a few weeks or months, pupils can observe the health of the animal. Other pupils may wish to take photographs of the animals before and after the experiments. Emphasis should also be given to the controls developed in each experiment so that one variable is studied at a given time.

Display of the Invisible Man, which is usually found in toy shops, will illustrate the circulatory, muscular, digestive, and skeletal systems.

Dissection of a frog can enhance a study of the digestive system (fig. 12.2).

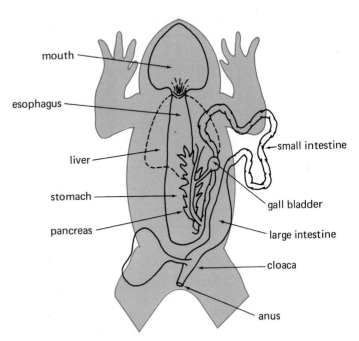

Fig. 12.2.   Digestion in a frog.

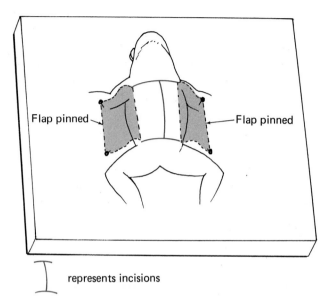

Flap pinned⁓   ⟵Flap pinned

⊥ represents incisions

Fig. 12.3.   Dissection of a frog.

For a laboratory session, large preserved frogs may be obtained from biological supply companies. If dissecting kits are not available, a small scissors and forceps are minimum requirements. A scalpel and probing needle would be helpful. Show the pupils how to make a flap by lifting the skin with a forceps, in the middle of the undersurface (ventral side). Place the scissors at the base of the abdomen near the top of the hind legs and cut the skin toward the head region (anteriorly). Make an incision across the chest between both forelegs. Repeat the incision at the base of the abdomen between both hind legs. It is now possible to expose the organs as the flaps are pulled out, extended, and pinned on a board as shown in fig. 12.3.

Audiovisual Aids

In the upper grades and in the intermediate school, the same frog may be used by the pupils in studying the structures of the circulatory, nervous, skeletal, excretory, reproductive, and respiratory systems. A ditto sheet with an outline of a frog can be given to each pupil at the beginning of the laboratory period. Each pupil can fill in the ditto sheet by drawing the system or organs studied and labeling all parts. *Models and charts* can be introduced to reinforce observations and recognition of the systems. Overlays or single transparencies may be used on the overhead projector to indicate the location of various organs in situ.

In the first part of this text, it was suggested that the teacher may influence the development of positive attitudes toward the study of various types of animals such as frogs, snakes, or rats. The teacher's positive facial expression during the dissection of the frog can aid in students' adopting positive attitudes toward dissection.

Protein digestion as a demonstration. A solution resembling gastric juice is prepared by mixing 10 drops of hydrochloric acid with 10 drops of lactated pepsin. Add a little egg white and observe the following day.

Microprojector demonstration. Prepared slides of blood cells, nerve, and muscle cells can be projected on the screen so that pupils can identify and differentiate several types of cells in the body.

Movie films and film loops are also available on various physiological systems: circulatory, digestive, respiratory, and so on. For a complete listing of current films, refer to Film Index and Film Guides in the library; also, see the appendix.

Consulting specialists such as local physicians and health agency officials are invited to speak to the class. Epidemics and contagious diseases would be of special concern to medical and other health officials. Pupils may wish to report on their individual conferences with such resource people in the community. The importance of guarding one's personal health and its relation to the community can be examined.

I. The nervous system
    A. Brain
        1. Contains billions of nerves enabling learning to occur and memory images to be stored.
        2. Contains connections to nerve network that controls body muscles.
            a. Afferent nerves carry incoming messages to the brain.
            b. Efferent nerves carry outgoing messages to tissues and organs.
        3. Adequate rest and sleep, good nutrition, and the avoidance of excess stimulants or depressants are needed for a healthy condition of the brain.
        4. Brain is divided into three parts.
            a. Cerebrum controls reasoning, memory, consciousness, imagination, and learning; receives sensations such as hearing, taste, smell, sight, pressure, and pain.
            b. Cerebellum controls muscular movements such as walking; and balancing is maintained in conjunction with the inner ear. Messages are sent to the brain to maintain body balance when jumping, running, turning, or stopping.
            c. Medulla controls automatic functions such as breathing, heart beating, and body temperature.

Background Information

B. Spinal cord
   1. Connects nerve impulses from body receptors and sense organs to the brain.
   2. Center for reflex actions (like touching something hot); no thinking is required to remove hand.

II. Eye—almost spherical, about 1 inch in diameter
   A. Millions of light-sensitive cells in retina send impulses to brain which interprets the image viewed.
   B. Cones and rods are specialized cells in the retina.
      1. Cones are sensitive to different colors in the bright light.
      2. Rods are sensitive to dim light and affect light intensity to produce different shades of gray.
   C. Sclera is the tough tissue that surrounds the eye; it is transparent over the iris and pupil and forms a bulge (cornea).
   D. Pupil is the hole through which light is admitted. In dim light, the pupil opening is larger than in bright light.
   E. Iris is the doughnut-shaped, colored portion of eye and surrounds the pupil.

III. Ear—three parts
   A. Outer ear consists of lobe and ear canal leading to eardrum.
   B. Middle ear contains hammer, anvil, and stirrup—"bones of hearing."
   C. Inner ear contains the semicircular canals (labyrinth) for balancing the body and the cochlea for transmitting sounds to the brain.
      1. Outer and middle ear conduct sound to the cochlea.

    2. Sound receptors are located in the cochlea.

D. Eustachian tube connects middle ear with the mouth.

    1. Air pressure decreases when an airplane climbs and air pressure in middle ear increases.

    2. Opening the Eustachian tube by yawning equalizes the internal and external pressure on the eardrum. This equalization of pressure is also developed by swallowing when an airplane ascends or descends.

IV. Digestion

A. Mouth

    1. Adult has 32 teeth (28 before wisdom teeth appear).

        a. 8 teeth in front (incisors) cut and chisel food.

        b. 4 sharply pointed canines rip food.

        c. 20 molars grind and mash food.

    2. Chewing and secreting saliva in the mouth prepares the food surfaces for chemical action—digestion.

        a. 3 pairs of salivary glands secrete saliva in the mouth.

        b. About half of the saliva in the mouth is an enzyme, ptyalin, which begins to digest about 5% to 10% of the starches and other carbohydrates in the mouth.

B. Gullet or esophagus

    1. Tube connecting mouth to stomach

    2. Food moved down by peristalsis (wavelike action) into the stomach

C. Stomach

    1. Gastric juice is secreted from gastric glands in the stomach.

       a. Small amounts of hydrochloric acid assist in digestion, that is, the breakdown of food from complex to simpler molecules.

       b. Pepsin, an enzyme, initiates the digestion of proteins.

       c. Very small amounts of gastric lipase begin the digestion of fats.

       d. A small quantity of rennin in the gastric secretion digests casein, a protein in milk.

D. Pancreas

  1. A large gland found beneath the stomach pours about 1,200 ml. of secretions into the upper portion of the small intestine.

  2. Pancreatic secretions contain enzymes and other chemical substances.

       a. Amylase (enzyme) digests carbohydrates.

       b. Trypsin and chymotrypsin (enzymes) digest proteins.

       c. Pancreatic lipase (enzyme) digests fats.

       d. Sodium bicarbonate is secreted, reacts with hydrochloric acid coming from the stomach, and increases the quantity of sodium chloride (a neutral salt in the intestine).

E. Liver

  1. Secretes bile which contains bile salts, cholesterol, and bilirubin.

  2. Bile salts act like detergents and are not enzymes.

  3. Bile is stored in the gall bladder and at various times is secreted into the gastrointestinal tract.

F. Small intestine
    1. The enzymes (sucrase, maltase, and lactase) split disaccharides into monosaccharides.
    2. Other enzymes secreted by the small intestine glands are peptidases for digestion of proteins and lipases for splitting fats.
    3. Almost all of the secretions with the digested food materials are absorbed.

G. Large intestine (colon)
    1. Secretes mucus for lubrication.
    2. Stores fecal wastes.

V. Respiration

A. Many factors regulate the respiratory centers:
    1. Concentration of carbon dioxide
    2. Concentration of hydrogen ions
    3. Available oxygen
    4. Exercise
    5. Arterial pressure
    6. Speech
    7. Sensory phenomena

B. Muscular contractions of breathing are regulated by the nervous system.
    1. Inspiration—breathing of air as thoracic cage expands
    2. Expiration—breathing out of air as thickness of chest decreases

C. Oxygen and carbon dioxide exchange
    1. Oxygen diffuses into the blood from the lungs, forming an unstable substance, oxyhemoglobin, when it combines with the hemoglobin of the red blood cells.
    2. The oxygen splits off from the hemoglobin as it diffuses into the tissues while passing through tissue capillaries.
    3. As metabolism takes place, carbon dioxide

is formed in the cells.

4. Carbon dioxide, transported in the form of carbaminohemoglobin in the blood, is released into the alveoli when the blood enters the pulmonary capillaries. This is the reverse of oxygen and oxyhemoglobin.

D. Breathing pathway—air
1. Air enters nose and mouth.
2. Air travels down the windpipe (trachea).
3. Air enters the bronchi (two branches off the trachea).
4. Air goes into bronchioles and alveoli, which are surrounded by capillaries.
5. Diffusion of gases as described in C above.

VI. Circulation
A. Functions of circulatory system
1. Nutrients and oxygen are supplied to all body cells.
2. Hormones and other chemical substances are also carried in the blood to various parts of the body.
3. Waste materials are transported by blood to appropriate organs and tissues for removal.
4. Blood carries antibodies and other chemicals to fight disease.

B. Composition of blood
1. Red blood cells contain hemoglobin which carries oxygen and carbon dioxide.
   a. Trillions of red cells are in the body.
   b. Millions of new cells are manufactured every second in red marrow of the bone.
2. White blood cells destroy harmful microorganisms.
3. Platelets assist in clotting.
4. Plasma
   a. Is 90% water.

b. Includes hormones, enzymes, minerals, wastes, proteins, fats, sugars, and antibodies.

C. Heart—keeps blood flowing through the circulatory system.

    1. Right side of heart receives blood from major veins.

        a. Blood enters right atrium when heart muscle relaxes.

        b. Atrium contracts, forcing blood through tricuspid valve into right ventricle.

        c. Right ventricle pumps blood into pulmonary artery to lungs.

    2. Left side of heart receives blood from lungs.

        a. Blood enters left atrium from pulmonary veins.

        b. Left atrium contracts, forcing blood into left ventricle.

        c. Left ventricle pumps blood into aorta and on through the systemic circulation.

D. Systemic circulation

    1. Venae cavae (two large veins) bring blood to right atrium down to right ventricle.

    2. From right ventricle, the blood goes through pulmonary artery to lungs.

    3. From lungs' (blood is now oxygenated), the blood goes to left atrium and down to left ventricle of heart.

    4. From left ventricle, the blood is pumped into large arteries going to head, chest, arms, and lower portion of the body.

    5. Oxygen is given off to the various organs and tissues via the capillaries that connect the arteries to the veins.

    6. Carbon dioxide is given off and carried in

the blood by the veins from all parts of the body back to the venae cavae.

7. The cycle repeats itself as blood enters the right atrium of the heart.

VII. Excretion

A. Wastes are disposed as follows:

1. Water, urea, salts, and other chemical wastes are removed through the kidneys and urinary bladder.

2. Carbon dioxide and water vapor are removed through the lungs.

3. Water and some salts are removed through sweat glands of the skin.

B. Solid, indigestible wastes are eliminated from rectum as fecal wastes.

C. Human urinary system

1. Kidneys (2)

a. Regulate volume of fluid in the body.

b. Remove urea and other waste materials from blood.

c. Return useful materials to the blood by reabsorption.

2. Ureters (2) conduct urine from the kidneys to the bladder.

3. Bladder stores urine and eliminates it through urethra.

VIII. Reproductive organs

A. Male

1. Testes (2) are enclosed in a saclike structure, the scrotum.

2. Sperm cells are produced in the testes.

3. Vas deferens is a tube through which sperm cells travel from testes to penis.

4. The urethral tube within the penis is the passageway for sperm cells during ejacula-

tion following sexual excitement.

B. Female

    1. Ovaries (2) produce eggs.

    2. Oviducts or Fallopian tubes carry the egg from ovary to womb.

    3. Womb or uterus is site where fertilized egg grows into a fetus.

    4. Vagina is the external opening of the uterus into which the penis enters and also where the baby passes through at birth.

IX. Endocrine system—ductless glands secreting hormones

A. Pituitary gland secretes hormones that affect size of the child and in special instances can produce dwarfism or giantism by lowered or excessive hormonal secretion, respectively. Also influences other endocrine glands.

B. Thyroid gland secretes the hormone thyroxin which controls body metabolism.

C. Adrenal glands (2) secrete hormones that influence blood pressure, heartbeat, and cellular oxidation.

D. Islets of Langerhans secrete the hormone insulin, which is needed for sugar oxidation in the cells.

E. Thymus gland stimulates antibodies and production of white blood corpuscles to fight against bacteria and viruses.

F. Gonads (testes and ovaries) secrete hormones.

    1. In male, hormones influence secondary sexual characteristics: manly voice, hair on chest, and beard.

    2. In female, hormones influence development of breasts, menstruation, and the cycle of producing eggs (ovulation).

13

OUR CHANGING ENVIRONMENT: AIR, WATER, AND WEATHER

Grades K–2   **Concepts**

1. Air is all around us.
2. Wind is air that is moving.
3. Air can do work.
4. Wind can dry things faster.
5. Air, like water, takes the shape of its container.
6. Water runs downhill.
7. Water is important for washing, drinking, cooking, and for all living things.

Grades 3–5

8. Air occupies space.
9. Water evaporates faster in the sunlight and by the wind.

10. Rainwater sinks into the ground and forms streams.
11. Living things need air for breathing.
12. Dew on the ground is formed from moisture in the air.
13. Fresh water can be removed from salt water by heating and then cooling the vapor.

Grades 6–8

14. Air is composed mainly of nitrogen and oxygen and small amounts of other gases.
15. Cold air is heavier than warm air.
16. Warm air rises, and cold air sinks.
17. The greater the amount of water moisture in air, the greater is the humidity.
18. A high humidity in a cooling environment of air will cause condensation and precipitation.
19. Precipitation is involved in such weather conditions as rain, sleet, fog, and snow.
20. The water cycle consists of the evaporation of water into the air, followed by a return of water to the ground after condensation.
21. High air pressure areas usually have good weather.
22. Low air pressure areas usually have unpleasant weather such as rain or snow.
23. Air is necessary for burning.
24. Clouds contain moisture.

Concept Formation

In order to understand weather phenomena, it is necessary to understand the properties and behavior of air and water. Concepts of air and water are very closely related and influence weather. For example, concepts 15 and 16—*Cold air is heavier than warm air,* and *Warm air rises, and cold air sinks*—and concept number 17 on moisture help us understand the behavior of air which influences weather.

In concepts 1, 2, 3, 5, 8, 11, 14, 15, and 16 the properties and behavior of air are important to interpret weather and its changes. Children can appreciate the action or motion of air such as wind. This signifies the presence of air more readily than merely stating that air is all around us. Stories told by children as to why their mothers insist that they wear certain clothing when weather is changing will also bring into focus air and its relation to weather.

Pupil Experiences

Some youngsters will relate how one of their balloons was carried away by wind or moving air. Other children will tell about the beach ball that was blown out to sea. One girl mentions that her father's hat was blown off his head. Many pupil experiences can be related to demonstrations, experiments, and discussions on air and wind.

Air that can do work is another concept that can be developed. Everyone is familiar with the windmill. Children can make toy windmills and blow on them. Encourage children to attach a pin to their homemade windmills. Ask them to design other materials that can be attached to the pin and the windmill. Other children may use a fan to show how moving air performs work.

Air, like water, takes the shape of its container. A child can blow air into a plastic bag. He observes how the air fills up the bag and the bag expands due to the air. He can pour a glass of water into the bag. Where does the air go?

What is the shape of the water in the plastic bag? A discussion of how fish are transported in a plastic container with water will provide a basis for understanding some properties of water. It will also raise questions about air in water as bubbles. This can serve as a means of encouraging new experiments to be designed by the pupils.

Why do we make two holes on the top of a can to make the liquid pour easily? What would happen if only one hole were made and the can were turned upside down in a vertical line? Pupils could discuss opening orange juice or soda pop cans and how air could be used to keep the liquid from pouring out or vice versa.

The concepts numbered 6, 7, 10, 13, and 17 are related to properties and behavior of water. Most children will have observed that water runs downhill. They can be asked to relate their observations and experiences in the home and at play. A discussion should follow on the uses of water. Where does water go? This will lead to water sinking into the ground and the formation of streams.

Water Cycle

In the upper grades and in the intermediate school, during hot days problems of perspiration and humidity may be introduced to stimulate discussions on evaporation and the cooling of the body. The showing of pictures, telling of anecdotes, and reading about air and water can serve as a basic introduction to the understanding of weather.

Concepts dealing directly with weather phenomena are numbered 4, 9, 12, 15, 18, 19, 20, 21, and 22. Why do people use electric fans? Why do some people take a piece of cardboard or a paper to fan themselves? These questions will not only develop an understanding of evaporation but also the weather (water) cycle (fig. 13.1). After water evaporates into the atmosphere, how does it return to lakes, rivers, and oceans? This suggests precipitation after condensation; the precipitation can take the form of rain, snow, sleet, and drizzle, among other forms of weather.

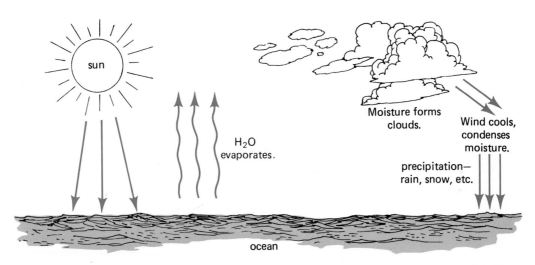

Fig. 13.1. Water cycle.

**Experiments
and Demonstrations**

For kindergarten and the lower grades the concept of *air being all around us* can be demonstrated by waving plastic bags and observing how they fill with air. Children can bring in paper bags and blow air into them to see how they fill with air. After a plastic bag is filled with air and is tied securely, place a book or some other object to show that air supports the object on top of the plastic bag. Repeat, substituting water for air in the plastic bag.

As a laboratory experience, children can make many folds in an $8\frac{1}{2}'' \times 11''$ piece of paper and use it as a fan. Moving the fan back and forth illustrates the presence of air and can be used to hasten the evaporation of moisture (pupils' exhalation on the chalkboard). The concept of *wind moving air* is also demonstrated by this activity.

Other learning activities involve the use of balloons in which air is blown. Note how air takes the shape of the balloon. Some balloons will be oval, cylindrical, or animal-shaped. Substitute water for air in the balloons and observe that water, like air, takes the shape of the balloon or any other container.

Concepts pertaining to evaporation can be developed through problem-solving activity. Anecdotes related to pupil experiences such as having wet socks can introduce a problem. The anecdote indicates that the fireplace, sunshine, and wind are available. The children are asked to state the problem. One youngster suggests that the problem is to find out which will dry wet socks faster. They design experiments using a fan for wind, some form of heat or a lighted candle for the fireplace, and sunshine outdoors. Skill in performing these experiments is needed to prevent burning the wet socks. Perhaps a miniature clothesline can be established to hold the wet socks.

In this problem-solving situation, it would be fruitful to raise questions about standardizing the conditions. Do the wet socks contain the same amount of water for each experiment? Is the humidity in the room or outside the same for each of the experiments? These questions should lead to a discussion of the importance of a control in making any conclusions. Thus the children will have a more accurate basis for comparing observations in the process of drawing conclusions.

For grades three to five the concept that *air occupies space* can be developed by several demonstrations or laboratory situations. Invert an "empty" glass containing a dry piece of cloth (see fig. 13.2). Place it in a large container of water so that the water covers the glass completely. Remove the upside-down glass from the water, and take out the piece of cloth. Allow pupils to touch the cloth. Why is it dry? What kept the water from rushing into the glass? Air occupied space in the glass and prevented the water from rushing into the glass. Thus the cloth remained dry.

Fig. 13.2.   Air keeps water out of glass.

Some children will ask if it is possible to let the air out of the glass so that the water can get in? Allow the children to place the inverted glass at a 45-degree angle instead of an upright position to illustrate the exit of air and the rushing in of water. Another youngster may decide to tilt the glass after it was completely submerged in an upright (inverted) position. Bubbles of air will be observed escaping from the glass as water rushes in. Such varied experiments should be encouraged to test the hypotheses proposed by the children.

Living things need air for breathing. Some living flies may be placed in a sealed jar (fig. 13.3A) and the same

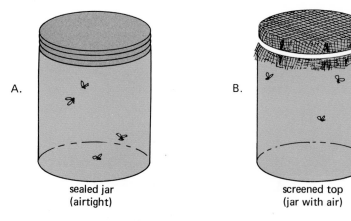

A.   B.

sealed jar   screened top
(airtight)   (jar with air)

Fig. 13.3.   Fruit flies in jars.

number of flies can be placed in a similar jar with a screened top (fig. 13.3*B*). In the first jar, air will be consumed during the breathing process with no source of fresh air. Pupils can keep a record of the behavior of the flies and note how long the flies live in both jars.

Rainwater sinks into the ground and forms streams. An empty 5-gallon aquarium can be filled with a bottom layer of rocks, 2 or 3 inches high. On top of this layer, add about 2 or 3 inches of gravel. On the uppermost layer, add about 1 or 2 inches of topsoil. Add water slowly into the topsoil. It will be observed that the water sinks into the topsoil (ground) and goes through the spaces between the gravel and rock to form puddles (stream) at the bottom (see fig. 13.4).

Water evaporates faster in the sunlight. This demonstration can be made by using two 4-inch, clear plastic round dishes. In one empty dish, a pupil may add just enough water to cover the bottom of the dish and place it in the sunlight for one or two days. In another dish he may add the same amount of water and place it in a closet away from sunlight for the same period of time. Discuss the observations.

Some children may suggest that the humidity in the room is an important factor. This splendid contribution could lead to other experiments; it should be encouraged. Other children will add that these dishes should be covered to see where the water goes if it leaves the bottom of the dish. Observations can be made that some droplets of water will *condense* on the upper surface of the covered dish.

Dew on the ground is formed from moisture in the air. Children have noticed that, on a cold glass of milk that remained on the table for 15 minutes or more on a hot summer day, moisture appeared on the outside of the glass. Where did the moisture come from? The concept of humidity or water vapor in the air that condenses to form liquid droplets on the outside of the glass is developed through such experience. This discussion emphasizes precipitation and makes for an understanding of weather.

In grades six to eight, air and water concepts are related to weather phenomena. A striking demonstration can be performed with the aid of a 1-gallon tin can with a screw cap. This can be purchased at a local hardware store. Place

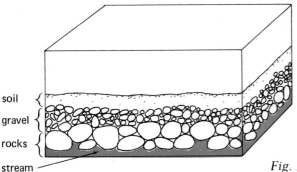

soil
gravel
rocks
stream

Fig. 13.4. Formation of a stream.

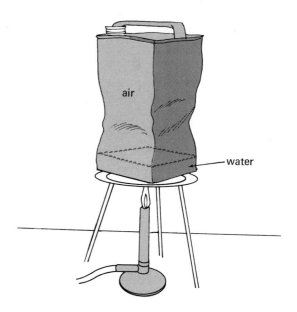

Fig. 13.5.   Air pressure crushes a can.

about 6 ounces of water in the can and, with the cover open, heat the water until it begins to boil. After boiling for about one minute, remove from the source of heat. Carefully place the screw cap tightly on the can. Immediately place the tightly covered can under a faucet of cold water or pour several glasses of cold water on the hot can. The can will be crushed on all sides as it is cooled (see fig. 13.5).

If the students are encouraged to propose explanations for how the can was crushed, the following ideas will probably appear:

1. Boiling of water forms vapor as the liquid water evaporates.
2. During boiling of water, air above the liquid water in the can is forced out.

3. A partial vacuum is formed inside the can when the lid is put on as the can is cooled.
4. The pressure inside the can is less than the pressure outside the can when the cold water is poured on the outside of the can.
5. The greater air pressure on the outside of the can crushes the can.

Air pressure is significantly associated with changes in weather. Frequently low air-pressure areas display forms of precipitation such as rain or snow. High pressure areas are usually found to have good weather. Hence observations of air pressure and its effects in the atmosphere are helpful in understanding weather conditions.

A worthwhile laboratory experience is the construction of a convection box to show how *warm air rises and cold air sinks.* A deductive inference can also be made that cold air

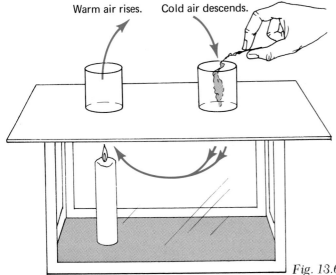

Warm air rises.　Cold air descends.

Fig. 13.6.　*Convection box.*

is heavier than warm air. A shoebox with a Plexiglass or substitute front panel can be used in the making of convection box to show the airflow (see fig. 13.6).

The water cycle can be demonstrated by boiling water in a teakettle. Allow the steam to strike a frying pan filled with ice cubes about 4 or 5 inches above the teakettle. Condensation will occur as the steam strikes the undersurface of the pan. The droplets of moisture will be cooled by the ice cubes, resulting in precipitation. Thus water in the atmosphere is evaporated, cooled, condensed, and precipitated back to the soil (fig. 13.7).

Will dark surfaces heat up faster than light surfaces? Make the following materials available: two tin cans of equal size containing equal amounts of water, two thermometers with equal initial readings, a brush, and a can of black paint. Ask the children to design an experiment using these

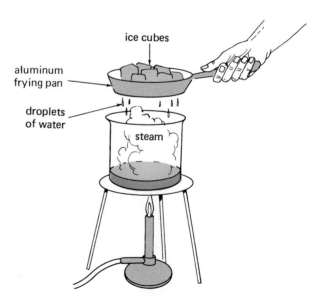

Fig. 13.7.   Forming rain.

materials to help them solve the problem. It is suggested that temperature readings be made of both cans every ten or fifteen minutes for at least one hour.

The radiation of sunlight and its effects on temperature changes can be related to light-colored vs. dark-colored surfaces. What are the advantages and disadvantages of having a light-colored roof in the summer and in the winter? During summer months, do people wear light-colored or dark-colored clothing? Pupils can design additional experiments by measuring temperature changes of light- and dark-colored cloths.

Environmental Pollution Experiments

If students understand the phenomena such as evaporation, condensation, precipitation, and humidity involved in weather changes, they should become involved in designing and performing environmental pollution experiments. What are common air pollutants? How many pollutant particles (solids) are deposited in our immediate surroundings? Open-air jars deposited on the school roof, at home, and in a park can be examined over a period of one week, two weeks, and one month to compare different qualities of air. Solid wastes such as soot and ashes can be weighed in each sample. The degree of acidity or alkalinity of the solution can be measured with pH paper and a color chart. With the aid of the chemistry department, tests for carbon, nitrogen, and hydrocarbon compounds can be made.

Rainwater can be collected in bottles with a large filter to catch the water. Not only is it possible to measure the amount of rainfall within a twenty-four-hour period, but also it is possible to evaporate it. The evaporation of rainwater in an evaporating dish will enable one to see if any salts or other solid particles remain. Such solid particles were probably washed down from the atmosphere by the rainwater.

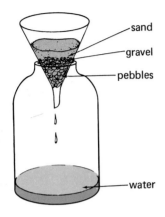

Fig. 13.8.   A water filter.

Samples of water taken from lakes, rivers, rain, and other places can be filtered to purify the water and to see what residues are left behind (see fig. 13.8). Water samples from lakes or ponds after filtering will still show many microscopic organisms in the filtered water. Place a drop or two of such pond water on a slide and use a cover slip. Examine it; it is likely that some protozoans and other microscopic organisms will be in this sample. Refer to the photo on the next page to see if any of these organisms (paramecia) appeared in the sample.

Children who have cameras may wish to photograph pollution in the environment. Litter and garbage on streets, on roadways, in lakes, in streams, and in rivers can be photographed. Likewise, smog and smoke from traffic, smokestacks, and incinerators can also be photographed for further study and report to the authorities. Many communities are instituting laws that protect the environment. Good photographic evidence can be most helpful in protecting our environment.

Background Information

I.   Air and weather
    A.   Most of the weather phenomena occur in the *troposphere layer*.
        1.   In the troposphere (under nonconvection conditions) there is usually a continuous lowering of temperature with an increase in altitude (3.5° F. per 1,000 ft.).
        2.   The amount of oxygen decreases as the altitude increases.
        3.   The troposphere is about 5 miles high at the poles and about 10 miles at the equator.
        4.   At the top of the troposphere, or tropopause,

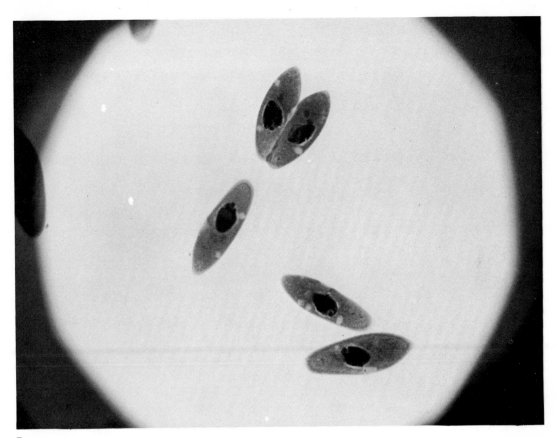

Paramecia

the temperature is approximately $-80°$ F. and the temperature no longer decreases with an increase in altitude; this is the beginning of the stratosphere.

B. The stratosphere extends from about 10 to 30 miles above sea level.

    1. The lower half of the stratosphere has a temperature at about $-80°$ F. and then the temperature rises to about $+32°$ F. at 30 miles above sea level.

    2. As the altitude increases, there is less wind in the stratosphere.

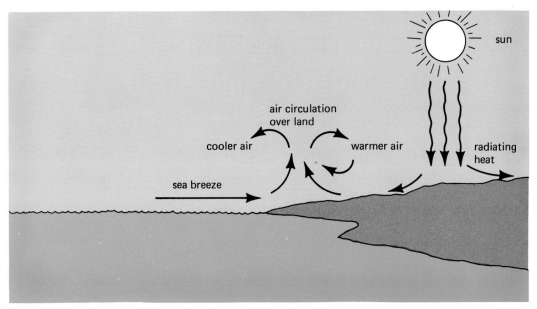

Fig. 13.9.   Air circulation.

    3.   There is little weather change and no turbulence or storms in the upper stratosphere.

C. Composition and behavior of air

    1.   Air is a mixture of several gases and pollutants, including solid dust particles.

       a.   About 78% or 79% of nitrogen is found in air.

       b.   About 20% or 21% of oxygen is found in air.

       c.   Varying amounts of water vapor are found in air, and a fraction of 1% of air contains carbon dioxide and such rare gases as argon, helium, krypton, neon, and xenon.

    2.   Cold air sinks because it is heavier than an equal volume of warm air.

    3.   Cool air is blown in from the ocean.

  4. The sun warms the ground that radiates the heat over the land and sets up a circulation with the sea breeze because the air over the land is warmed to a higher degree than that over the water (see fig. 13.9).

D. Air pollution—man-made contamination of the atmosphere, including industrial contamination

  1. Air currents such as convection carry smoke away from a given environment and also bring in pollutants from other places.

  2. The up-and-down mix of air currents dilute pollutants in a given part of the atmosphere (fig. 13.10).

  3. Severe pollution occurs with an inversion: the cool surface air cannot rise and is trapped by the warm air layer above (fig. 13.11).

  4. Air is contaminated by attrition, vaporization, and combustion.

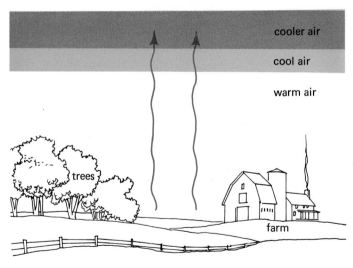

Fig. 13.10. Normal convection air currents—day.

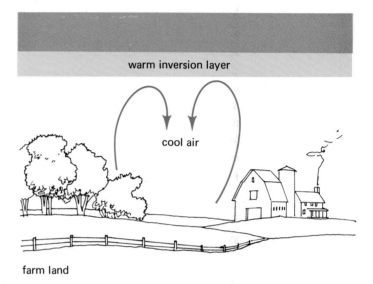

Fig. 13.11.   Inversion—night.

      a.   Attrition—friction such as grinding and wearing down of auto tires and soles of shoes, drilling, spraying, demolishing, and sanding are all part of attrition producing solid and liquid particles in the atmosphere.

      b.   Vaporization—liquids such as gasoline give off vapors (gases) that pollute the atmosphere.

      c.   Combustion—burning of fossil fuels such as coal, gas, and oil, all hydrocarbons, pollutes the atmosphere by their emissions.

  5.   Transportation, industry, power plants, space heating, and refuse disposal give off the following pollutants in millions of tons per year:

      a.   Carbon monoxide

      b.   Sulfur oxides

    c.   Hydrocarbons

    d.   Nitrogen oxides

    e.   Particulate matter

6.   Pollutants in the air can cause eye irritation, breathing difficulty, vegetation damage, skin irritation, inflammation of the respiratory tract, and decreased visibility.

7.   Excessive amounts of lead, beryllium, arsenic, and asbestos are poisonous when inhaled or ingested with food.

8.   Pollution accidents

    a.   In Poza Rica, Mexico, in November 1950, hydrogen sulfide spilled from a sulfur producing factory into the atmosphere during an inversion; within a half hour 22 people were dead and 320 hospitalized.

    b.   In Meuse River Valley, Belgium, a heavily industrialized area, in December 1930, pollutants trapped by an inversion for several days caused 60 deaths from poisoned air, and thousands of people were sick.

    c.   In Donora, Pennsylvania, an industrial town with a population of 14,000, in October 1948, a pollutant-filled inversion caused 20 deaths instead of the average two, and about 6,000 people were ill.

    d.   In London in December 1952, a five-day inversion caused about 4,000 people to die because of noxious air. London has had several such incidents.

    e.   Some people claim that several episodes took place in 1953, 1962, 1963, and 1966 in New York City. It is believed that during a three-day period of inversion, air pollution caused 168 deaths. It was also

(left) Cirrus clouds.
(center) Cumulus clouds.
(right) Stratus clouds.

suggested that this number would have been greater if it had not been the Thanksgiving holiday when many pollution-producing activities were curtailed.

II. Water and weather
  A. Water is in constant circulation because of evaporation and condensation, the water cycle.
      1. Water vapor is given off by plant leaves, oceans, lakes, ponds, animal skin, soil, and animal lungs.
      2. Droplets of water vapor in the atmosphere are chilled to form clouds in the atmosphere.
      3. Moisture that leaves the ground and escapes (evaporates) into the atmosphere leaves behind the impurities; the returning or condensed water is usually pure or free from impurities.
  B. Clouds—the result of moisture which condenses on tiny particles such as dust

1. Cirrus clouds—high clouds about 6 miles in altitude; composed of ice crystals, look white and feathery.
2. Cumulus clouds—dense clouds seen in rising currents of air built up into huge heaps, they are white and fluffy.
3. Stratus clouds—smooth gray skies that black out the sun; in summer they consist of water droplets; in winter, ice crystals.

C. Precipitation takes the form of fog, rain, snow, sleet, hail, glaze, and other types of weather. Essentially the moisture condenses and travels through different altitudes and through varying temperatures. At freezing temperatures aloft, the moisture can become ice, snow, hail, or other solid forms of water. This precipitation can melt if it travels through warmer temperatures before reaching the ground.

III. Weather instruments

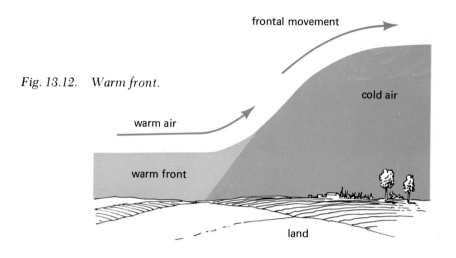

Fig. 13.12. Warm front.

A. For wind
  1. Wind vane measures direction from which wind comes.
  2. Anemometer measures the velocity or speed of wind.
B. For temperature
  1. Thermometer measures minimum and maximum daily temperature, as well as temperature at any given time.
  2. Thermograph records temperature over a period of time, day, or week on graph paper.
C. For air pressure
  1. Mercurial barometer measures in inches, centimeters, or millimeters the length of a column of mercury supported by the pressure of the air.
  2. Aneroid barometer measures air pressure; usually appears on instrument face as inches. A disc that has the air inside removed and pres-

frontal movement

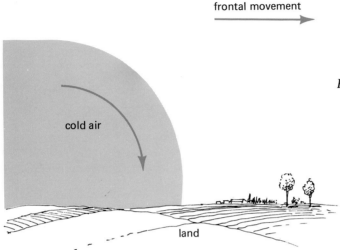

Fig. 13.13. **Cold front.**

sure changes on the disc cause the indicator to move accordingly.

D. For humidity

    1. Psychrometer or wet-and-dry-bulb thermometer measures water vapor content by the difference in the temperatures of the two thermometers as a result of evaporation.

    2. Hair hygrometer—hair shortens in a dry atmosphere and stretches when moist and moves an indicator to show the percentage of water vapor present.

E. For precipitation

    1. Rain gauge measures inches of rainfall.

    2. Radar locates areas of precipitation.

F. For several weather elements, a radiosonde is employed to measure temperature, pressure, and humidity at given intervals as it rises into the atmosphere.

G. Space satellites through television produce pictures of the atmosphere in various parts of the earth and

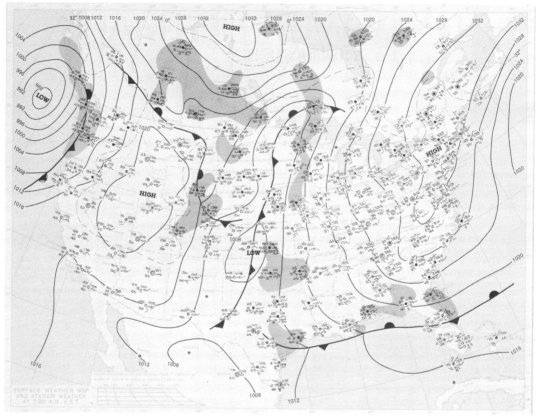

Fig. 13.14.   U.S. Weather Bureau weather map.

is especially noteworthy in showing characteristic storm-system cloud patterns.

IV.   Air masses

    A.   An air mass consists of a large portion of air, many miles long, wide, and high.

    B.   An air mass aloft usually has the properties or conditions, such as temperature and humidity, of the air on the surface below.

    C.   The properties of an air mass, its direction, location, and movement can be used to forecast weather changes.

D. Fronts are lines of contact between two air masses.
   1. Refer to fig. 13.12 and note the warm air in contact with and rising over the cold air; as the warm air moves upward, it is cooled. Condensation occurs, forming a cloud, and precipitation results.
   2. A cold front moves more rapidly and more vigorously than a warm front. Refer to fig. 13.13 and note that the cold front is steeper than the warm front and noses under the warm air mass, causing it to rise rapidly.
V. High, low, and weather map (see fig. 13.14)
   A. The *H* in the weather map area signifies a high air-pressure area. Usually the high pressure areas have clear, dry weather.
   B. The *L* in the weather map area signifies a low air-pressure area which usually brings cloudy weather with precipitation and perhaps storms.
   C. Isobars connect points of equal air pressure on the weather map; they are indicated in inches and millibars.
   D. Isotherms connect points of equal temperature on the weather map, reported in degrees Fahrenheit.

14

THE EARTH'S
CHANGING SURFACE

Grades K–2

1. The earth is a planet and has a shape like a large ball.
2. Water covers about three-fourths of the earth's surface.
3. Water changes the surface of the earth.
4. Air surrounds the earth.
5. Many kinds of minerals are found in rocks.

Grades 3–5

6. The earth is made up of three parts: solid (lithosphere), liquid (hydrosphere), and gaseous (atmosphere).

7. The earth's surface is always changing.
8. Rocks and soil are worn away by such forces as wind, water, man, plants, and animals.
9. Minerals are useful materials found in the earth.
10. Deserts are part of the solid earth that has little rainfall.

Grades 6–8

11. Rocks and soil are carried by rapidly flowing water.
12. Rocks contain one or more kinds of minerals.
13. Oceans, like soil, provide the necessary chemicals to support living things in obtaining their food.
14. When the earth's crust buckles, mountains are formed.
15. Volcanoes change the earth's surface by building mountains.
16. Earthquakes occur either at the surface or deep within the earth's crust.

Concept Formation

In kindergarten through grade two, the emphasis on concept formation is usually *descriptive*. In grades three to five, the emphasis frequently pertains to *uses, relationships,* and *values* in the development of concepts. *Cause-and-effect* as well as *operational* aspects in forming concepts are stressed in grades six to eight. However, all these factors appear in all grade levels to varying degrees.

The descriptive features of the earth's surface are generalized in concepts numbered 1, 2, 4, 6, 10, 12, and 13. The shape of the earth, the amount of water, air, parts of the earth, deserts, and oceans require various observations and experiences both in the surroundings as well as in the class-room.

Relationships, values, and uses of materials in the earth appear in concepts 5, 9, 11, and 16. Thus rocks and minerals and their uses, soil and flowing water, and earthquakes are discussed.

Cause-and-effect relationships and operational aspects of the changing earth's surface, a major concern throughout all levels, are stressed in concepts 3, 7, 8, 14, and 15. Hence the effects of water on earth, the forces that wear away soil, the formation of mountains, and the work of volcanoes and earthquakes receive much discussion, demonstration, and ex-perimentation.

Preschool children have experienced playing with sand and water, either at the beach, backyard, or vacant lot. A child makes an important discovery the first time he feels water as being wet and sand as being dry. As sand or soil becomes moist, an intermediate sensation appears. Soon, the child adds more water and more sand. The mud-pie creation comes into play. Thereafter the youngster may build castles from sand and water on the beach. These experiences can serve as a basis for developing concepts of the physical fea-tures and phenomena of the earth's surface.

Collecting Rocks and Minerals

Kindergarten children enjoy playing with clay and other workable materials that enable them to mold and create. Building a mountain, a cave, a lake, a desert out of clay may introduce the idea of what the earth is made of. Collecting pebbles, rocks, minerals, and different samples of soil be-comes a most interesting experience for pupils of all ages. Such collecting activities stimulate interest in finding out where they came from. It is the kind of activity that adults

Collecting specimens pro-
motes discussion.

carry over when they cannot throw away items in the home that were collected over a period of many years. Collecting stamps, coins, dolls, or antiques are basic traits in most people.

The mere collection and display of various rocks and minerals found in the earth constitute useful learning experiences. Children in the lower grades will soon show and tell about the names, color, and other features of the specimens collected. Field trips can be made to construction sites. Usually some common rocks such as granite, sandstone, and various types of pebbles such as marble chips may be found.

Samples of clay may be found to show the differences in particle size found in soil.

Rocks contain minerals. The collection of granite, marble chips, or sandstone contains the mineral quartz. Granite, for example, consists of quartz and feldspar, light-colored minerals; the dark grains are chiefly mica. Pupils at all grade levels will enjoy identifying different types of minerals. A discussion of the use of marble and other rocks for constructing homes will also add significance to the study of rocks and minerals.

Shape of the Earth

It is difficult to visualize the shape of the earth unless it were viewed from space. Hence pupils in grades three to five may study a softball, basketball, handball, grapefruit, and a grapefruit with bulges on it. There are approximately three possibilities to the shape of the earth: sphere, spheroid, geoid (fig. 14.1). The grapefruit with bulges on it or *geoid* appears to be the most widely accepted concept of the earth's shape.

In grades three to five, children can relate their experiences of seeing what water and wind do to the soil. Watering flowers or plants in pots or in the garden can illustrate a change in the appearance of the soil. What happens when a high-pressure hose is directed at a mound of soil? What is the difference in the appearance of the same mound when a sprinkler can is used to water it? These experiences can be related to a strong downpour of a heavy rain and contrasted with a fine drizzle. Similarly the earth's surface changes its appearance as these forces strike it.

A discussion of dry and wet soil will reveal the great effect of wind on earth. Pictures of deserts illustrate sand dunes. Demonstrations of a fan blowing toward a dry mound of soil compared with a wet mound of soil can show the effects of water and wind.

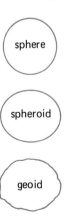

Fig. 14.1. Shape of the earth.

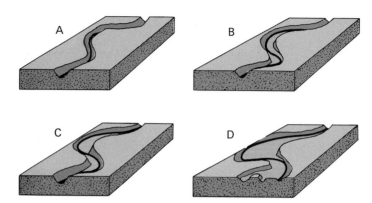

Fig. 14.2. Showing meandering originating accidentally in A and finally becoming a winding pattern in D.

Meandering

For grades six to eight, field trips to streams, ponds, lakes, and rivers will help to demonstrate the effects of water and wind on rock and soil. Meandering (fig. 14.2), for example, might be noted along the edges of some streams. Erosion and weathering can also be observed on field trips.

Oceanography

Units of instruction pertaining to oceanography become very meaningful when field trips to the beach and on boats are made. Mapping the ocean bottom through the use of modern instruments shows how vastly different the bottom of the sea is from what had been previously believed. Deep gullies and high mountains are detected in various places. Mountain ranges and valleys were made as a result of molten rock moving beneath the sea.

In grades six through eight, pupils on a fishing trip may take samples of water and temperature at different levels.

Studies are made of plant and animal life found in varied temperatures and depths. Perhaps samples of the sea floor might be procured in the right places and with proper equipment. The nature of soil and rock at the sea bottom will be of interest when compared with the earth's surface. From the flat part of the ocean floor arise volcanoes whose peaks reach above the water and form islands. Some of these islands, such as Hawaii, serve to anchor land for coral growths.

Experiments and Demonstrations

In kindergarten through grade two, children can perform experiments with mud and clay. What is the shape of the earth? Using clay or mud, the children can make an approximation of the earth as a miniature model. Ask them to show mountains, rivers, lakes, and oceans on their models. This type of exercise can prove a most creative experience. The concept that the earth is shaped like a large ball will evolve. It will not come out as a completely round ball, especially at both poles and where mountains and other irregularities occur.

Weathering and Erosion

If mud pies represent mountains, what will wear away the mountains faster, heavy rain or drizzle? Using a 20-gallon fish tank or similar container, have some of the children make a mud pie in the tank. Using a hose, allow a strong current of water to strike the mud pie "mountain." Repeat the exercise using a watering can or sprinkler to strike the "mountain."

Does the earth act like a sponge? Can it soak up endless amounts of water? How deep does one dig to find water?

Constructing a model of the changing earth's surface.

Will large sizes of pebbles hold more water than finer particles of soil, such as sand? These questions can lead to several experiments or demonstrations. Using a large fish tank or similar container place a 1-inch layer of large pebbles at the bottom. On the top of this layer, add a 1-inch layer of smaller pebbles. Finally, add a top layer of exactly 1 inch of top soil. Measure the amount of water that is needed to cover the top layer of soil. Keep a record of this amount of water.

Repeat the experiment, but reverse the order of the layers of pebbles so that the fine soil is at the bottom and the larger pebbles are on the top. How much water is needed now to cover the top layer of pebbles? Compare results and discuss. Relate this to water tables. What happens to water tables during a drought?

Water can be placed in a small jar to the top, sealed, and placed overnight in a freezer. For safety, wrap tin foil around the glass. The observation that the glass jar broke because of the expansion of freezing water can be compared with freezing rain going into the cracks of large rocks or boulders. The freezing rain expands as ice and pushes the rock apart. This process is a part of weathering. As a result of weathering, large boulders or rocks are finally pulverized into small particles of soil. (*Note:* water is an exception; it expands on freezing, whereas other substances contract.)

In the upper grades, demonstrations that show the gully formation and erosion are very effective. Models of mountains and varied slopes with and without grass and other plant ground cover can be designed by the pupils. The effect of running water to demonstrate erosion is seen when a watering can is applied at the summit of the mountain to form streams.

Pupils who have cameras can be asked to take photographs showing erosion compared with soil conservation. Bare soil versus soil containing plants can be discussed in local areas. The major difference between weathering and erosion can be developed when photographs or movies show erosion as the *movement* of the rock and soil being carried away by water. Both weathering and erosion break rocks down into ultimate soil particles.

Volcano

To demonstrate volcano eruption, prepare a model (fig. 14.3) from either papier-mâché or clay. The model could be about 1 foot high and on a base 2 feet long. The model could be prepared by some of the pupils. Place 2 heaping tablespoonfuls of ammonium dichromate into a small plastic

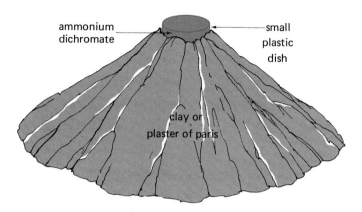

Fig. 14.3.   Model of volcano.

dish, for example, one that is frequently used to measure coffee. Place the plastic dish on top of the cone. Ignite the orange ammonium dichromate with a match. In a darkened room the smoke, fire, and colorful display of shooting green powder into the air which soon falls along the slope of the cone can be seen. The green powder slides along the sides as though molten lava were flowing.

If a more dramatic, sparkling effect is desired, place 1 inch of magnesium ribbon into the ammonium dichromate before igniting the mixture. However, exercise care that the sprinkles do not reach any of the observers.

Open-ended Laboratory to Identify Several Minerals

Museums and scientific supply companies usually sell boxes or packets containing common minerals. Each pupil can be provided with five or six common minerals in addition to the following: unglazed porcelain plate, glass plate, steel nail, magnet, copper penny, magnifying glass, *dilute* hydrochloric acid *(caution: if acid comes in contact with clothing or the body; wash promptly with water),* beam balance, and a "black" light if available.

Each student or student group has a different set of minerals. Have him determine the physical properties of each mineral and complete the following chart.

PROPERTIES OF MINERALS

	1	*2*	*3*	*4*	*5*
Color Degree of shine Weight Color it writes Magnetism Reaction with acid Hardness					

Depending on the ability of the class, the teacher will determine how detailed the laboratory directions have to be. If the emphasis is on process, then fewer teacher-directed instructions are given. In a slower class, the teacher usually needs to give very specific directions.

For a class where more teacher directions are required, a different approach ("closed-ended" laboratory) may be employed. Place a set of minerals and a "mineral identification chart" before each student and provide him with laboratory instructions for testing the various minerals. Ask the students to write the name for each unknown mineral by inspecting the chart, and then test each one to verify it.

The following anecdote was mimeographed and given to the pupils who were performing an open-ended laboratory experiment:

Tom and Jack are on an ocean cruise. There are two swimming pools: fresh and salt water. Both brothers were told not to go swimming. They went for a swim, each in a different pool, when their parents took a nap. Later, one of the brother's swimsuits was still wet.

The concept the teacher wanted to develop as a result of this open-ended laboratory was that *sea salt is hygroscopic* (absorbs moisture from the air). After each pupil read the anecdote, the teacher asked, "What is the problem?" The pupils suggested the following problems: Which type of water (fresh or salt) leaves a detectable trace? Which brother was punished? How did the parents know that one of the boys went into the salt water pool? Which swimsuit dried faster?

The pupils were asked for their ideas (hypotheses) which they could test. The following were some of the hypotheses proposed:

1. Salt water leaves a residue of salt.
2. You can smell salt water.
3. The swimsuit would be stiff from the salt water.
4. Both swimsuits would be wrinkled.

During discussion of the design of experiments to test hypotheses, the following were suggested: Take samples of cloth from which swimsuits are made and immerse one in salt water and another in fresh water. Weigh each sample before they are immersed. Weigh each sample again when soaked. After one sample is completely dry through evaporation, weigh each sample again and compare. Other students suggested that the wet samples should be weighed at fifteen-minute intervals and recorded on a chart (see following page):

Frequently an "open-ended" laboratory such as this may require more than one laboratory period. Sometimes the laboratory procedure is continued after school or at home. In this laboratory situation the pupils came to the conclusion in observing the hygroscopic property of sea salt.

WEIGHT OF SAMPLES

	Fresh Water	Salt Water
Wet 15 minutes 30 minutes 45 minutes Dry		

I. Physical features of the earth   **Background**
    A. Size and shape   **Information**

1. Speculation that the earth was a sphere was made in the fifth century B.C. by Parmenides of Elea.
2. Pythagoras taught that the earth was a globe.
3. Newton predicted that the earth had a slight bulge at the equator and was a little flattened at the poles.
4. The shape of earth resembles a grapefruit.
5. It is estimated that the earth is a little over 13 miles wider than its height; its circumference is about 24,860 miles.

    B. Composition
1. Four layers in the earth
    a. Thin crust (outermost)
    b. Solid mantle
    c. Liquid outer core
    d. Central probably solid body (innermost)
        (1) Scientists guess at the interior composition.
        (2) Probably iron and nickel are found.
        (3) For every 60-foot descent, there is about 1° F. increase in the temperature; at this rate, it is estimated that

the temperature may be as high as 350,000° F.

C. Minerals and rocks

  1. Rocks—aggregates of minerals

    a. Igneous rocks became solid rock from their original molten state and are crystalline in structure. Examples are granite and basalt.

      (1) They are found at bottom of other rocks located in the ocean floor.

      (2) Some igneous rocks are exposed and may be found in mountainous regions.

    b. Sedimentary or layered rocks

      (1) Originally most of them were deposited under water.

      (2) Examples are sandstone, shale, limestone, and conglomerates.

      (3) Conglomerates resemble concrete, which is consolidated gravel cemented together.

    c. Metamorphic rocks were formed as a result of changes by heat or a combination of heat and pressure in the earth.

      (1) Originally metamorphic rock was either igneous or sedimentary rock that was changed by pressure and/or heat.

      (2) Limestone was changed into marble by heat and pressure.

      (3) Gneiss was changed from granite.

      (4) Slate was changed from shale.

      (5) Metamorphic rocks may be found in the roots of old mountains and in the volcanic activity areas.

2. Minerals—occur in nature as inorganic compounds and can be expressed by a chemical formula.

    a. Color, hardness, and cleavage are properties used to identify a mineral in the field. Many field guides to common rocks and minerals are available (see bibliography, appendix).

    b. The following chart shows the metal that is extracted from the mineral.

Metal	Mineral
(1) aluminum	bauxite, cryolite
(2) calcium	gypsum, chalk
(3) chromium	chromite
(4) copper	chalcocite, cuprite
(5) iron	pyrite, magnetite, hematite
(6) lead	galena
(7) lithium	spodumene
(8) magnesium	magnesite
(9) mercury	cinnabar
(10) potassium	sylvite
(11) silver	silver sulfide
(12) sodium	common salt
(13) tin	cassiterite
(14) zinc	sphalerite

    c. Uses of rocks and minerals

        (1) Construction of homes, factories, and so on

        (2) Medicines

        (3) Fertilizers for better agricultural production

        (4) Extraction of metals for various parts in airplane, automotive, and other vehicles

        (5) Manufacture of glass and glass products

        (6) Medical and dental instruments

        (7) Development of communication and radar systems

II.   Processes that change the earth's surface

    A.   Erosion—the disintegration, wearing away, and removal of rock material

        1. Weathering—the disintegration brought about by gases in the air such as carbon dioxide and by rainwater and ice

           a. Chemical weathering—limestone is attacked because calcite is soluble in carbonic acid. The carbonic acid is formed when the carbon dioxide from the atmosphere combines with the rainwater. Chemical changes also affect the colors; minerals containing iron and magnesium appear as red and brown stains in rocks.

           b. Mechanical weathering—freezing water in crevices breaks up rocks and causes disintegration; the same is achieved by the growth of plant roots as well as extreme temperature changes. Ultimately rock is changed to pebbles and sand.

           c. Stream erosion—running water of streams is a most important agent; it cuts the sides and bottom of its pathway. The volume of water and the slope affect the changing shape of the stream. Cutting, scraping, ramming, grinding, and pounding of rocks, debris, boulders, sand grains, and pebbles are responsible for the changes in the appearance of a stream, its banks, and its bottom. Theoretically, though not in reality, stream erosion wears away a land surface to almost a flat plain at sea level.

2. Glaciers—moving ice as glacial erosion
   a. Valley glaciers are found in the Alps, western United States, and on the Alaska coast.
   b. Ice caps are located over most of Greenland and Antarctica.
3. Groundwater—dissolving action
   a. Upper surface of the saturated area is known as the water table.
   b. Groundwater moves rapidly through coarse material like gravel or sand and slowly through fine substances like clay.
   c. It dissolves much material and carries away minerals to cause hardness in water wells.
   d. It forms caves.

B. Vulcanism—movement of liquid rock
   1. Warning of earthquakes or minor shocks frequently precede an eruption of a volcano.
   2. Underground gases and liquids cause explosions as fragments of solid materials, water droplets, and gases are hurled into space.
   3. Molten rock (magma) pours out above ground and is known as lava.
   4. Volcanoes build up mountains.
   5. Molten lava solidifies into various volcanic rocks such as:
      (a) Basalt
      (b) Obsidian

Earthquakes.

       (c) Pumice

6. Heat and pressure built up in the interior of the earth melt rocks that work their way up.

7. Radioactive elements in the earth's interior supply much of the heat energy.

C. Diastrophism—mechanical changes such as folding, warping, jointing, and faulting in the earth's crust

D. Earthquakes—and the earth's structure

    1. Seismology—the science of earthquakes

        a. Seismograph is the instrument that measures intensity, shock effects, speed, and direction of earthquakes.

        b. The shocks travel by wave motion in the various parts of the earth.

(1) Primary (longitudinal) waves (P) are fast waves recorded on the seismograph.

(2) Secondary (transverse) waves (S) are recorded on the seismograph seconds after the primary waves.

(3) The center of the earthquake is located by a process involving the interval between the arrival of P- and S-waves.

(4) Earthquake studies enable scientists to learn about the interior of the earth's surface.

2. Causes of earthquakes

    a. Artificial explosions

    b. Landslides

    c. Movement of magma before and during volcanic eruptions

    d. Dislocation of solid rocks along faults

III. Earth's characteristics—estimates

    A. Average density—345 lb./cubic foot

    B. Average speed in orbit—18.5 miles/second

    C. Circumference at equator—24,902 miles

    D. Equatorial radius—3963.34 miles

    E. Land area—55,222,000 square miles

    F. Polar radius—3949.99 miles

    G. Radius (if a perfect sphere)—3958.9 miles

    H. Speed of rotation at equator—0.29 miles/second

    I. Surface area—196,940,000 square miles

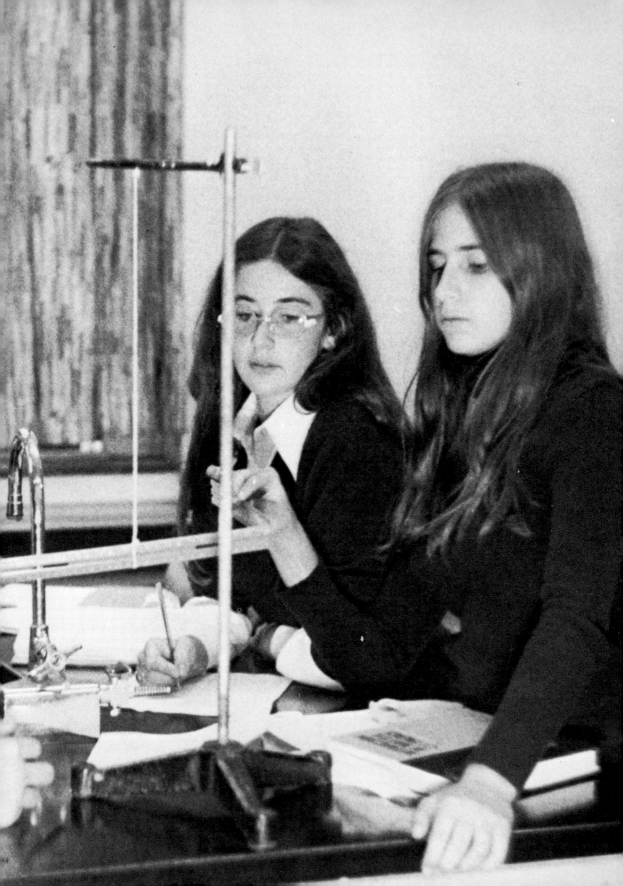

15

THE SOLAR SYSTEM

Grades K–2

Concepts

1. The sun is far away from the earth.
2. The sun gives light and heat.
3. The earth spins like a top, making day and night.
4. Stars are far away and look small.

Grades 3–5

5. Gravity keeps us from floating into space.
6. Planets move around the sun, and their "circular" paths (ellipses) are called orbits.
7. The sun is a star that gives off light directly.
8. The moon and planets give off reflected light.
9. The earth rotates every twenty-four hours and only part of it receives light from the sun at one time.

10. As the earth revolves around the sun each year, seasons change.

Grades 6–8

11. The tilt of the earth's axis makes for differences in the heat absorbed by the earth from the sun.
12. The Northern and Southern Hemispheres have opposite seasons.
13. Each planet is different in size and distance from the sun.
14. The sun, planets, satellites, planetoids, meteors, and comets make up the solar system.
15. A group of stars that appears to outline a figure is known as a constellation.
16. Time is determined by the rotation of the earth on its axis.

Concept Formation

The *descriptive* concepts pertaining to the solar system are numbered 1, 2, 4, 6, 7, 12, 13, and 14 and refer to distance, shape, pathway, and properties that make up the solar system.

Cause-and-effect relations are emphasized in concepts 3, 5, 8, and 16. In addition to cause and effect, there is a greater degree of *operational interrelationships*, along with cause and effect in concepts 9, 10, 11, and 15. In most instances, it appears that more experience in and out of class is usually required to develop concepts pertaining to the solar system.

The Sun

Children in the lower grades, kindergarten through

grade two, may have difficulty in visualizing the concept of distance such as *the sun is far away from the earth*. The measurement of distance such as one block or one street away has meaning. Children walk one or more blocks to school and are thus able to relate such distances. However, the unit as large as *mile* would present instructional problems unless related to children's experiences.

A discussion of how long it takes to travel by car, train, or plane to visit grandparents or other family members might serve as an introduction. Children who have taken long airplane trips with their parents might relate the fact that a whole day was spent traveling on the plane to Europe. Gradually, by relating a week or month with how far you could travel in that time, the concept can be developed that the sun is far away from the earth.

The sun gives light and heat. The concept that light is given off by the sun needs little discussion. However, the fact that heat is given off by the sun can be determined experimentally. An open-ended laboratory approach to determine if there is a difference in the temperature of two glasses of water when one glass is placed in direct sunlight and another in the shade will help develop the concept that heat is given off by the sun.

For purposes of inquiry children should ask questions of how to design these experiments. Questions of equal volumes of water and their importance, as well as why one glass should be kept in the shade, should be discussed in detail. If children have not yet learned to read thermometers, what means of temperature change can be used? For second graders who can see the increase in temperature in a thermometer, discuss whether several temperature readings every five minutes would be helpful.

Day and Night

The concept, *the earth spins like a top, making day and*

night, may evolve by the use of such toys as a top or a gyroscope in the class. Children enjoy playing with a spinning top. A flashlight can show how about half of the top receives light from it at any given time. A basketball may also be turned slowly in connection with a flashlight. The basketball and the spinning top represent the earth rotating on its axis while the flashlight acts as the sun.

Stars

Stars are far away and look small. Place a lighted flashlight in a closed shoebox with a small opening to permit light to leave the box. Have the children observe the light from the shoebox at close range. Compare the light when viewed many feet away at the end of a long corridor (fig. 15.1).

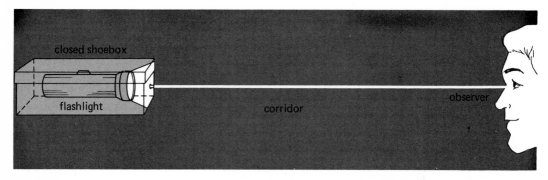

Fig. 15.1. Viewing light from a flashlight in a long corridor.

Planets

In grades three to five, children can make models using clay, papier-mâché, and other materials to demonstrate how planets move and reflect light. They can also play games in which different pupils represent a planet, a star (sun), or a

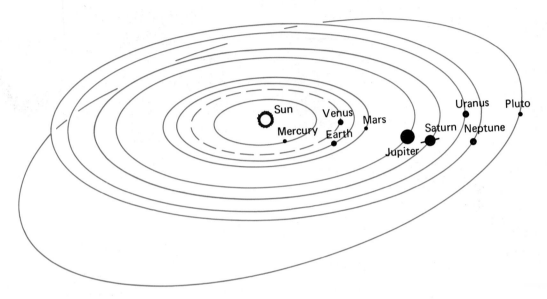

Fig. 15.2.   Solar system.

moon. Picture books can be used from kindergarten through the upper grades to visualize the appearance, size, shape, and relationships of the solar system.

Planets move around the sun and their "circular" paths (ellipses) are called orbits. Each pupil may represent a specific planet. He can have a poster pinned on his shirt to give the name of the planet or the sun. Each of the pupils at the signal will be asked to rotate and revolve in the classroom around the sun. The diagram in fig. 15.2 may serve as a guide.

Questions such as why Mercury is the brightest planet in the sky can be discussed while the game of how the solar system operates is being played. Discussions of space, distance, and movements of planets will enhance the imagination of the solar system.

Children can make models of planets or bring in different-size objects to represent planets. In a dark closet or a

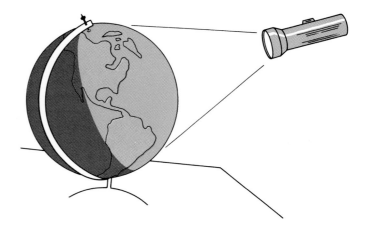

Fig. 15.3.   One side of earth receives sunlight at one time.

darkencd room, place the models and compare their visibility with and without a flashlight being used as a source of light. Discuss other objects in a darkened room and their visibility when another source of light such as a candle or electric bulb is used. These activities and discussions should lead to the development of the following concepts: *The moon and planets give off reflected light. The sun is a star that gives off light directly.*

What causes day and night? This question can initiate the design of how to show that only one side of the earth receives the sun's rays at a given time. A globe to represent the earth and a source of light will demonstrate that when it is day on one part of the earth, it is night on another. By rotating the globe, daylight and darkness can be observed. Thus the following concept is taught: *the earth rotates every twenty-four hours and only part of it receives light from the sun* (refer to fig. 15.3).

Light cannot pass through solid objects and thus forms shadows. The formation of shadows can be demonstrated easily. Ask the pupils how the following materials could be used: a projector, a screen, black construction paper, and chalk. "Sit on a chair between the lamp and the screen," is a common suggestion. After one or more children do this, ask others to indicate what they observe on the screen. A pupil's face or head is observed. "What happened to the light?" "Susan's face is blocking the light." A series of pupil questions and answers will develop the understanding of how shadows are formed. Change the position of the chair and the pupil. Pupils should be encouraged to raise other questions and make predictions. Such predictions should be tested and discussed.

Some children will make profiles using the chalk on the black construction paper. Questions on whether the size of the profile could be varied should be discussed and tested. The enlargement of profiles or pictures and varying the intensity of the light will also evolve from these discussions and experiments. Ultimately these experiences should be related to the intensity of the sun's rays, surface area covered, and their effect on the earth.

Problem Solving

A problem-solving approach may be used to develop the concept, *the Northern and Southern Hemispheres have opposite seasons* (see figs. 15.4 and 15.5). The same materials used for day and night can be used again, namely, a globe and a lamp on a table.

The following anecdote is presented by the teacher: "It is three weeks before Christmas in New York. Your older sister wants to send your cousin a swimsuit for a Christmas gift. Your cousin lives in Australia and you think it a terrible idea because the beaches in New York are extremely cold around Christmas. Your older sister knows much, and she has very good taste. What is the problem?"

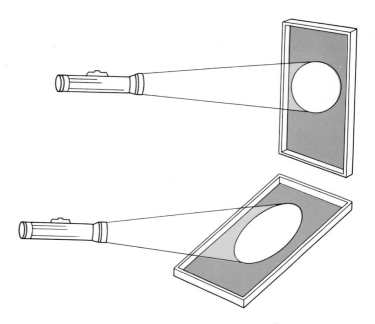

Fig. 15.4.   Direct and oblique sun rays on surface area.

The concept of seasonal changes with relation to the Northern and Southern Hemispheres is tested as a result of solving this problem. The pupils are encouraged to propose, screen, and test their hypotheses. The identification and statement of the problem should be made at the very beginning. A globe of the world and a lamp should be available. Encourage discussion by asking pupils if they agree or disagree with the hypotheses before they are tested.

When possible encourage pupils to ask questions such as, "Which hemisphere receives more direct sunlight during December?" Questions and answers pertaining to oblique (slanted) rays, the intensive or extensive sun's rays in terms of covered surface area (fig. 15.4) should also arise from the pupils. The effects of action by the sun, weather, and climate should also be discussed.

In grades five through eight, the concept, *each planet is different in size and distance from the sun,* can evolve from a study of the characteristics of the various planets. Pupils can make models of the solar system, showing approximate relative sizes of the planets.

Note the following two concepts: (1) *the sun, planets, satellites, planetoids, meteors, and comets make up the solar system;* and (2) *a group of stars that appears to outline a figure is known as a constellation.* The pupils may be asked to make observations in the sky during the evening. Students who have telescopes should use them for their observations. Shoeboxes or other paper boxes and construction paper can be used to cut out the stars that make up the more common constellations. Lighting arrangements can facilitate the study of these constellations. The construction paper with holes representing stars may be placed against a bright window for class study. An old umbrella with cutouts can also be used to represent constellations. Creative projects of this type frequently develop much interest in astronomy.

Fig. 15.5. Sun rays on Northern and Southern hemispheres.

Time and Earth

In establishing the concept that *time is determined by the rotation of the earth on its axis,* several activities can be

CHARACTERISTICS OF PLANETS

	Millions of Miles from Sun	Mass (earth = 1)	Density (water = 1)	Rotation (days)	Radius (earth = 1)	Temperature (°F)
Mercury	36	.054	5.46	88	.38	(Light side) 780
Venus	67	.814	4.96	15–30	.967	(Dark side) −9
Earth	93	1.000	5.52	1.00	1.000	(Light side) 135
Mars	140	.107	4.12	1.03	.523	(Mean) 57
Jupiter	480	318	1.33	.41	10.97	(Warmest) 54
Saturn	890	95.3	.71	.43	9.03	−36
Uranus	1,800	14.6	1.56	.45	3.72	−225
Neptune	2,800	17.3	2.47	.66	3.38	−300
Pluto	3,700	.1	5.5	?	.45	?

performed. For a problem-solving lesson the teacher may display an unmarked globe of the earth with meridian lines shown only at the poles and at the equator with a number of strings attached to the North Pole. One of the pupils locates 0 degree meridian at the equator. Another pupil pulls one of the strings to that point, fastens it, and continues to connect the string to the South Pole. The central meridian for Eastern Standard Time is located by another pupil who connects the string through the corresponding point at the equator and continues attaching it to the South Pole. If in New York City, another pupil is asked to tell in which central meridian New York is located.

In using problem-solving situations the teacher can present anecdotes or situations such as, "Your parents or friends are in London, England. They wish to telephone you before 10 P.M., EST on May 1. What time and day should they place their call in order to reach you shortly before your bedtime in New York City?" The pupils will learn how to use the globe, counting 15 degrees for each longitude and allowing an hour for each 15 degrees on the globe. Several children can pose their own problems by suggesting where their relatives live in distant places and solving their own problems.

Laboratory and Demonstration Activities

Developing a planetarium. You have just volunteered to set up a planetarium for the school science fair. You wish to show a model of the solar system that demonstrates the distances between the planets and their proper proportion. The information on the top of the next page (see list of planets) is available to you.

The pupils were asked to state the problem. One pupil said, "To show the distance between planets using a scale model." A discussion was held on what is the meaning of a scale model, how to make measurements, and what materi-

Planet	Distance from Sun (in miles)
Mercury	36,000,000
Venus	67,000,000
Earth	93,000,000
Mars	142,000,000
Jupiter	483,000,000
Saturn	886,000,000
Uranus	1,702,000,000
Neptune	2,793,000,000
Pluto	3,670,000,000

als could be used. Some pupils suggested different-size beads, marbles, Ping-Pong balls, softballs, or basketballs; other children proposed to use a cash-register tape. One group of pupils used varied sizes of register tape, while another group used different kinds of balls.

After constructing the planetarium, the pupils recognized the vast difference in distance Pluto and Neptune are from the sun compared with the earth–sun distance.

Discussion

1. How far would the moon be from the earth if the average distance of the moon from the earth is 240,000 miles?

2. If the Apollo astronauts traveled to Mars, how long would the trip take? Assume they are traveling at the same speed when it took them three days to travel to the moon (a distance of 240,000 miles). How long would it take to go to Venus and return to the earth?

3. Would you like to travel to Pluto at the same speed the Apollo astronauts traveled to the moon? Why?

**Reading
and Scientific
Thinking**

An excerpt from an article such as the following can be used to provoke scientific thinking as scientists make measurements and predictions:

> By comparing data from the space probes of Venera 4 and Mariner 5, a value of about 6085 ± 10 km. was deduced for the radius of Venus.
>
> The Mariner experimenters pointed out their value differs strikingly from the radius of 6056 ± 1 km. obtained in mid-1966 from an analysis of Earth-Venus and Earth-Mercury radar data.
>
> The scientists checked, of course, for various causes for the discrepancies. For example, "The slowing down of radar waves in the atmosphere of Venus has been estimated for rather extreme atmospheric conditions and found to be insignificant in its effect on the radar radius."
>
> The article concludes, "It is obviously of considerable importance to resolve this question of the radius of Venus not only because of the implications concerning atmospheric and surface conditions, but because the accuracy with which radar and radio observations can be used to test gravitational theories is also thrown into doubt."[1]

Students in grades six, seven, or eight can read the above excerpt or similar ones with a view to arguing the importance of scientists' rechecking their measurements and related data. How much confidence does a scientist place in an instrument such as radar? How accurate are observations? What are the possible sources of error? These kinds of questions will evoke responses that relate to the ways in which scientists work.

[1]From W. G. Melbourne, "Radar Detection of the Radius of Venus," *Science* 130 (31 May 1969): 985–87.

Concepts that are developed from a study of the different phases of the moon are:

1. We see the moon as a result of reflected sunlight.
2. It takes the same time for the moon to rotate on its axis as it does to revolve in its orbit around the earth.
3. Differences in the appearance of the moon are caused by changing positions of the moon with respect to the earth and the sun.

To develop an understanding of the third concept, the following problem can be introduced to the class via an anecdote: "John and Susan were walking in the park on a pleasant evening. John remembered seeing a full moon several days ago. He was disappointed when he failed to see a full moon."

When the teacher asked the class to state John's problem, a pupil said: "What made the moon change its appearance?" The teacher asked for various hypotheses and the following three were suggested: The clouds change the appearance of the moon; there must be an obstruction that changes the form and appearance of the moon; changing the position of the moon with relation to the earth and sun makes the moon look different.

In testing the last hypothesis, students were used to simulate models of the earth, sun, and moon. A projector was used as a source of light. The pupil acting like a moon (holding a globe) walked around the classroom (earth). A chart was placed on the board and discussed as the pupils completed the columns under appearance and phase of the moon.

As a result of using the globe showing the map of the world, pupils may wonder about the heights of various places. This can be accomplished through the use of maps. The concept of a contour line that connects points of equal elevation above sea level was taught by the problem-solving method, illustrated as follows:

> Mayday! Mayday! Somewhere over Chelan National Forest . . . engine trouble . . . heading NE . . . passed over a large glacier . . . am following small stream . . . passing over a small lake . . . there is a fork in the stream . . . altitude about 7,200 ft. . . . a mountain is ahead . . . can't make it over . . . Help!

Equipment necessary: Contour map of Chelan National Forest.

A. Identify and state the problem.
   1. The airplane is in trouble. (True, but we cannot solve this problem.)
   2. The plane must find a safe place to land. (No, from the message, the implication is that it crashed.)
   3. The plane must be located before the blizzard sets into the area.
B. Select and screen the hypotheses.
   1. Divide the area of the Chelan National Forest and search by plane. (It might take too much time.)
   2. Try to locate the area according to the last message by plane and by foot. (This, too, would take too much time.)
   3. Use a map to locate the position of the plane. (Fine, what kind of map would be used?)
C. Elicit from the students the idea of a relief or topographic map.
   1. Distribute maps to students.
   2. What is the significance of the curved lines? What do the numbers mean?
   Discuss the relationship of the contour lines and

the elevation. The contour interval is indicated on the map. Only every fifth line is indicated by the actual elevation.

D.   Have each student locate the probable crash area by using the map and information given.

(Lesson developed by Mrs. Dorothy Webster, a graduate student at Queens College.)

I.   Planets

   A.   Mercury
1. Called "the twinkle" by the Greeks
2. Smallest in size and mass of all the planets
3. Receives the most heat and light from the sun
4. Has phases like those of the moon and its illuminated hemisphere can be seen from all angles
5. Brightest in the crescent phase
6. Has no moons
7. No evidence of an atmosphere
8. Hottest on one side; the other side, in eternal darkness, is coldest planet in the solar system.

   B.   Venus
1. With the exception of the sun and moon, the brightest object in the sky
2. Most nearly circular orbit of all the planets
3. Mass of Venus about 82% that of earth
4. Has no moons
5. Covered by a thick layer of opaque cloud
6. Atmosphere largely carbon dioxide
7. Takes at least a month to turn on her axis and receives the sun on all parts at different times

   C.   Earth
1. Has a satellite, the moon

 2. Is densest body in the solar system with the possible exception of Pluto whose value has not been determined
 3. Makes a revolution in a nearly circular path
 4. Is fifth in diameter and fifth in mass among all the planets
 5. Unique planet in that it supports life well

D. Mars
 1. Some scientists report that living things exist on this red planet.
 2. Appears red because it reflects less blue light
 3. Reflects light poorly
 4. Mars day about one-half hour longer than the earth's day
 5. Has an atmosphere
 6. Has seasonal changes as noted from polar caps
 7. Has two moons

E. Jupiter
 1. Brightest of all planets except Venus and sometimes Mars
 2. Larger than all other planets put together
 3. Density about one-fourth less than that of the earth
 4. Has the smallest day of all planets, nine hours, fifty minutes
 5. Atmosphere—contains hydrogen, nitrogen, and carbon; gases methane (CH_4) and ammonia (NH_3) identified
 6. Light—reflected sunlight
 7. System of twelve moons
 8. Some scientists speculate that Jupiter may have many more moons than can be observed at present.

F. Saturn
 1. Most oblate of all the planets

2. Density so low that it could float on water
3. Hydrogen atmosphere
4. A short day, about ten hours, thirty-eight minutes
5. Nine satellites identified; most larger than the moons of Jupiter
6. Unique characteristic—system of rings that can be observed through a telescope
7. Rings probably rocky fragments, pebbles, and dust

G. Uranus
   1. Varying degree of brightness as it turns on its axis
   2. Resembles Saturn and Jupiter in its structure
   3. Five moons observed

H. Neptune
   1. Considered almost a twin of Uranus
   2. Not visible to the naked eye
   3. Bluish green appearance
   4. Mass about 17.3 times that of the earth
   5. Two satellites identified

I. Pluto
   1. Outermost of known planets
   2. Probably no atmosphere
   3. Part of its orbit lies within the orbit of Neptune, but a collision is practically impossible.

I. The sun
   A. Dimensions
      1. Average distance from the earth to the sun—93 million miles
      2. Size—109.3 times the mean diameter of the earth.
      3. More than 1 million times the volume of the earth

    4. A little more than 300,000 times the earth's mass

    5. Surface temperature from about 6,000° K. to about 20,000,000° K.

    6. Gravity on surface of sun approximately twenty-eight times as much as on the earth

B. Face of the sun

    1. Observations report swirling, boiling, and violent motions.

    2. Sunspots appear as markings through the telescope.

    3. Clouds of glowing gas are observed as prominences.

    4. Photosphere is the visible sphere of light and is believed to be opaque and contain great amounts of hydrogen atoms.

C. Sunspots

    1. Sunspots are large areas of the solar surface about 800 to 80,000 kilometers across and are not as brilliant as the surrounding areas.

    2. They occur in groups.

    3. Most exist for less than four days.

    4. Disturbances resembling tornadoes break through the photosphere.

    5. Affect and disturb electrical (radio, TV) communication by affecting ionization layers in the atmosphere by ejecting high-speed electrical particles from the sun.

    6. Speculations are made about relationships to weather cycles, business activity, wars, and other human problems.

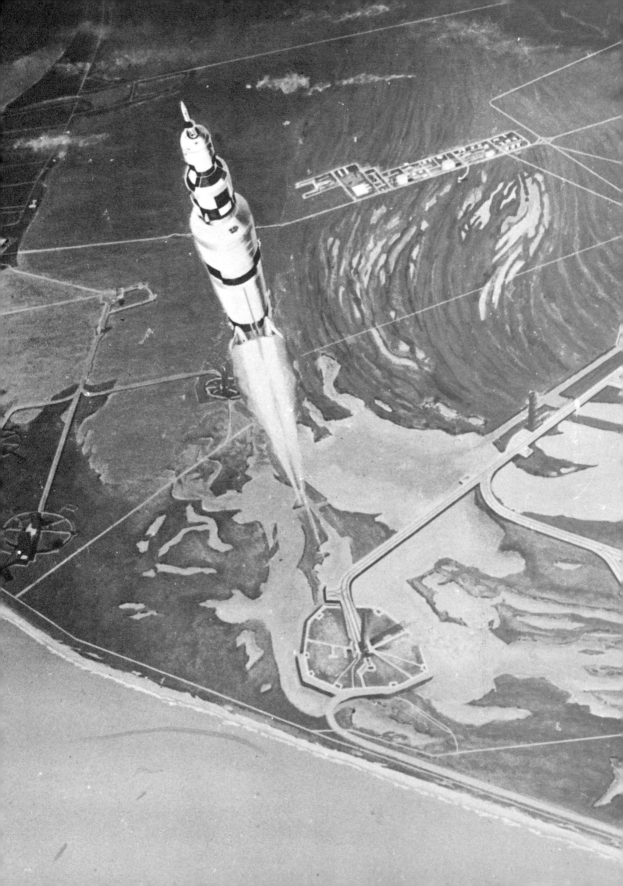

16

SPACE TRAVEL: AIRPLANES, JETS, ROCKETS, AND SPACE VEHICLES

Grades K–2

Concepts

1. We can travel all over the earth with an airplane.
2. Rockets help push astronauts in space to travel to the moon.
3. Jets travel much faster than propeller-type airplanes.
4. Radar helps an airplane land safely in bad weather.
5. Astronauts have special clothing to wear on the moon.

Grades 3–5

6. We learned to travel faster in air and in space from the balloon to jet to space vehicle.
7. Air pressure holds the airplane up.

8. Thrust is a force that moves the airplane forward.
9. To raise an airplane off the ground, an upward force called lift is needed to overcome gravity.

Grades 6–8

10. A satellite will orbit the earth when no air resistance is present to slow it down.
11. Retro-rockets act like brakes in slowing down a satellite, causing the satellite to fall from its orbit.
12. Satellites collect and transmit information on temperature, intensity of radiation such as cosmic and ultraviolet rays, and the size and shape of the earth's magnetic field.
13. Satellites benefit man by worldwide communications, weather and climate conditions forecasts, and navigational aids to ships.
14. Astronauts who land on the moon provide us with samples of rocks and minerals to show its composition and structure and provide information about space and the universe.
15. Rocket propulsion is an example of Newton's third law of motion—action and reaction.

Concept Formation

The concepts numbered 1 through 9 deal chiefly with aviation, especially the principles of flight. These are primarily descriptive ideas that have appeal on lower grade levels from kindergarten through grade five. In grades three to five more specific concepts pertaining to the principles of flight appear in the form of four forces that operate on an airplane in flight: lift, thrust, drag, and gravity.

In grades six through eight, concepts 10 through 15 pertain to satellites and space travel. The emphasis is not only on cause and effect as given in grades three to five but also on uses and implications for man.

History of Flight

Children and adults still marvel at seeing an airplane in the sky. The sudden appearance of loud, booming noise and its immediate disappearance still cause us to be curious about the nature of flight. Telling stories about the history of flying and the ultimate discovery of how to fly can be a stimulating experience for children in the lower grades. This can be followed by a series of aerospace and flight film-strips, film loops, or movies. Such materials are readily available for rental or purchase from commercial sources. Many aircraft companies and airlines will gladly furnish movies at no cost to schools.

We can begin our story of flying with the legends handed down by the ancient Greeks. One idea that prevailed was that a man was carried through the sky on the back of a huge eagle. Another story was told that Daedalus and Icarus escaped from an island prison by attaching feathers to their arms with wax. They both plunged to their deaths when the wax melted when they flew too close to the sun. In the ancient Orient interesting tales were told about how people wanted very much to fly.

Not until about the time Columbus discovered America did the groundwork for applying scientific principles appear. The famous Italian artist and inventor, Leonardo da Vinci, sketched an airplane with flapping wings. He also sketched a helicopter that used an air screw. About eighteen hundred years earlier, Archimedes found that when an object is lighter than the water it displaces, the surrounding water pushes the object upward. This caused many people to inquire why

The Wright Brothers.   this could not be true in the air as well as in water. In 1783 two French brothers, Montgolfier, filled a cloth bag with hot air. Because hot air is lighter than the surrounding colder air, the bag rose. Others substituted hydrogen gas for the hot air.

Thus the beginning of lighter-than-air craft, or balloons, came into existence. Sandbags were taken aloft and were dropped to control upward movement. To descend, gas was released from the balloon. At the beginning the fliers of balloons depended on the ocean of air or winds for horizontal movement. Finally, a French engineer, Henri Giffard, by adding propellers and streamlining the balloon, was able to control horizontal movement.

Many people were still not satisfied with only lighter-than-air flight. They conducted many experiments such as imitating birds by flapping wings but were unsuccessful. Steam-driven propellers on gliders were used by the end of the nineteenth century. This plane would get off the ground briefly but could not stay aloft. Batlike wings were unsatisfactorily employed. Englishmen, Germans, Frenchmen, and others experimented. Otto Lilienthal, a German engineer, was about to add a lightweight gas engine when he was killed in a crash. Finally, following the studies on gliders made by Lilienthal, two American brothers, Orville and Wilbur Wright, used a wind tunnel to conduct their experiments in their bicycle store in Dayton, Ohio. They discovered how to maintain level flight and make turns by twisting the wings. On 17 December 1903 at Kitty Hawk, North Carolina, they flew an airplane of their design for which they built their own powerful engine.

Experiments

The following activities will aid in formulating several concepts on flying. How does air lift things? It may be helpful to review the fact that air occupies space. A glass which is half filled with water is covered tightly with a piece of cardboard. The glass is inverted in a large jar of water and, while immersed, the cardboard is removed. Move the inverted glass at an angle of about 45 degrees and observe the bubbles of air from the glass escaping through the water in the jar. Through questions and discussion, the children will become aware of the fact that the half-filled glass of water contained a half-glass of air (fig. 16.1).

To show how air supports water in a glass, the same materials can be used. Fill the glass to the brim with water, making certain that no air is in the glass. Place the cardboard on top of the glass tightly, making certain again that no air bubbles or air spaces are in the glass. Invert the glass, supporting the cardboard with your hand. The column of air under the cardboard will exert enough pressure on the card-

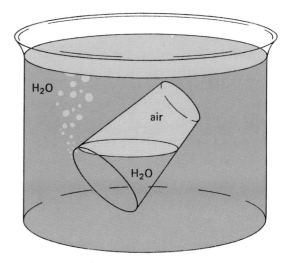

Fig. 16.1.   Air bubbles escaping from glass.

board so that the water will remain in the upside-down glass when your hand is removed from the cardboard.

Gliders

Invite children to design different types of gliders from paper. Some of the designs will look like those in fig. 16.2. Indoors or outdoors the flight of these paper gliders will develop into interesting discussions about the size, shape, and folds in the paper. The children can measure the distances and durations of flight in the different types of gliders they made. The game idea of creating a glider that will stay aloft and travel a great distance can be a fun activity in or out of class.

How do we slow down something that is traveling through the air? In a discussion the parachute will be mentioned. As a laboratory activity the children can make their own parachutes by connecting four pieces of thread to the edges of a piece of facial tissue. The other ends of the four pieces of thread are connected together to a piece of chalk or other object which will bring down the parachute (tissue). Observations are made on how air fills up the parachute and how it floats as it touches the ground.

Flight and Airplane Forces

In grades three to five, the following activities are useful in developing concepts on flight. Bernoulli's principle (see fig. 16.3) is demonstrated to show the lifting effect. Take an 8½″ × 11″ sheet of paper and place one of the

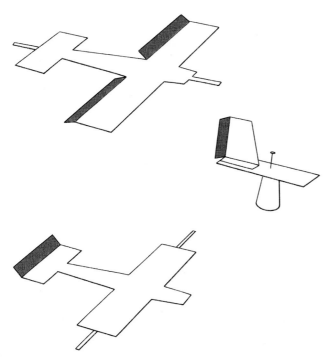

Fig. 16.2.   Gliders.

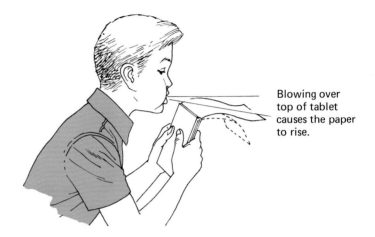

Blowing over top of tablet causes the paper to rise.

Fig. 16.3.   Bernoulli s principle.

edges of the paper under the lips about 1 inch away from the mouth. Blow vigorously on top of the edge of the paper and note how the paper lifts upward. The speed of the moving air on top of the paper is faster, and the air pressure is lower. Because the air pressure under the wing is greater than that above the wing, it supports the weight of the airplane. The wings of airplanes are curved on the upper surface to provide a greater surface area or greater distance for the air to travel as compared with the undersurface. Yet the air from the engine striking the wings will reach the opposite end of the wings at the same time. Hence the air on the upper surface of the wing would move faster and its pressure reduced.

To demonstrate how air pressure can lift things, have children bring in different-sized paper bags. Each pupil can place a book on top of the bag. By blowing up the bag, the book will be lifted (see fig. 16.4). Note how air supports the wing because of higher air pressure under it (fig. 16.5).

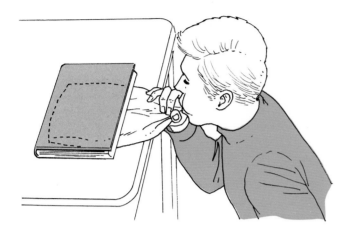

Fig. 16.4.   Moving air lifts objects.

Fig. 16.5.   Air flow around wing.

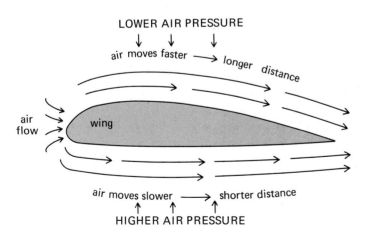

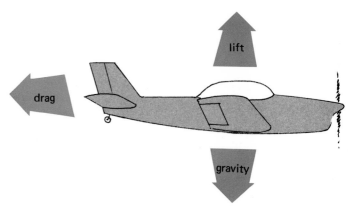

Fig. 16.6.   Airplane forces.

To overcome drag and cause an airplane to move, thrust is needed. When the forces of lift and thrust are greater than the forces of drag and gravity, an airplane will fly (see fig. 16.6). Thrust is provided by an engine. Jet propulsion or a propeller moves the plane forward. The engine either drives a propeller or provides jet propulsion.

Thrust in a jet can be studied by using a toy balloon. In a jet, thrust is produced by directing high-velocity gases to

Fig. 16.7.   Action-Reaction.

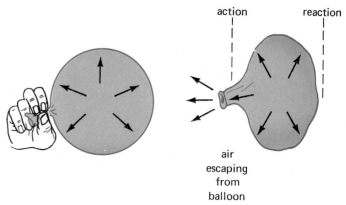

the rear. Similarly a balloon travels forward as the escaping air is released in a backward direction. This is an illustration of Newton's third law: "For every action, there is an equal and opposite reaction" (see fig. 16.7).

Encourage pupils to design an experiment that illustrates how a jet flies. Stretch string or wire across in a room. Using balloons, paper clips, and straws, or other suggested materials, pupils should attempt to create a thrust situation with a balloon that resembles a jet. This type of activity becomes a problem-solving situation, especially if the first trial does not work perfectly. The action-reaction law can be demonstrated through this problem-solving activity and at the same time the children can visualize a flying jet.

Launching a Rocket

The law of action-reaction is also applied in the launching of a rocket. One of the major problems in the development of launching a space vehicle into orbit was that the old single-stage rockets would melt before they reached the stratosphere. The friction produced by the high-speed rocket traveling in air was very great. This caused an excessive amount of heat that melted the rocket. For many years before Sputnik was launched, the thermal barrier was a problem that hindered the launching of a satellite into space. Finally through research scientists found that a multistage or three-stage rocket is needed. As a result, the speed required for a space vehicle to go into orbit would gradually be attained without causing the rocket and the vehicle to melt.

Different stages were used to increase the velocity slowly. Friction was reduced so that the rocket would not burn up. With each stage, as the rocket went higher in space, it traveled faster. The higher in altitude and in space, the less was the friction, because little air was available.

The original rocket engines used solid fuel and carried

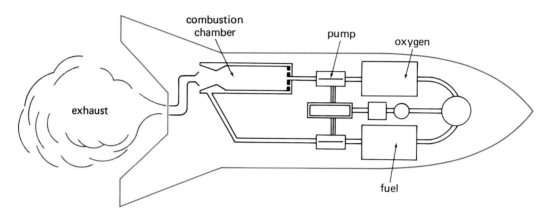

Fig. 16.8. Liquid propellant rocket.

their own sources of oxygen. Liquid-fuel rockets have two tanks: In one of the tanks, liquid hydrogen is stored, and the second tank contains a liquid oxidizer. With the aid of a pump, the fuel and oxygen is forced into a combustion chamber (see fig. 16.8). The speed with which the fuel flows into the combustion chamber is controlled by valves. This determines the speed of the rocket and the required velocity needed to go into orbit. When the propellant is ignited in the combustion chamber, hot gases form and exit through the exhaust. The exhaust gases cause the forward motion of the rocket. By changing the stream of the exhaust, the rocket's direction can be changed.

Getting Satellites into Orbit

To launch a satellite into orbit, it must attain a speed of 17,500 miles per hour. The weight of the fuel slows down a rocket. By using three stages, where the first two stages drop off during flight, the decrease in weight of fuel increases the speed of the rocket. The first-stage booster burns out and drops off after three minutes, when the launch vehicle attains a speed of about 7,000 miles per hour at an altitude of about 38 miles. The nose cone separates during the second stage, which burns off when the launch vehicle is about 300 miles above the earth. It is now traveling at about 10,000 miles per hour. The third-stage rocket detaches from the satellite when the speed is about 17,500 miles per hour, the speed required for the satellite to stay in orbit.

Sir Isaac Newton described an imaginary man-made satellite. Imagine a huge mountain that extended above the atmosphere and had a gigantic cannon on its summit. If the cannon were fired, what would happen to its missile? Newton's first law of motion states that an object moves in a straight line at a constant speed unless a force acts on it. Gravity is the force that acts on the missile and pulls it toward the center of the earth, resembling the curved path A in fig. 16.9. By placing a greater explosive charge in the cannon, the velocity of the missile would increase. The missile would travel farther out into space before falling to earth. This might look like path B or C in fig. 16.9, depending on its velocity. By making the explosive still stronger, the velocity of the cannon would further increase, and it might move along path D in the diagram. Along path D the satellite continues to fall but does not land on the earth. The curved path of D matches the curve of the earth. The satellite would continue to orbit the earth indefinitely because no air resistance is present to slow it down. This would now be a satellite instead of a missile. When the rocket's third stage is fired above most of the earth's atmosphere, it would act like Newton's cannon following path D in fig. 16.9.

Instead of traveling in a perfect circle, rockets are made to provide an extra margin of speed. The pull of gravity slows the satellite, and when it falls back to earth, it climbs outward again. Hence an elliptical orbit is formed. When the satellite is closer to the earth, that point of the ellipse is called the *perigee*. The *apogee* is the farthest point. To orbit indefinitely, the satellite's perigee must be well above the atmosphere. If the perigee lies inside the atmosphere, friction of air will slow the satellite.

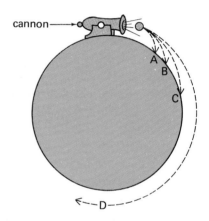

Fig. 16.9. Getting a satellite into orbit.

Care must be taken to avoid high speeds on reentering the atmosphere, or the satellite might burn like a meteor. A group of rockets known as retro-rockets are in front of the capsule. The jets of gas from the retro-rockets change the position of the satellite and act like brakes. It falls from orbit and returns to earth. A heat shield absorbs most of the heat produced by friction. Friction also decreases the speed of the satellite as it returns to splashdown or some solid part of the earth.

How is oxygen needed for combustion? Using glass jars of different sizes, invert them over lighted candles of equal size on a smooth surface such as glass. Which candles are extinguished first? How is this related to the problem of rockets getting an adequate supply of oxygen in outer space?

Instead of using lighted candles of equal size, vary the length of candles and use several glass jars of equal size. What differences are observed in both experiments? What is the control factor in each experiment? What would happen if the sizes of candles and glass jars were different and used in the same experiment?

1. Make models of a propeller-type airplane, a jet, and a rocket.
2. Visit an airport and arrange to tour a cabin with instruments used for flying.
3. Write to the National Aeronautics and Space Administration (NASA) and ask for information about the latest rockets and space vehicles.
4. How do getting into a rowboat, firing a rifle, and letting go of an inflated balloon illustrate Newton's action-reaction principle?

Numerous movie films, filmstrips, and film loops demonstrate the theory of flight and the operation of jets, rockets, satellites, and space vehicles. Excellent photographs are available from the National Aeronautics and Space Administration. These films and photographs can be used to discuss the concepts related to aerospace developments.

For example in the film *Jets and Rockets: How They Work* (Coronet), pupils see how a cart moves when a man pushes against it. Then the man climbs into the cart and moves it by pushing against a stationary wall. When he pushes against a movable wall, both the wall and the cart move. Next he shows that he can move the cart by throwing sandbags from it; and last, he uses gas under pressure, released from a large cylinder mounted on the cart. This series of demonstrations leads to an intuitive understanding of the action-reaction principle, which is the basis for understanding the motion of jets and rockets.

Such a film is very helpful when it shows experiments too dangerous to perform in the classroom. For example, an oxyacetylene torch demonstrates the importance of oxygen in combustion, and gunpowder is used to show the operation of solid-fuel rockets.

Filmstrips and movies on satellites and their work are stimulating as a prelude to discussions on what we had to discover about space before we could send astronauts to the moon. Problems of dangers in space such as temperature, lack of oxygen, pressure changes, falling bodies such as meteors, electrical and ionizing radiation particles, solar flares and winds, and weather changes, as well as taking photographs and communicating from space to the moon and the earth had to be studied. Launching satellites with sufficient scientific instruments to probe space for this information made it possible to send man to the moon.

In discussing satellites and their uses, it should be emphasized that we did benefit by learning to improve weather forecasting around the world, making worldwide navigation systems more efficient, to improve television and communication systems around the world, and ultimately to establish space stations. These space stations will enable us to learn much about how man can travel and survive in space.

I. Operation of a jet engine

    A. Parts and functions

        1. Compressor.

        2. Burning chamber with fuel injectors.

        3. Turbine.

        4. Compressor draws air into engine.

        5. Air and fuel are mixed in burning chamber.

        6. Burning fuel produces hot expanding gases.

        7. Unbalanced force produced by the hot gases pushes the jet forward.

           Demonstration. Burn four or five matches in a small test tube and seal it with a cork. Hot expanding gas is produced when matches ignite. Like the jet, the hot gases exert action forces. Simultaneously, reaction forces are produced by the sides of the tube and the cork in which the gas is held. Action forces cause movement of the jet. Action forces are unbalanced as the cork pops out. There are no longer backward-action forces to balance the forward-action forces. Hence, the unbalanced force pushes the test tube or the jet forward.

        8. Gases shooting out the rear pass the turbine and set it in motion.

        9. The turbine turns and operates the compressor as gases rush out.

      10. Hot, rapid-moving, expanding gases move the engine and airplane forward.

    B. Liquid fuels—jets and rockets

        1. Jet engines need air as a source of oxygen to burn fuel.

        2. Jets fly within the earth's atmosphere.

        3. Rockets fly above the earth's atmosphere.

Background Information

4.   Rockets contain their own source of oxygen and can be stopped and restarted in flight.

5.   Some rockets contain liquid oxygen and liquid fuel and burn to produce hot gases.

C.   Solid fuels—rockets

1.   Chemical compounds that contain oxygen are used to burn fuel.

2.   An increase in fuel increases the power of the rocket engine.

3.   Increasing the weight by increasing the fuel limits the maximum speed.

4.   Stacking engines in stages, where the bottom one falls off after a short period of time, increases the speed.

5.   Thus several stages are used in rockets to launch a space vehicle or satellite.

II.   Apollo missions to the moon

A.   Lift-off

1.   Rocket engines provide full thrust of 8 million or more pounds.

2.   After 2 minutes rockets and vehicle are 20 or more miles up, and first stage of rocket engine is dropped.

3.   About 9.5 minutes after lift-off the second stage rocket is dropped.

4.   In about 2.5 minutes into the third stage the spaceship is around 117 miles in high orbit around the earth.

5.   The speed in orbit is about 17,500 miles per hour and can be increased when heading toward the moon.

B.   On the moon—discoveries

1.   Collection of rock samples containing important minerals

2.   Placing and recording by instruments of:

Placing instruments on the moon.

a. Moonquakes
b. Electrically charged particles on moon—
   ions, solar wind
c. Magnetic measurements and variations
d. Temperature changes of rocks and other
   substances on the moon
e. Radioactive plutonium 238, which is used
   to generate electric power on the moon

3. Craters
4. Zero-gravity experiments
5. Liquid and heat flow
6. Separation of molecules in solution

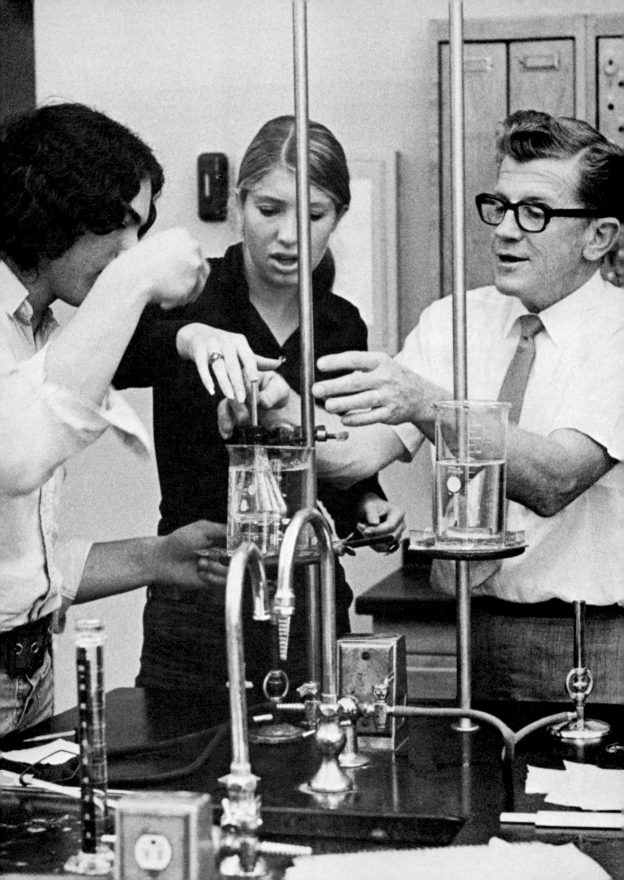

17

MATTER AND ENERGY

Grades K–2   **Concepts**

1. Things (matter) exist as solids, liquids, and gases.
2. Some objects may look different, but they are made of the same material.
3. Different kinds of materials make up the world.
4. Things slide better on smooth or wet surfaces than on rough or dry ones.
5. Round things roll faster than flat ones.

Grades 3–5

6. Heat can change solids into liquids and liquids into gases.
7. Matter is made up of small particles called atoms.
8. Groups of atoms form molecules.

9. An element contains one kind of atom.
10. Even when the physical state changes, the molecules may remain the same.
11. In a chemical change, the molecules change.

Grades 6–8

12. All matter is made up of chemical elements that are represented by symbols.
13. In a mixture original substances can be identified and separated.
14. In a compound the original substances no longer remain the same as they form the compound or new substance.
15. A chemical formula of a compound shows the definite proportions of the elements that make up the substance (compound).
16. The three basic particles that are found in all atoms are protons, neutrons, and electrons.

Concept Formation

As the concepts in the lower grades are examined, the observation is evident of the emphasis on description or appearance. An introduction to relationships and cause and effect are introduced, such as *round things roll faster than flat ones.* As the concepts in grades three through five are studied, the conceptual hierarchy emphasizes some abstract ideas such as *groups of atoms form molecules* or *an element contains one kind of atom.* The movement from concrete visual and actual experiences shifts to the nonvisual or abstract. Definitions with meanings are needed to establish these abstract concepts.

In the intermediate school, grades six through eight, the

concepts are abstract and may sometimes be expressed through symbols and formulae. In addition, cause-and-effect relationships are established when chemical change is introduced by heating substances to form compounds.

Although many syllabi will treat magnetism and electricity, machines, and heat energy under the major topic of matter and energy, these will be given individual attention in subsequent chapters. However, the concept of friction is introduced in the lower grades with: *things slide better on smooth or wet surfaces than on rough or dry ones* and *round things roll faster than flat ones.* Although heat will be treated in another chapter, the concept *heat can change solids into liquids and liquids into gases* is suggested herein for the third through the fifth grades. It is difficult to develop sharp lines of demarcation between matter and energy changes.

Life processes depend on the interactions between matter and energy. In order to understand much of man's achievement, it is necessary to understand the nature of matter in terms of molecules and how they change in our environment. Such changes are evident in weather from clouds in the sky to oceans, rivers, rocks, minerals, air, clothing, homes, and living things. Transformation of matter into energy and changes in the properties of matter should be observed as a result of pupil demonstrations and experiments. Inquiry and open-ended laboratory procedures in grades five through eight can be fostered by using a series of *Laboratory-Theory Sequence of Instruction* outlined in the following brief lesson plans.

LABORATORY-THEORY
SEQUENCE OF INSTRUCTION

Lesson Plans

SOURCE: Submitted by Charles M. Emslie, Professor of Physics, Graceland College, Lamoni, Iowa.

Period I

Lesson objective:

Given a box containing samples of ten different items, a magnifying glass, and a magnet, the students should be able to describe orally the physical characteristics of each item, using identifying terms such as hardness, brittleness, color, luster, weight, magnetism, etc.

Concepts developed:

1. All materials have identifying characteristics.
2. Classes of materials have common characteristics.
3. Materials can be identified by these characteristics.

Activities:

1. Four beakers with earth, air, fire, and water as ancient theory of elements.
2. Students inspected items in a box (three students per box) with magnifier and magnet.
3. Described materials with such terms as hardness, color, luster, brittleness, weight, magnetic, etc.
4. Each group selected one item from their box and listed its characteristics. The remainder of the class was asked to identify the item from this description.

Period II

Lesson objective:

Using a periodic chart, a flame, and selected chemicals, the students should be able to identify five chemical elements by a flame test or color change and describe these changes orally.

Concepts developed:

1. Each element has been named and given a chemical symbol.
2. There are about 103 known elements and 90 appear in nature.
3. Elements can be identified by certain tests (flame, color change, precipitation, etc.).

Activities:

1. Have one student at a time build a structure with wooden blocks and identify his structure for the class.
2. Use letters of alphabet and musical scale analogy of building blocks for language and music.
3. Perform flame test for chemical elements.
4. Two students demonstrated iodine and cornstarch test.
5. Students demonstrated ammonia and commercial detector (phenolphthalein).
6. Summary and review.

Period III

Lesson objective:

Using a magnifier, a magnet, a toothpick, water, and a chromatograph, the students should be able to separate three mixtures of two or more materials.

Concepts developed:

1. Mixtures can be separated mechanically.
2. Compounds are new materials and cannot be separated mechanically.

Activities:

1. Each student given a magnifier, a mixture of salt and sand, a mixture of iron filings and sand, and a toothpick and asked to separate the salt and iron filings from the sand.
2. Each student given chromatograph kit and observed separation of materials by color.
3. Sharing time, summary, and review.

Period IV

Lesson objective:

Given several common materials, a flame, and some water, the students should be able to identify and describe orally some of the characteristics associated with chemical changes and be capable of writing simple chemical compound formulas.

Concepts developed:

1. Chemical change always produces new materials.
2. Exchange of energy is associated with chemical change.

Activities:

1. Film, *Chemical Change* (11 min.), was shown.
2. Teacher demonstration of burning bread, wood, paper, and sugar.
3. Steel wool over water experiment was set up; students predicted what would happen.
4. Sharing time, summary, and review.

Period V

Lesson objective:

Given a carbon dioxide indicator and a water indicator, the students should be capable of identifying these two chemical compounds and describing their observations verbally.

Concepts developed:

1. Water is in most dry materials.
2. One test for water is color change of dry copper sulfate.
3. The two elements in water can be separated by electrolysis.
4. Two methods of identifying the compound carbon dioxide.

Activities:

1. Set up electrolysis experiment and observe decomposition.
2. Dry copper sulfate on hot plate and note color change.
3. Dry pieces of chalk and collect water evaporated.
4. Have each child make the carbon dioxide test with either lime water or commercial indicator.
5. Set up long-range balloon and plastic bag for leakage experiments.
6. Observe steel wool experiment and discuss results.

Period VI

Lesson objective:

Given several different materials the students should be able to divide each item into smaller and smaller pieces and describe orally the continuation of this dividing process down to the atomic level.

Concepts developed:

1. The particulate nature of matter.
2. All matter is composed of atoms and molecules.

Activities:

1. A different student performed each of the following as a demonstration for the class:
   (a) Cut iron wire in half and throw away half until remainder was too small to hold.
   (b) Same cutting process with a sugar lump.
   (c) Oil in water.
   (d) Oil with detergent in water.
   (e) Water in atomizer.
   (f) Dissolve sugar, copper sulfate, potassium permanganate, and Nestle's Quick in water, and filter solution.
2. Set up long-range evaporation experiments using water, alcohol, and oil.
3. Damp sponge balanced on a meter stick experiment.
4. Set up long-range solids for sublimation experiments.
5. Discussed the concepts of atoms and molecules as building blocks of matter.

Period VII

Lesson objective:

Using large crystalline models and a raft of soap bubbles, the students should be able to describe orally the structures of simple solids using the concepts of atoms and molecules.

Concepts developed:

1. Many solids have crystalline shapes.
2. Six basic crystalline structures.
3. Atoms and molecules are very, very small.

Activities:

1. View film, *The World of Molecules* (11 min.).
2. Set up sugar crystal growing experiment.
3. Each student had a small dish to perform the bubble raft experiment.
4. Passed out samples of six crystalline structures.
5. Listed and discussed size of atoms and molecules using a series of examples of common materials (sand, water, raindrop, etc.).

Period VIII

Lesson objective:

Using inflated balloons and plastic bags held in an atmosphere of perfume, vanilla extract, etc., and mixing sugar with water, the students should be able to describe verbally how these materials could penetrate and mix without a corresponding change in volume.

Concepts developed:

There are tiny spaces between the molecules that make up a substance.

Activities:

1. Inflated balloons and plastic bags with air over perfume, ammonia water, vanilla extract, and chlorine water.

2. Set up ammonia indicator in plastic bag over ammonia water.
3. Passed out samples of marbles, B-B shot, and sand as indications of spaces between molecules.
4. Performed experiment of dissolving 50 cc. of sugar in 300 cc. of water for a total volume change of 325 cc. of solution.
5. Observed changes in length of inflated balloon and plastic bag experiment set up during period 5.
6. Sharing student collections and lesson review.

Period IX

Lesson objective:

Using the concept of the particulate nature of matter the students should be able to describe verbally a theoretical atomic structure consistent with their observations.

Concepts developed:

1. Atoms are composed of two different kinds of charged particles.
2. Individual charged particles exert forces on other charged particles.
3. Charged particles are named electrons and protons.
4. A third particle exists called a neutron.

Activities:

1. Observed and discussed the observed changes in all the extended time experiments (balloons, plastic bags, evaporation, etc.).
2. Slide projector as model of electron microscope for looking at tiny particles.

3. Each student performed the charged paper strips experiment.
4. Students demonstrated hard rubber, glass, fur, and silk charging experiments.
5. Discussed atomic theories and handed out sheet describing atomic structure of first eight elements on periodic chart.
6. Summary of concepts developed.

Period X

Lesson objective:

Given styrofoam balls and pipe stem cleaners, the students should be able to build an atomic model of one of the first eight elements on the periodic chart and describe their structure verbally.

Concepts developed:

1. The basic forces in our world.
2. The structure of atoms.
3. The significance of the atomic number, atomic weight, number of electrons, protons and neutrons in an atom.
4. The relative size of electrons, protons, and neutrons.
5. The structure of simple molecules.

Activities:

1. Viewed film, *Forces* (12 min.).
2. Each student constructed an atom using styrofoam balls and pipe stem cleaners.
3. Performed heated ball and ring experiment.
4. Built water molecule with styrofoam balls and pipe stem cleaners.

5. Discussed method of writing chemical formulas for simple compounds.
6. Passed out sheet describing the proton and showing molecular models.
7. Summary and description evaluation procedure.

LABORATORY-THEORY
SEQUENCE OF INSTRUCTION

Period I

Lesson objective:

Using familiar examples of common forces and the film entitled *Forces* the students should be able to identify and describe verbally at least three of the fundamental forces of the universe.

Concepts developed:

1. The concept of a fundamental force.
2. The fundamental forces of our world (gravity, electric, magnetic, nuclear).

Activities:

1. Gave each student a folder for science materials.
2. Introduced the topic and explained classroom procedure.
3. Students listed fundamental forces on a sheet of paper. (Students shared their list with the class, one at a time.)
4. Film entitled *Forces* was shown and reviewed.
5. Instructor demonstrated electric, magnetic, and gravitational forces.

Period II

Lesson objective:

Using the modern description of electrons, protons, and neutrons, the students should be capable of describing the interacting characteristics of these three fundamental particles.

Concepts developed:

1. Identify the fundamental particles of matter (proton, neutron, electron).
2. The relative weight or mass of each particle.
3. The magnitude and sign of the charge on each particle.

Activities:

1. Reviewed fundamental forces.
2. Looked at beakers of air, earth, fire, and water as ancient view of elements.
3. Explained modern theory of matter.
4. Described characteristics of three elementary particles (mass and charge).
5. Shared student collections, summary, and review.

Period III

Lesson objective:

Using the fundamental particles and the periodic chart the students should be able to verbally describe the composition of the first eight elements on the periodic chart.

Concepts developed:

1. The atomic model of the atom.

2. Definitions of element, atom, molecule, ion nucleus, etc.
3. The systematic way the particles are organized to form the 103 elements on the periodic chart. (Include interpreting the various numbers.)

Activities:

1. Conducted a review session of forces and particles.
2. Described possible arrangements of fundamental particles.
3. Described elements and the meaning of the numbers on the periodic chart.
4. Gave each student a small periodic chart for their science folder.

Period IV

Lesson objective:

Given a list and description of the known chemical elements, the students should be capable of verbally describing elements, compounds, and mixtures and be able to write simple compound formulas.

Concepts developed:

1. The molecule as a combination of two or more atoms.
2. Molecular motion in gases, liquids, and solids.
3. Chemical compounds and mixtures.

Activities:

1. Reviewed forces, particles, and atomic structure theory.

2. Described the three states of matter (gas, liquid, and solid).
3. Described the differences between mixtures and compounds.
4. Described atomic structure of compounds.
5. Described shorthand method of writing formulas for chemical compounds.
6. Showed film, *World of Molecules* (11 min.).
7. Gave each student a description of the proton and sketches of molecular structure.

Period V

Lesson objective:

Given styrofoam balls and pipe stem cleaners the students should be able to construct an atomic model of one of the first eight elements on the periodic chart and describe their structure verbally.

Concepts developed:

1. The size and number of molecules in a drop of water and grain of sand.
2. Size of the spaces between atoms and molecules in a gas, liquid, and solid.
3. Increased molecular motion with temperature rise.

Activities:

1. Reviewed atomic structure.
2. Listed approximate number of molecules in drop of water, grain of sand, etc.
3. Passed around samples of marbles, B-B shot, and sand as example of spaces between molecules.

4. Heated ball and ring and discussed what parts of the atomic structure were expanding.
5. Each student constructed a model of a simple chemical element using stryofoam balls and pipe stem cleaners. (A water molecule was also built.)

Period VI

Lesson objective:

Using a magnifier, a magnet, a toothpick, water, and a chromatograph, the students should be able to separate three mixtures of two or more materials.

Concepts developed:

1. Different materials have different physical characteristics.
2. Mixture can be separated mechanically.
3. No new material is formed in a mixture.

Activities:

1. Each student separated sand from sugar and iron filings from sand with toothpick and magnifier.
2. Each child asked to describe physical characteristics of a sample of material.
3. Class performed the chromatograph experiment as method of separating mixtures.
4. Long-range balloon experiment was set up.
5. Summary and lesson review.

Period VII

Lesson objective:

Using a flame and selected chemical compounds the students should be capable of identifying chemical elements by the flame test or color change and should be able to describe orally some of the characteristics associated with chemical change.

Concepts developed:

1. Specific elements can be identified by certain tests.
2. A new and different material is formed in a chemical change.
3. The original material is used up in a chemical change.

Activities:

1. Used wooden blocks, musical notes, and letters of alphabet as examples of fundamental building block for a particular system.
2. Identified several chemical elements using the flame test.
3. Two students demonstrated cornstarch and iodine identification.
4. Identified ammonia using phenolphthalein indicator.
5. Burned wood, bread, paper, and sugar as examples of chemical change.
6. Each student performed the carbon dioxide test with either lime water or commercial indicator.
7. Set up the steel wool over water experiment.
8. Summary and discussion of theories associated with observations.

Period VIII

Lesson objective:

Given a carbon dioxide indicator and a water indicator and several materials that evaporate readily, the students should be capable of identifying water and carbon dioxide and verbally explaining evaporation and sublimation.

Concepts developed:

1. One method of identifying water.
2. One method of separating water into two gases.
3. Water is in *dry* materials.

Activities:

1. Separated water by electrolysis.
2. Damp sponge balanced on metal stick experiment.
3. Dry copper sulfate water indicator test.
4. Set up sugar crystal growing experiment.
5. Set up inflated balloon and plastic bag experiments over perfume, ammonia, vanilla, etc.
6. Set up evaporation and sublimation experiments.
7. Summary and discussion (questions and answers) of relationship of atomic theory to observations in this lesson.

Period IX

Lesson objective:

Given several different materials the students should be able to divide these materials into smaller and smaller pieces and then verbally describe the continuation of this process to the atomic level.

Concepts developed:

1. The particulate nature of matter.

2. Dissolved particles and spaces between molecules.
3. The differences between physical and chemical changes.

Activities:

1. Viewed film, *Chemical Change* (11 min.), and discussed important concepts presented.
2. Student demonstration of cutting iron wire, sugar cube, water, etc., in one-half and discarding half until too small to continue.
3. Dissolved 50 cc. of sugar in 300 cc. of water and measured 325 cc. of solution.
4. Dissolved sugar, potassium permanganate, copper sulfate, and Nestle's Quick in water and filtered.
5. Discussed steel wool over water experiment and discussed the atomic level considerations associated with the experiment.
6. Summary and review with student sharing collections and other science interests.

Period X

Lesson objective:

Using large crystalline models and a raft of soap bubbles the students should be able to describe orally the structures of simple solids using the concepts of atoms and molecules.

Concepts developed:

1. There are spaces between the particles of all matter.
2. Molecules of some solids are arranged in certain crystalline structures.
3. Evidences of atomic structure are indirect.

Activities:

1. Observed and discussed all the long-range experiments.
2. Described ways scientists look at tiny particles.
3. Described samples of six basic crystalline structures.
4. Students performed bubble raft experiment as model of crystalline structure.
5. Summary and review of entire unit.
6. Discussed evaluation instrument (purpose and method of administration).

Problem Solving

The following concept is taught via the problem-solving method: *Substances in a mixture can be separated by physical means such as solution, filtration, and evaporation depending on the properties of the substances that make up the mixture.*

An anecdote is written on the board or mimeographed for distribution: "You wish to put salt on an egg that you cooked over the camp stove near the beach. By accident you spill the salt into the sand. You still would like to have some salt on your egg."

The teacher shows a mixture of salt and sand and displays the following materials: magnet, tweezers, paper towels, pots, jars, funnel (cone-shaped cup), camp stove. After having the pupils read the anecdote and observe the displayed materials, the teacher asks the pupils to state the problem.

After two or three pupil statements, the problem is stated: "How can the salt be separated from the sand so that it can be used on the egg?"

The children are invited to state their hypotheses:

1. A tweezer can be used to pick out the salt grains.
2. A magnet can attract and lift out the salt grains.

3. In solution, the sand can be filtered using paper towels and a funnel. The salt solution can be heated on the camp stove and the salt would be left behind as the water evaporates (fig. 17.1, *A* and *B*).

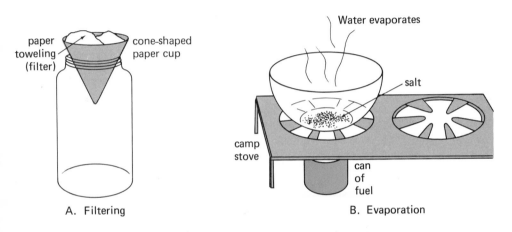

A. Filtering   B. Evaporation

Fig. 17.1.   Filtering and evaporation.

After performing these experiments to test the three hypotheses it was found that salt was left behind in the evaporating dish. The tweezers and the magnets were found to be unsatisfactory. The pupils concluded that solution, filtration, and evaporation were the physical means of separating the mixture of salt from sand.

A seventh-grade teacher wanted the students to separate the components of a mixture in an open-ended laboratory situation. The teacher explained that the following materials were available: a mixture of sand and iron filings, a test tube

**Open-ended
Laboratory**

containing iron filings and water, a test tube containing sugar dissolved in water, a test tube containing copper sulfate dissolved in water, beakers, wire gauze, Bunsen burners, evaporating dishes, tongs, ring stands and clamps, magnets, funnels, filter paper, and test tubes.

In a previous classroom experience, the pupils learned the properties of mixtures. They were also taught the different types of combinations of mixtures: two solids, a solid that is dissolved in a liquid, and a solid that is insoluble in a liquid.

The pupils were asked to design experiments for separating the components in these mixtures. Each student recorded the results of each experiment. Written results were submitted to the teacher.

The amount of preliminary information and instructions for these experiments will vary from class to class and from teacher to teacher. In some classes the open-ended laboratory may begin to resemble the conventional "follow-the-directions" type of laboratory. In other classes the open-ended laboratory resembles the problem-solving or inquiry approach. In the problem-solving approach used in separating a mixture the pupils had to identify and state the problem. In the open-ended laboratory the problem was stated for the pupils.

Both procedures, problem solving and open-ended laboratory, emphasize formation and screening of hypotheses, design and testing of experiments, evaluation of data, deductive and inductive reasoning, observations, written reports, and conclusion. Various degrees of creativity can be emphasized in both of these methods. In an open-ended laboratory the conditions become more ideal when each student performs experiments slightly different from those of his neighbor. Also, the results cannot be obtained merely from reading the answers in the textbook. Some topics and concepts lend themselves to more effective instruction by a single method that should be selected by the teacher.

I. Nature of matter

    A. Structure

        1. All matter is composed of molecules.
        2. All molecules consist of atoms, which in turn contain protons, neutrons, and electrons.

    B. Properties

        1. Gravity
        2. Electric charges
        3. Magnetic fields
        4. Color
        5. Density
        6. Solubility
        7. Melting point
        8. Boiling point
        9. Hardness
        10. Ability to burn

    C. Elements

        1. At least 103 known elements appear on the periodic table.
        2. Each element has its own atomic structure and atomic number (see fig. 17.2).

            a. The number of protons in the nucleus of an atom is the atomic number of the element listed on the periodic table.
            b. The number of protons found in the nucleus is usually equal to the total number of electrons in the atom.

                (1) Protons are positively charged particles of electricity.
                (2) Electrons are negatively charged particles of electricity.

            c. The sum of the number of protons and neutrons in the nucleus is the atomic mass (weight) of the element.

Background Information

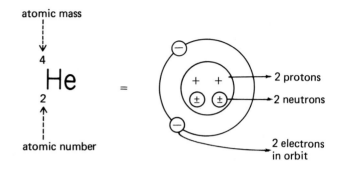

Fig. 17.2.   Helium atom.

(1) The neutron is considered to be similar to a proton and electron held together with no electrical charge.

(2) The mass of an electron is about 1/2000 the mass of a proton and is therefore not considered in determining the atomic mass (weight) of an element.

(3) The protons and neutrons are known collectively as nucleons, because they are found in the nucleus of the atom.

D. Mixtures
1. Two or more different substances where each substance retains its original properties and can be separated by physical means such as solution, filtration, evaporation, or magnetism.
2. Examples of mixtures
a. Sugar and water are two different compounds, but the water can be separated (evaporated) from the sugar.

      b.   Iron filings and sand represent a mixture of an element (iron) and a compound (sand).

      c.   Iron filings and lead pellets are illustrative of a mixture consisting of two different elements.

  E. Compound

    1. Two or more different substances where each substance no longer retains its original properties, and none of the constituents can be separated by physical means.

    2. Examples of compounds

      a.   Water is a liquid compound that consists of two gaseous elements, hydrogen and oxygen. Water does not resemble either of its constituents.

      b.   Sand is a compound that consists of two different elements, silicon and oxygen. The properties of silicon are different from sand; the same is true for oxygen.

II. Kinetic molecular theory

  A. Matter consists of molecules.

  B. Molecules are in a constant state of motion.

  C. Molecules are far apart from each other and collide with each other.

  D. The speed of molecules is related to temperature. An increase in temperature will be accompanied by an increase in the speed of molecules.

III. Conservation of matter and energy

  A. Matter can neither be created nor destroyed.

  B. Energy can neither be created nor destroyed.

  C. Matter can be converted into energy.

    1. Heating of coal or another fuel such as oil or gas converts it into energy along with the by-products formed.

    2. A form of energy such as mechanical energy

can be transformed into other forms of energy such as electrical energy. A storage battery of an automobile converts chemical energy into electrical energy.

3. In a closed system the transfer of energy among objects will still keep the total energy of the system constant.

4. Potential energy is the energy contained in a body because of its state or position.

5. Kinetic energy is the energy of a body in motion.

6. Energy is the ability to do work.

7. Disturbing matter at the nuclear level involves greater energies than that at the molecular level.

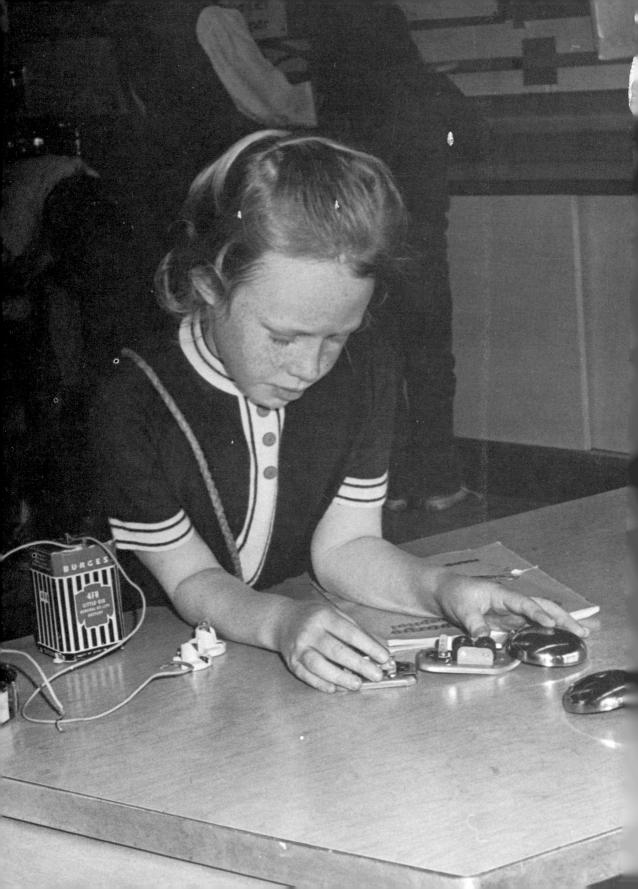

18

MAGNETISM
AND ELECTRICITY

Grades K–2

1. Magnets pick up different things.
2. Magnets pick up, push, or pull iron and steel objects.
3. Magnets help us in the home and other places.
4. Magnets have different shapes and sizes.
5. Magnets lose much of their energy when they are dropped, pounded, or heated.
6. Magnets can pull through water, glass, paper, and other media.

Grades 3–5

7. Magnets have two poles, north and south.

8. The earth is a large magnet and also has two poles.
9. A compass needle can be made with a bar magnet.
10. A compass needle is a magnet.
11. Like poles repel and unlike poles attract each other.
12. Permanent magnets are made from cobalt, nickel, and iron.
13. Iron filings can help to make a magnetic field visible.
14. Magnets are important in navigation and industry.

Grades 6–8

15. Magnetism is a form of energy.
16. Electricity is induced in a coil when a magnet is moved back and forth through a coil of wire.
17. Electromagnets receive current pulsations and help to produce sound in telephones.
18. The magnetic force between two poles depends on their strength and distance from each other.

Concept Formation

Magnetism and electricity are closely related to each other when electrical appliances are discussed or demonstrated. Although the concepts for magnetism and electricity are listed separately, many demonstrations and experiments will show the interrelationship.

The following learning activities are suggested for the lower grades. Many children have magnetic toys—fishing sets, dancing dolls, and alphabet and number sets. These toys can be brought to class for observation, play, and discussion. Can openers, pot openers, auto dashboard trays, and other useful materials that contain magnets can also contribute to the class discussion.

To discover which materials are attracted by magnets, children are invited to bring to class such items as nails, buttons, keys, clips, hairpins, wood, rubber, and thumbtacks. A group is formed for all objects that are attracted to the magnet and another group for those not attracted. Another possibility is to label two sheets of paper: one for "yes" (attracts), another for "no" (does not attract).

Questions can be elicited from the children. For example, ask, "What happens when a magnet is placed in the middle of a mixture of buttons and paper clips?" "Will each part of a magnet pick up with the same number of clips?" "How many paper clips can a magnet hold?" "Will all magnets pick up the same number of paper clips?"

Encourage pupil creativity by providing bobby pins, slices of cork, and small triangular pieces of paper. Invite students to design small boats that can float on water. In a large pan of water, place a number of the sailboats made from bobby pins, cork, and paper. Using a magnet, show how the boat will move as it is attracted to the magnet. Perhaps a sailing contest could be developed using several boats and each student using a different magnet.

A fishing game can also be made. Children can cut out cardboard to resemble fish. Paper clips can be attached to each fish. Attaching a magnet to a fishing rod, children can go fishing in a barrel. Perhaps each fish can be colored differently and a fun game can be developed.

The demonstration illustrated in fig. 18.1 can be set up. Pupils will be amazed at how the paper clip is suspended in mid-air. They will ask and answer questions as they offer various explanations. Test different sample materials between the magnet and the clip. Encourage pupil questions,

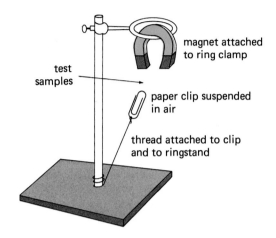

Fig. 18.1. Paper clip suspended in air.

hypotheses, and explanations as different materials are tested. This demonstration via *inquiry* can be done for the
lower grades up through the fifth grade. As the children
gain new experiences, they will offer more detailed explanations about the magnetic effects observed in this demonstration.

Fig. 18.2. Magnetic lines of force.

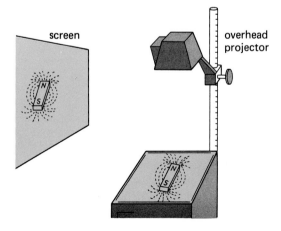

Using an overhead projector, place a Petri dish or a 4-inch circular transparent plastic dish on it for projection on the screen. Insert a bar magnet under the empty dish so that the magnet can be observed on the screen. Very gently sprinkle iron filings into the empty dish so that the lines of force can be viewed (fig. 18.2).

After viewing the demonstration on the magnetic lines of force, the pupils can perform a series of experiments illustrating the appearance of the lines of force. If plastic dishes are not available, use ordinary writing paper and have the children place a magnet under the paper. Using a salt shaker carefully sprinkle iron filings on the paper, and the same observations will be made as noted in the demonstration. Other problems to be tested with the magnets are: Will magnets attract iron from a glass of water? How can this be done without getting the magnet wet? What happens when two magnets are used?

A compass needle is a magnet. Pupils are asked to bring in to class any type compass that may be in the home. They experiment by moving the compass in different parts of the room to determine north, south, east, and west.

As a laboratory experience the children make their own magnets. Use a bar magnet and give a sewing needle ten or more strokes in only one direction. This will usually magnetize the needle. If the magnet is not highly magnetized, it may be necessary to stroke the needle several additional times.

Making a Compass

A magnetized sewing needle can be placed on a thin

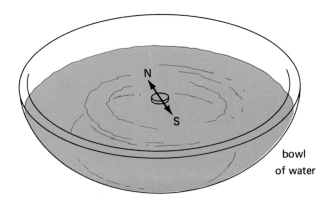

Fig. 18.3.   Floating a compass needle.

slice of cork, which is floated in a bowl of water (fig. 18.3). The compass needles made in the classroom should be compared with a regular compass. Move the floating compass in various directions of the room to determine the extent of its accuracy.

Static Electricity

We all experience static electricity at one time or another. If our hair is very dry, it will practically stand up when we use a plastic or hard rubber comb. If we walk across a carpet in a dry room and touch a metal door handle, we may receive a shock. As friction is produced by rubbing, combing, or fast walking in a very dry situation, electrons are removed from one object to another. Neutral objects contain the same number of protons and electrons. When friction occurs, an electric charge is produced as electrons are removed from one object and flow to the other object (see fig. 18.4).

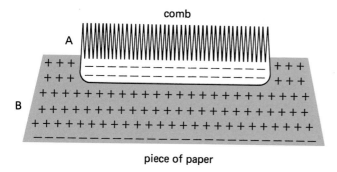

Fig. 18.4. Electrons travel from one object to another.

In fig. 18.4*A* electrons flow to fig. 18.4*B*. The removal
of electrons from object one makes the object positively
charged because of the excess number of protons or positively charged particles of electricity that remain behind.
Object two, which picked up the electrons, receives the additional number of electrons, making it negatively charged; it
now has a greater number of electrons than protons. Hence
the opposite charges on both of these objects causes them to
be attracted.

Lightning

In lightning, two oppositely charged clouds may cause a
spark to jump from one cloud to another or from a cloud to
something on the ground. During thunderstorms the falling
of water droplets that are pushed upward by rushing air become electrically charged. These water droplets make up the
clouds, and there is usually a difference in the electrical
charge between two neighboring clouds, between ground
and cloud, and between parts of the same cloud.

Demonstration   Rub a plastic rod with a piece of wool or fur. Place the charged rod in a pile of small pieces of paper. Pupils will observe the attraction of paper pieces, which will soon fall off. This can initiate a discussion of static electricity. How do we explain the slight shock we receive when sliding in and out of automobile seats? When we rub a balloon on our clothing and the balloon sticks to it, we illustrate static electricity.

Experiment   How can a sheet of paper be made to stick to a blackboard without using glue or tape? Discuss conditions of dryness and wetness, the amount of time devoted to friction, and the length of time the paper adheres to the board. How does the quality of paper affect the adhesion? Does the size of the paper influence the static electricity?

Magnetism and Electricity

To show the relationship between magnetism and electricity, children in the lower grades can make electromagnets. They will soon discover that *electricity can produce magnetism* and that the *electromagnet is a temporary magnet*. The materials needed are: one dry cell—1.5 volts, a thin electric wire, a 2-inch-long nail, paper clips, and thumbtacks. Wind a piece of wire (center) around the nail (fig. 18.5). The thin electric (bell-type) wire, which has a number of turns around the nail, is connected to a dry cell.

Problem Solving   How does the number of turns of wire around the nail

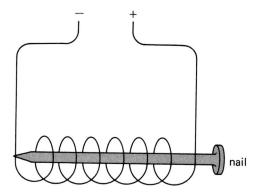

Fig. 18.5. Preparing an electromagnet.

influence the number of thumbtacks or paper clips that can be picked up by the nail which is now an electromagnet? Is there a difference in the strength of the electromagnet when the turns of wire are close together or far apart? What happens if one of the terminals is disconnected from the dry cell while thumbtacks are attached to the nail (electromagnet)? Pupils should experiment, by the trial-and-error approach, to determine answers to these questions. They may wish to test other materials as well as different sizes and thicknesses of wire.

Grades K–2

Concepts in Electricity

1. Electricity has many uses in the home, school, and neighborhood.
2. Electricity flows through wires from the power plant to the home.
3. Electricity creates heat, light, sound, and movement.

4. We should not plug in electrical appliances into outlets unless we learn how to do so correctly.

Grades 3–5

5. Friction or rubbing things together causes static electricity.
6. Static electricity causes lightning.
7. Current electricity is electricity that flows through wires.
8. When electricity travels in a complete path, the path is called a circuit.
9. Most metals are good conductors of electricity.
10. Usually nonmetals are poor conductors of electricity.
11. A switch makes or breaks an electrical circuit.

Grades 6–8

12. Electricity is a form of energy that can be related to heat and light.
13. Electric current is the flow of electrons through a conductor.
14. Fuses protect circuits from overheating when the fuses melt and break the circuit.
15. Electrical circuits may be in series or in parallel or both.
16. Electromagnets are used in electrical motors.

Concept Formation   The concepts pertaining to static electricity and electromagnets were partially introduced earlier in this chapter (refer to "Magnetism.") The study of electromagnets relates the concepts of magnetism with electricity in a very useful manner. Discussions of uses of electricity in the home, especially with appliances that are familiar to children, are helpful. The radio, TV, electric clock, hair dryer, tape recorder, and phonograph are good examples to use in class.

The importance and uses of electrical energy are not fully appreciated until we are forced to do without it under temporary emergency conditions. A few years ago, in the early evening of November 9, a major part of the eastern United States was without electricity. Suddenly all the lights in the home, schools, factory, and streets went out. Darkness prevailed in and out of homes. People who were driving cars at night depended on their own headlights from the cars to see where to travel. Traffic lights were out; and traffic jams were massive. Some citizens used flashlights and attempted to direct traffic at major intersections.

The sudden impact of darkness was also felt in the home. In homes with electrical stoves, millions of families ate cold dinners. Flashlights, candles, and liquid fuel lamps were used to maneuver in the home. Many people were afraid of accidents. Others had fears of being burglarized. Members of a family who needed to iron clothing or use electrical appliances found themselves unable to perform their tasks. For most people the adjustment to darkness and lack of electrical power was almost disastrous. Thus the important role that electrical energy plays in our daily lives came to light when electricity was restored in the major part of the United States.

Learning Activities

For children in kindergarten through second grade, a good laboratory experience is to have them examine a flashlight. After asking the children to bring flashlights to class,

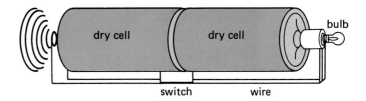

Fig. 18.6.   Flashlight.

an interesting collection will be found: pen lights, lanterns, small and large flashlights. They will soon discover that electricity provides light through the flashlight. By taking a flashlight apart, children will observe the dry cell or cells (battery), a bulb, a case, and a switch. By removing any one of these parts the pathway of electrons will be open or broken and no light can come from the flashlight. Children should have the experience of changing positions of the dry cells to determine if they work (fig. 18.6).

Pupils can study the parts of a flashlight (fig. 18.6) and trace the connections that permit electrons to flow through the simple series circuit. A careful study of the filament of the bulb will show that it does not burn. The filament (wire) in the bulb gets hot because of the electron flow. When it becomes very hot, it glows and "throws off' light.

Laboratory Experience

In grades three to five and above, pupils can develop concepts pertaining to series circuits, parallel circuits, and the use of a switch to open and close a circuit. Provide each pupil with three sockets, three bulbs, connecting wires, a switch, and a large 1.5-volt dry cell. Allow them to experiment with connecting the bulbs in series and in parallel cir-

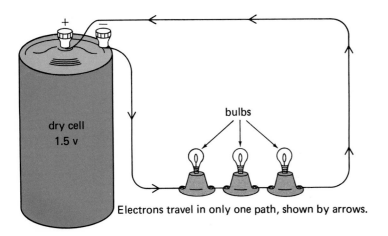

bulbs

Electrons travel in only one path, shown by arrows.

Fig. 18.7. Series circuit.

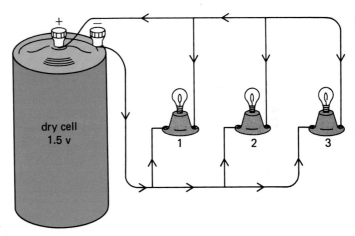

Fig. 18.8. Parallel circuit.

cuits. They should learn the difference between a series circuit in which the electrons (electricity) flow in a singular
path (fig. 18.7), and a parallel circuit in which electrons flow
in more than one path (fig. 18.8). In the series circuit each
bulb can act as a switch. If one bulb is removed, all the
lights go out. The bulb that is removed prevents the electricity from completing its circuit; this breaks open the circuit.

To close the circuit, return the bulb and observe all lights go on. Also the intensity of light in the bulbs should be noted as electrons flow from the dry cell to the first bulb and so on. This observation should be compared with the bulbs in a parallel circuit.

After experimenting with various possibilities of connecting wires to the bulbs in the sockets, the pupils should make an arrangement similar to those shown in figs. 18.7 and 18.8. Some of the children may need some direction to construct these circuits. However, as much as possible they should be encouraged to be experimental and use the trial-and-error approach.

In the parallel circuit, the children should note what happens when one bulb is removed. This should be followed by removing the adjacent bulb. The pupils will observe that the third bulb is still lit. They should make the deductive inference that in a parallel circuit, the bulb does not act as a switch when one of several bulbs is removed. They should also compare the intensity of light that is given off by each of the bulbs in a parallel circuit.

Pupils should also experiment by inserting a knife-type or button switch in various places along the series and parallel circuits. A discussion on the advantages and disadvantages of each type of circuit should be held. Children may wish to bring in Christmas tree lights and study the kinds of circuits they have. Dangers of household electricity should also be discussed. Fuses and circuit breakers should be discussed in terms of fire prevention. If too much electricity is loaded on a given circuit, a fuse melts or a circuit breaker operates to stop the flow of electricity.

Problem Solving   In grades six through eight, a problem-solving lesson to teach the concepts related to series and parallel circuits can be performed as a class demonstration in which the teacher asks the pupils to identify the problem and involves a few students at a time in suggesting hypotheses, testing them through experimentation, evaluating the observations, and making deductive inferences. The teacher displays the following materials: two 1.5-volt dry cells, bulbs, sockets, bell wire, switch, screwdriver, and a light-bulb tester. The teacher writes the following anecdote on the board: "Mr. Simpson and his neighbor bought Christmas tree lights. In a few days the neighbor's lights went out. Mr. Simpson had only one bulb that burned out."

Problem. Why did all the lights go out on the neighbor's string of lights?

Hypotheses:
1. The bulbs were all burned out.
2. The wires were cut or torn.
3. There is a short circuit, not enough electricity.
4. The wires are connected differently to the light sockets.

Materials. Two 1.5-V dry cells, sockets, lights, bell wire, switch, screwdriver, light-bulb tester.

Experiments to verify hypotheses:
1. To test hypothesis 1, remove all bulbs from the unit string and test each in bulb tester. All but one bulb should work.
2. To test hypotheses 2, replace each burned-out bulb with a good one, and screw them into each socket on string; all should light up, showing that wires were not cut or torn.
3. Set up a demonstration model of a short circuit, using dry cells, minilights, and sockets to show that this situation could not exist, as wires were not broken (refer to step 2).

4. Set up a simple circuit with dry cell, one bulb and socket, and switch. Ask class to hypothesize what will happen when a second light is added to the circuit. Show that both light up but more weakly than the one did. Add second dry cell to circuit; brightness should be restored. Remove one bulb; other light goes out. Have class suggest that neighbor's lights were wired this way.

5. Let class suggest different methods of wiring these lights, that is, one to each outlet, two wires to each socket, and so on. Set up each and let class accept or reject each hypothesis; parallel circuit is only one which works.

Concepts to be taught:
1. Electrons flow from the negative pole to the positive pole of the dry cell.
2. Dry cells connected to each other in series increase the amount of E.M.F. (volts) available to the circuit.
3. In a series circuit the electrons must flow through all loads; in turn hence if one light bulb is removed, no further current will flow.
4. In a parallel circuit the electrons split up and flow through each part separately; removal of one bulb does not affect rest of circuit.
5. Connecting dry cells in parallel does not increase the E.M.F.; it merely extends the life of the cells.
6. Parallel circuits are used in the home, so that lights can be operated independently.

For more advanced students in the intermediate schools (grades six to eight), the following problem-solving lesson was developed by one of the teachers:

Teacher writes the anecdote on the board and displays batteries, lengths of #22 and #28 nichrome wire, #28 copper wire, small light bulbs and sockets, alligator clips, and lamp wire. The teacher plans to have the pupils formulate the concept, *resistance in a conductor is dependent on the con-*

ductor's length, temperature, cross-sectional area, and the material from which it is made. This concept should be formed as a result of solving the problem.

Anecdote. "Peter needed to make a resistor in the form of a coiled heating element for part of his science project. The directions called for 6 feet of nichrome wire, but all he had was 4 feet of copper wire. When he wound the wire up and connected it to a 9-volt battery, it did not become hot."

Student activities:

1.   Identify and state the problem: Why didn't the resistor become hot?

2.   Suggest hypotheses:
  a.   Using a different type of wire changed the resistance.
  b.   An incorrect length of wire was used.
  c.   The copper wire is thicker than the nichrome wire (as observed by inspection).
  d.   A higher voltage is needed.
  e.   The circuit was not connected properly.

3.   Design and perform experiments. Students determine the resistance of the different types of wires available. Since no meters are present, resistance can be qualitatively measured by comparing the brightness of a light bulb when different types of wire are used.
  a.   Connect the batteries and bulbs in a series circuit and then connect the different wires to determine which offers the least resistance.
  b.   Vary the length of the different wires by sliding the alligator clips along the wire. By watching the brightness of the bulb, the relationships of length of wire to resistance can be determined.
  c.   Determine whether thick or thin wires offer the least resistance by observing the brightness in

the light bulb. (Students will have to look up the term "gauge" to learn that the higher the gauge number, the smaller the wire's diameter.)

4. Evaluate the data and formulate the generalization: As a result of the experiments, students should observe that resistance of wire (conductor) will:

a. Increase with increasing length
b. Increase with decreasing diameter
c. Vary, depending on the composition of the wire used

Background Information

I. Magnets and magnetism

A. Substances that contain iron, steel, nickel, and cobalt are attracted by magnets.

1. Two ends of a magnet are called north (+) and south (−) poles, respectively.

2. Opposite poles attract each other; like poles repel each other.

3. A freely suspended magnet turns until it points in an approximately north–south direction, the basis of the magnetic compass.

a. The end of a bar magnet that points in a northerly direction is known as the north pole of the magnet.

b. The end of the magnet that points in a southerly direction is known as the south pole.

4. Behavior of some of the electrons is used to explain the magnetic properties of different substances.

a. Spinning electrons produce a magnetic field.

b. Electrons may be visualized as small spherical clouds of negative charge that spin like a top.

c. Electrons that spin in opposite directions in a substance cancel out the magnetic field.

5. It is believed that the molecules of magnetic substances are arranged in linear order or a straight line; molecules of nonmagnetic sub-substances are arranged in a zigzag fashion.

6. If a magnet is cut into several pieces, each piece has opposite poles at the ends. Thus a magnet is conceived to contain many tiny magnets.

7. Sprinkling iron filings on a piece of paper placed on top of a bar magnet displays magnetic lines of force.

8. Magnets can lose their magnetic properties by:

a. Heating them

b. Keeping two magnets side by side or on top of each other for a long time

c. Dropping or hitting them

9. Magnets are very important in making electric motors, generators, telephones, compasses, and many toys.

II. Electromagnets

A. Made by passing electricity through a wire

1. Electromagnets are made stronger by increasing the number of turns of wire around the core.

2. Electromagnets are made stronger by using more dry cells (battery), which increases the current of electricity.

3. Electromagnets are temporary magnets, be-

cause the electricity can be turned on or off to create or break a magnetic field.

III.   Static electricity
    A.   Friction produces static electricity.
    B.   All matter is made up of atoms that contain protons, neutrons, and electrons.
        1.   The mass of an atom is determined by the number of protons and neutrons found in its nucleus.
        2.   Protons are positive electrical charges.
        3.   Neutrons are neither positive nor negative in electrical charge.
    C.   Oppositely charged particles attract each other.
        1.   Usually there are the same number of electrons as there are protons in an atom.
        2.   By rubbing two different substances it is possible to move electrons from one substance to the other.
        3.   Removal of electrons from a substance that is initially neutral results in a positive charge because of the greater number of protons that remain.
            a.   Rubbing a glass rod with a piece of silk will remove some electrons from the glass onto the silk.
            b.   A positively charged glass rod attracts a small piece of paper that has an opposite charge.
            c.   Insulators do not conduct electricity; they work best for producing static electricity.

IV.   Electricity
    A.   Electricity is defined as the flow of electrons through a conductor.

1. Most metals are good conductors that enable electrons to move easily from atom to atom.
2. Nonconductors or insulators do not permit electrons to flow through them easily.

B. Series circuit
   1. Electricity has only one path through which it travels in a closed circuit.
   2. All bulbs or appliances are hooked up to each other in a "straight" line.
   3. The current flows through and across the sockets and the bulbs.
   4. Removal or burning out of a bulb leads to all the bulbs or appliances going off; each bulb acts like a switch.

C. Parallel circuit
   1. Electricity has more than one pathway through which it travels in a closed circuit.
   2. Most household wiring is done in parallel.
      a. If one bulb goes out in the parallel circuit, all the other bulbs still function.
      b. If an overload occurs and the fuse burns out, not all of the electrical appliances go off unless it is the main line fuse.

D. Electrical safety
   1. Teach how to insert a plug into a receptacle without making direct contact with electricity.
   2. Demonstrate a simple series circuit with one or two bulbs, using thin bare copper wires, and compare with another circuit using insulated bell wire. Observe heat generated by exposed wire, which is a cause of fire.
   3. Emphasize importance of replacing wires which begin to fray.

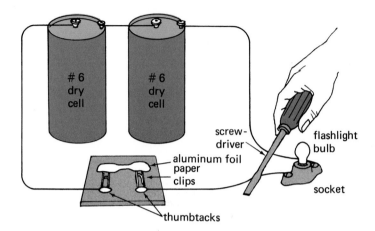

Fig. 18.9. *Fuse and overload.*

4. Demonstrate dangers of an overload or short circuit, following fig. 18.9.
5. Indicate the importance of having good fuses and dangers when a fuse is burned.
6. Experiment in using different types of aluminum or tin foil.

19

MACHINES AT WORK

Grades K–2

1. Rubbing two things together makes them hot.
2. Machines help us make work easier.
3. A push or pull is a force.
4. Cranes and dump trucks are examples of machines.

Grades 3–5

5. A knife, screwdriver, and doorknob are examples of simple machines.
6. Wind is a force that makes a sailboat move.
7. Although at times friction is a hindrance to machines, it is also helpful.
8. Machines develop power for us by using wind, using falling water, and burning fuels.

Grades 6–8

9. The two major types of simple machines are the lever and the inclined plane.
10. The lever includes the wheel and axle, and the pulley.
11. The inclined plane includes special forms such as the wedge and the screw.
12. A machine changes the amount, speed, or direction of a force.
13. Work is the product of force times the distance.
14. The mechanical advantage is a number that indicates how much our machine multiplies the force we put into it.

$$\frac{W}{E} \left(\frac{\text{weight or resistance}}{\text{effort}} \right) = \text{mechanical advantage}$$

Concept Formation

Friction is an interesting concept that is introduced in the lower grades by everyday phenomena such as rubbing hands together, blocks, rocks, or other objects. Children will observe that heat is generated and they may explore which objects become hotter as a result of friction. Concepts numbered 1 and 7 pertain to friction. In grades three to five the concept is extended to show the hindrance as well as the usefulness of friction. Practical illustrations for children such as ice skating, walking, and running show the importance of friction. We slip and fall when there is no or little friction; as a surface, ice for example, becomes smoother, friction is decreased.

In relating friction to machines, children are familiar with ball bearings in roller skates. The rubbing surface of the inside of the wheel against the axle is reduced when ball

bearings are used (see fig. 19.1). With less surface contact, a
lesser amount of friction is produced.

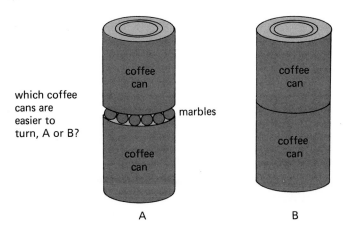

which coffee
cans are
easier to
turn, A or B?

Fig. 19.1.   *Ball bearings (marbles) reduce friction.*

The types of simple machines, how they work for us,
and how we get power are suggested in the concepts numbered 2, 4, 5, 9, 10, and 11. Although younger children may
have little access to tools, they all have toys that are made
up of at least one or more types of simple machines: shovels, toy hammers, autos, doll carriages, and many others.
These are illustrations of simple machines that are related to
these concepts.

Concepts numbered 3, 6, 8, 12, 13, and 14 pertain to
force, work, and mechanical advantage. Wherever possible,
pupil experiences with force should be introduced. If a pupil
sails or rows a boat, force can be taught with meaning.
Objects that are too heavy to lift without the help of a machine can be discussed in terms of actual pupil experiences.

Friction. Because a certain amount of friction is always present when any machine is working, it is useful to develop this concept along with the understanding of how simple machines operate. Ask younger children to bring in marbles, dominoes, tinker toys, rocks, pieces of flint, a small spring that can be attached to tinker toy wood, small carts, and toy autos. Place all of these materials in the center of a classroom.

Encourage the children to suggest how they can use some of these things to demonstrate and overcome friction. For example, some children will note that marbles are easy to play with because they roll very fast. The question could be asked, "Would dominoes move just as fast as marbles?" The design of an experiment by using a tinker toy set to make a homemade pinball machine could prove effective. Using the same force applied to the plunger, compare the speed of and distance traveled by the marble as compared with a domino. How much surface of the domino comes in contact with the floor of the box of the pinball machine? Compare this surface contact with that of a marble.

Roller skates use ball bearings resembling marbles to reduce friction. This makes for faster and smoother travel. Have the children test the toy carts and toy autos. Do some of these toys reduce friction? What kind of tires are found on these autos? How can less rubber on the tire be made to touch the ground when the car is moving? Overinflation and underinflation of tires with discussion on friction and wear and tear on tires will prove interesting.

Problems

For each of the following, indicate whether friction is being added or removed:

1. Removing top snow from an ice skating rink.

2. Pitcher uses rosin before making a pitch.
3. Batter rubs hands in dirt before holding the baseball bat.
4. Throwing sand on an icy street.
5. Putting a few drops of oil in the wheel near axle of the bicycle.
6. Putting some wax on a dance floor.

Lever. The seesaw or teeter-totter in the school playground is a good illustration of a lever. The center where the board pivots or turns is called the fulcrum. If two children sit at opposite ends of the teeter-totter, at equal distances from the fulcrum, they will balance it if each child is of equal weight. If one child is heavier, he will bring down the teeter-totter. If the heavier child wishes to balance the seesaw, he needs to move closer to the fulcrum while the lighter child remains at the same place at the opposite end (see figs. 19.2 and 19.3).

Simple Machines

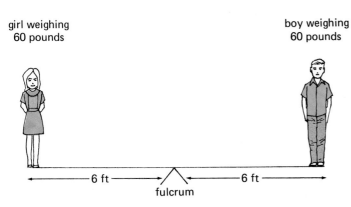

girl weighing
60 pounds

boy weighing
60 pounds

6 ft   6 ft
fulcrum

Fig. 19.2. Equal weights, equal distance. Balance.

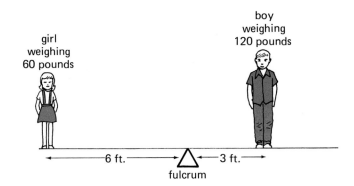

Fig. 19.3.   Twice the weight requires half the distance from the fulcrum to balance.

To demonstrate this ratio, select two children who together equal the weight of one child. Ask the pupils to propose the distance from the fulcrum at which each child should sit.

Experiment. Using two cardboard boxes about 2 or more feet apart on the desk, place a yardstick between them so that a string can be attached to the yardstick that holds a suspended rule (see fig. 19.4). At each end of the suspended rule, attach a piece of string (equal length) and a paper clip to balance it. The string that supports the rule should have a loop to permit the rule to be moved from side to side. Encourage the children to propose what changes should be made to balance the rule as different conditions are suggested.

For example, if three paper clips are attached at one end, what must be done to balance the teeter-totter at the other end? Soon it will be discovered that three clips need to be moved one-third of the distance from the fulcrum to balance the one clip at the opposite end. This is the mechanical advantage of three. It represents the relationship between the weight (or force) and the weight (or force) that it lifts or balances the teeter-totter. In other simple machines

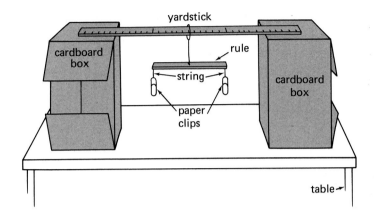

Fig. 19.4. *Balancing the rule.*

the mechanical advantage will suggest proportionately how much less effort is needed to do the same amount of work. Thus a mechanical advantage of three means that this machine will require only one-third the amount of effort to get the work done.

A pair of pliers is an example of a first-class lever. The longer the handles are on a pair of pliers (fig. 19.5), the less effort force is required. This is similar to the teeter-totter case where the lighter child who is a greater distance from the fulcrum balances the heavier child.

In a second-class lever, the fulcrum, instead of being in the center, is at one end, and the resistance is between the fulcrum and the effort. Invite the children to bring in nutcrackers, good examples of second-class levers. In both first- and second-class levers, a small force is required to move through a greater distance than a larger force. It would be stimulating for the children to attempt to break some nuts by using their fingers and compare with the little effort required when a nutcracker is used.

Another illustration of a second-class lever is a door.

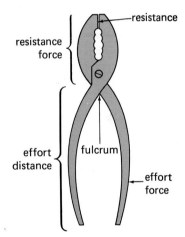

Fig. 19.5. *Example of first-class lever.*

Little effort is needed when applied to the doorknob; the hinges serve as fulcrums. The door acts as the resistance.

First- and second-class levers, like most machines, can overcome a greater force or resistance by applying a small force. Screwdrivers, can openers, and bottle openers are other examples of simple machines that require less effort force.

In the case of a third-class lever, such as a broom, a larger effort force is used in order to increase the speed and the distance of a force. In fig. 19.6, note how the right hand acts as the fulcrum while the left hand is used to apply the effort force. Other examples of a third-class lever are baseball bats, golf clubs, and paddles. In each case of a third-class lever, the effort is between the fulcrum and the resistance.

Fig. 19.6. Broom: A third-class lever.

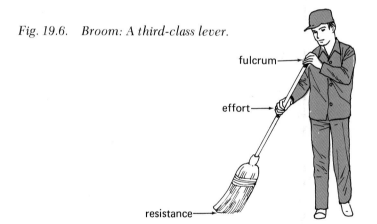

The location of the fulcrum thus determines the class of the lever.

In the first-class lever (fig. 19.7) the fulcrum is between the effort and the weight (resistance).

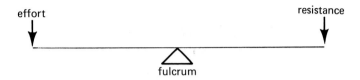

Fig. 19.7. First-class lever.

In the second-class lever (fig. 19.8) the fulcrum is at the end but not too far from the resistance.

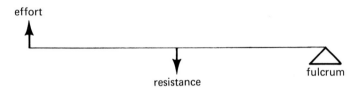

Fig. 19.8. Second-class lever.

In the third-class lever (fig. 19.9) the fulcrum is at the end but not too far from the effort.

Fig. 19.9. Third-class lever.

By using weights, a spring balance, a 12-inch rule, and a small piece of wood as a fulcrum, ask the students to experiment by using all three types of levers. The problem is

Problem Solving

to determine the relationship between the weight and its distance to the fulcrum. The pupils will soon discover that the greater the distance of the weight from the fulcrum, the more difficult the object is to lift.

In a seventh-grade class, a problem-solving lesson was given by writing the following anecdote on the board: "In the back yard where Jim lives, huge boulders landed a few years ago. After a heavy rainfall, Jim noticed a small piece of a $10 bill under a boulder that probably weighed over 300 pounds. Jim found it impossible to lift the rock."

Very quickly, the pupils identified and stated the problem: "How can Bill lift the rock to get the ten dollar bill?" The suggested hypotheses included the use of a pulley to move the rock, the use of a lever, and two or three boys trying to move the rock. Using the lever and pulleys, the pupils designed experiments to test these hypotheses. After performing the laboratory work and following a stimulating discussion, the pupils realized that the lever was the most effective tool to use in solving this problem.

Problem Solving

In grades three to five, a problem-solving situation dealing with friction can be very interesting. In a fifth-grade class, the following anecdote was provided on the board: "Jane's mother, Mrs. Peterson, needed a very heavy comfortable chair to be moved from the bedroom to the living room. She could only lift a corner of the chair and it was too heavy for Jane and her mother to move. No other help was around."

The proposed hypotheses were:

1. A rope could be tied around the chair and the chair pulled into the living room.
2. A crowbar could be applied to the chair to push it a

little bit each time the crowbar was applied.

3. A small rug or plastic could be placed under the chair, and the chair could be slipped into the living room.

After a serious discussion of what experiments to do, a box containing several heavy books was used in the classroom to represent the heavy chair. A large piece of plastic and a small bathroom rug were also used, one at a time. In raising the question, "Why did the plastic and the rug make it easier to move the heavy box with books," the pupils observed that a smoother surface was provided. In discussing a smooth versus a rough surface, the concept that reducing friction increases the efficiency of work was established.

The wheel-and-axle machine is a large wheel to which **Demonstrations**
is attached a smaller wheel or axle. It may be considered a **and Experiments**

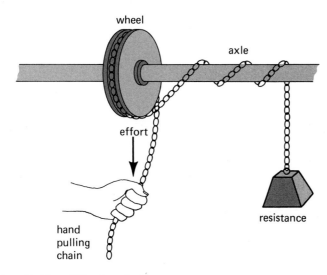

Fig. 19.10.   Wheel and axle.

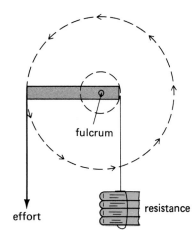

effort

fulcrum

resistance

Fig. 19.11.
Side view of wheel and axle.

first-class lever because its fulcrum (point of rest) is at the center. The steering wheel of an automobile is a common example. The force is transmitted by the axle through the gears and the car moves. In the case of a bicycle the effort is applied to a small wheel which makes for an increase in speed. Fig. 19.10 is a diagram of a simple wheel-and-axle machine.

In fig. 19.11 note that the side view of the wheel and axle resembles the lever. In determining the mechanical advantage, the radius of the large wheel or the *resistance* is divided by the radius of the axle *(effort)*.

In the lower grades, kindergarten through three, the concepts on the use of the wheel and axle can be developed gradually by using books, rubber bands, and round pencils. The effort force required to move a book is measured by the stretch of the rubber band. See figs. 19.12, *A* and *B*, and observe how much the rubber band stretches when three round pencils are placed under the book to be moved. Have some of the children perform these experiments using objects other than books.

In the demonstrations with books, a discussion of rolling friction (using round pencils) and sliding friction will be helpful. Toys such as cars, trucks, and carts on wheels can be used for demonstration and experimentation. Allow the children to place different objects in a cart on wheels and have them pull them with a rubber band to measure the effort force. In upper grades a spring balance can be used to measure actually the force effort required to move the resistance or weight of objects in the cart on wheels.

In grades six through eight the pulley may be introduced as a very useful machine. Moving pianos, office furniture, and other very heavy objects to another level in a building frequently requires the use of pulleys. Perhaps a pulley may be visualized as a circular lever; the fulcrum is in the center as the wheel turns on its axis. When a single fixed

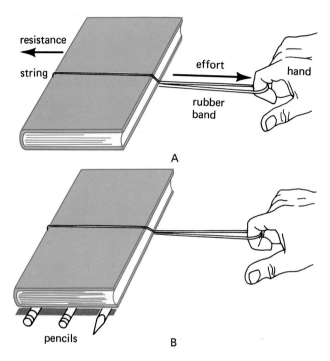

resistance

string

effort

hand

rubber
band

A

pencils

B

*Fig. 19.12. Comparing effort to move a book with and
without rollers.*

pulley is used, there is no gain in force or distance. It is simply more convenient to change the direction of the force
such as pulling the line down instead of up. As an illustration it is convenient to raise a flag on a pole with the help
of a single fixed pulley. When a system of pulleys is used to
lift heavy weights, it is called a block and tackle.

Following the illustrations in figs. 19.13–19.15, encourage pupils to determine by experiments:

1. The relationship between the distance the force pulls
   down (on rope) and the distance that the resistance
   (flag) moves up.

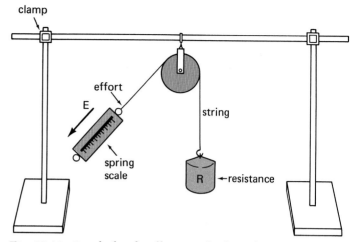

Fig. 19.13. *Single fixed pulley attached to a bar.*

Fig. 19.14. *Single movable pulley.*

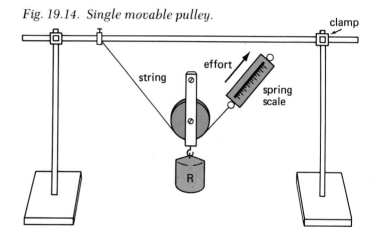

2. Is there a change in direction of effort force?
3. Is there an increase in distance or speed of resistance?
4. Is the effort force multiplied?
5. Remembering that the mechanical advantage equals resistance (grams) divided by effort (grams), state the mechanical advantage (M.A.) for each of the setups in figs. 19.13–19.15.

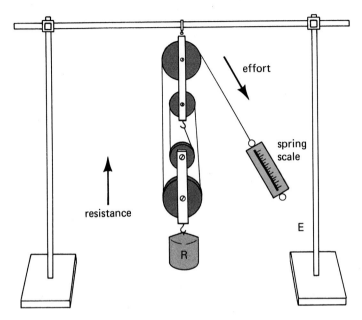

effort

spring
scale

resistance

E

R

Fig. 19.15. Block and tackle.

It is always a problem to lift an object weighing two or more times the weight of the person attempting to lift it. Anecdotes, actual situations, and demonstrations may be given in class to enable children at all levels to identify this type of problem. Although a choice in selecting the best machine to do the work becomes a secondary problem, it is common to use the inclined plane.

Children will frequently observe how wooden planks are placed from the edge of the truck platform to the street in order to facilitate the lifting of a piano or other heavy object. To reduce friction, wheels are placed under the piano so that less force need be applied. Discussions based

Problem Solving

on these observations and actual pupil experiences can serve as effective stimulants in having children solve problems by individual and group experimentation.

To lift a 160-lb. box onto a table that is 4 ft. above the ground, how much work will be done?

First, the concept that *work equals force times the distance* should be established. Second, the application of the information is made in this equation:

$$\text{work} = \text{force} \times \text{distance}$$
$$W = 160 \text{ lbs.} \times 4 \text{ ft.}$$
$$W = 640 \text{ ft.-lbs.}$$

Instead of lifting the 160-lb. object 4 ft., let us use for an inclined plane a wooden board 8 ft. long (see fig. 19.16).

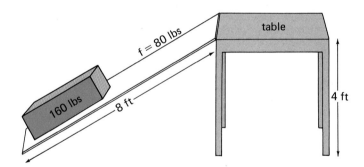

Fig. 19.16. Inclined plane.

The problem is to determine how much force is required to move the object (160 lbs.) through the distance (8 ft.) on the inclined plane. The same equation of work is used; namely, force exerted × distance force moves on the inclined plane equals the load × distance to be lifted off the ground. Substituting the values in order to find out the force exerted, the equation is:

$f \times 8$ ft. $= 160$ lbs. $\times 4$ ft.

$f \times 8$ ft. $= 640$ ft.-lbs.

$f \qquad = \dfrac{640 \text{ ft.-lbs.}}{8 \text{ ft.}}$

$f \qquad = 80$ lbs. (the force exerted)

The amount of work done by pushing the 160-lb. object up the inclined plane is now determined by the actual force exerted, or 80 lbs. Thus the work equals force times distance, or 80 lbs. times 8 ft., or 640 ft.-lbs. The amount of work done with or without the simple machine (inclined plane) is the same. However, it is easier to do the same amount of work because in this case only half the amount of effort force (80 lbs.) is needed to do the same amount of work. Actually the distance was increased in order to decrease the effort force. Frequently this is referred to as trading distance for force.

The concept of mechanical advantage can be developed by recognizing that only one-half the amount of effort force is needed in this case, and so the machine has the mechanical advantage of two. This inclined plane gave two times the force compared with the use of no machine. The mechanical advantage can be determined as follows:

M.A. = length/height = 8/4 = 2 *or*

M.A. = load/force $\quad$ = 160/80 = 2

Laboratory Experiments

Pupils can be provided with a spring balance, objects to be lifted such as roller skates, and wooden boards to be used as inclined planes. Comparing the weight of different objects lifted with the force required to move each object on an inclined plane will develop many of the concepts of an inclined plane (see figs. 19.17 and 19.18).

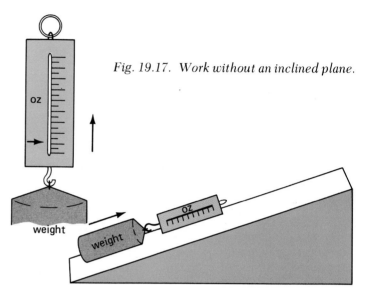

Fig. 19.17. Work without an inclined plane.

Fig. 19.18. Work with an inclined plane.

The wedge. Shaped like the letter V, a wedge consists of two surfaces of inclined planes back to back. Wedges cut and split objects by pushing and prying. The knife, ax, and chisel are examples of wedges. They are not so efficient as the lever, pulley, or wheel and axle because much sliding friction is involved in the use of a wedge.

The screw. The screw may be considered an inclined plane that is rolled around a cylindrical object such as a pencil. As an illustration note in figs. 19.19 and 19.20 the relationship in appearance between the inclined plane and the screw. The inclined plane winds around to resemble a spiral object, the screw. Although there is a gain in force by using the screw, speed and distance are sacrificed. Observe a piano stool that operates on the principle of the screw. Although an auto jack is a complex machine consisting of more than one simple machine, it is worthwhile to observe a jack as it lifts an auto.

Field trips to the farm, the garage, the hardware store, the kitchen, toy stores, and building construction sites will reveal various types of simple and complex machines. Some pupils may take photographs of these machines and bring them in to class for discussion. Which of these machines are really helpful? Do some of them pollute the environment? Can anything be done to minimize such pollution? Interesting discussions on machines, technology, and environment will relate science to social science in a very effective manner.

Machines and the Environment

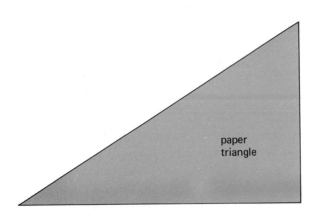

Fig. 19.19. Triangular paper resembling an inclined plane.

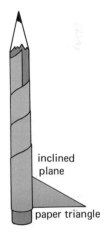

Fig. 19.20. Same paper rolled around a pencil.

How have machines changed our way of life? Imagine if the only means of transportation today were the horse and buggy. Could we manage in today's world without autos, airplanes, boats, and trains? How do machines give us power? How would we live without electricity today? Have our foods, shelter, and clothing been changed by machines? These questions can provide stimulating activity in discussions, reading, and field investigations.

"Give me a fulcrum on which to rest, and I will move the earth."—Archimedes

I. Development of machines and man
   A. Prehistoric man: bow and arrow
   B. Ancient Greeks: wheels and the lever
   C. Surface transportation in America: steam locomotive, autos, and buses
   D. Air travel
   E. Transportation of food and clothing for a better economy
      1. Railroads, trucks, and steamships: transported machinery, tools, food, and clothing
      2. Wooden plow, sickle, and cradle: replaced by steel plows, reapers, and threshers
      3. Muscle work by human, ox, and horse: replaced by complex machines

II. Simple machines
   A. Lever—three classes of levers; each class is determined by the relative location of the fulcrum with respect to the effort force and the applied force.
   B. Modified levers—pulley and wheel and axle
      1. Pulley—movable pulleys are very convenient for making work easier; usually the more pulleys, the less effort force is needed to get the work done.
      2. Wheel and axle—operates on the principle of a lever but allows the resistance or load to move through greater distances than the lever.
   C. Inclined plane
      1. Used for loading barrels, machines, and other heavy objects onto trucks and cars.
      2. Permits the lifting of an object with less

weight (force) than the weight of the object itself.

D. Special cases of the inclined plane
1. Wedge—a pair of inclined planes, back to back, split and cut objects.
2. Screw—an inclined plane that is spirally wound around a cone or cylinder.
   a. Holds objects firmly together
   b. Lifts heavy objects, as in the case of an automobile jack

III. Mechanical advantage = load/force or resistance/ effort
A. Ideal mechanical advantage—neglects friction and the weight of the simple machine as in the case of a pulley. If a motor weighing 400 lbs. is raised by a force of 100 lbs., the ideal M.A. is 4.

$$\frac{400}{100} = 4$$

B. Actual mechanical advantage—if in the same load as above, the actual effort force was 125 lbs., then the actual M.A. would be 3.2.

$$\frac{400}{125} = 3.2$$

IV. Complex machines
A. Most complicated machines consist of various combinations of simple machines.
B. Examples of complex machines are automobiles, typewriters, steam engines, cranes, printing presses, and knitting machines.

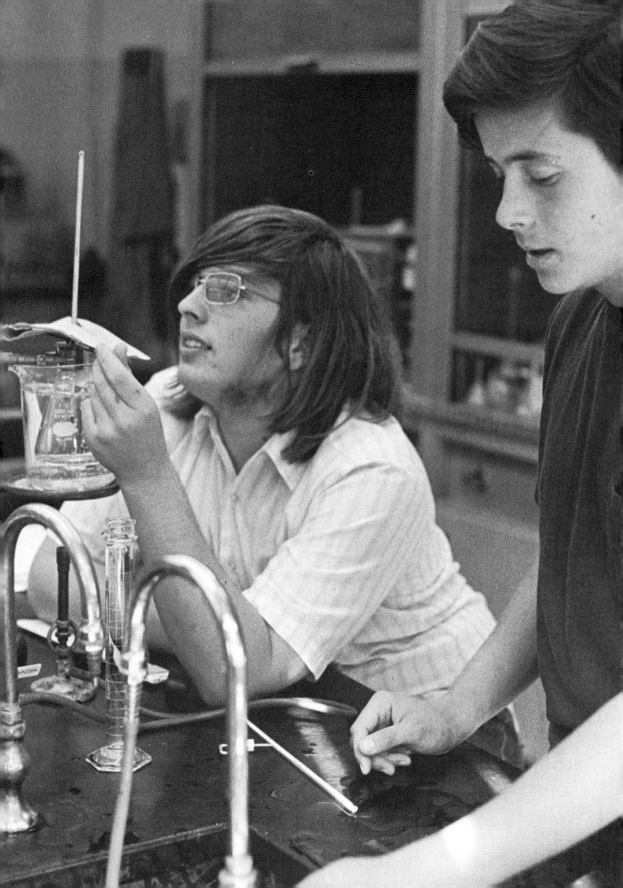

20

HEAT AND
ITS BEHAVIOR

Grades K–2   **Concepts**

1. Sun's rays heat the earth.
2. The amount of heat received on the ground changes during different hours of the day.
3. A thermometer is used to measure temperature.
4. The sun warms some things faster than others.
5. The temperature will change from day to day.

Grades 3–5

6. During chemical changes heat is either released or absorbed.
7. Molecules move faster when heated.

8. During expansion molecules move apart and during contraction molecules come closer together.
9. Heat causes expansion in solids, liquids, and gases.
10. Metals are conductors of heat; air is a good insulator.

Grades 6–8

11. Different metals expand at different rates, and each type has its own rate of expansion.
12. Three methods by which heat is transferred from one object to another are conduction, convection, and radiation.
13. Heat is absorbed by dark-colored surfaces and reflected by light-colored ones.
14. A special characteristic of water is that it expands when cooled from 4° to 0° C.
15. In freezing water to ice, 80 calories of heat are lost by each gram at 0° C.
16. In boiling water to steam, 540 calories of heat are added to each gram at 100° C.

Concept Formation

The concepts numbered 1, 2, 5, 7, 10, and 12 pertain to descriptive aspects or properties of heat. At all grade levels children experience the warmth produced by the sun's rays. When it is very cold people without gloves will rub their hands to produce the heat of friction. Older pupils will recall burning themselves on touching a spoon handle that was left in a hot bowl of soup.

It is difficult to imagine anyone escaping from touching something hot. Everyone experiences hot and cold weather during seasonal changes. Most families burn some type of fuel to obtain heat in the home during cold weather. Children make campfires and use heat for cooking purposes. The dangers of excessive heat in electrical wires, heat exhaustion, or smoking that causes fires are known to people of all ages. Such experiences may serve as a basis for discussion in establishing current concepts of heat. From this discussion, demonstrations, laboratory work, and problem-solving activity can extend the meaning of concepts related to heat energy.

The concepts numbered 3, 8, 11, and 14 pertain to measurement factors of heat such as the thermometer, molecular motion, and measurement changes in expansion of metals. The concepts 4, 6, 9, 13, 15, and 16 emphasize the cause-and-effect relations of heat energy.

Learning Activities

In the lower grades children usually bring a magnifying glass to school. They frequently enjoy using it on pictures and reading material. Occasionally a youngster in the lower grades may use a magnifying lens to burn a piece of paper. If the teacher emphasizes the dangers of making a fire and demonstrates it by a sink or bucket of water, it may serve a very useful purpose. The concentration and magnification of the sun's rays on a piece of paper that suddenly catches fire can be both interesting and dangerous. Hence fire safety precautions should be stressed with this type of demonstration.

A discussion of children's toys that become extremely hot when used for a long period of time will prove stimulating and helpful. Motors and projectors need to be cooled. Objects that operate on batteries to produce electricity also produce heat. How does the side effect of heat energy affect the life of the toy? What measures can be taken to minimize the heat effects? Resource people such as engineers and firemen in the community can be asked to relate their knowledge to children on problems of heat energy and toys. Safety precautions need to be stressed along with activities involving heat.

Demonstrations

Assuming that children have learned to read a thermometer, the mere agitation of water with a spoon in a glass for about five minutes will produce a change in temperature. The temperature should be taken before the stirring of the water and after it has been stirred continuously for about five minutes.

A half cup of water at room temperature is poured into a blender. The temperature of the water is taken before and after the blender is turned on for one minute. This type of mechanical energy produces heat energy.

Experiments

Children already experienced friction in rubbing their hands together to produce heat. Provide them with sandpaper and a board, and have them feel the board before rubbing sandpaper on it. After rubbing the board with sandpaper for about two or three minutes, they can feel the heat on the board.

Some pupils may wish to rub two rocks together. Other children may hammer a nail many times into a board and note the temperature change on the head of the nail. Discuss the importance of using oil or another lubricant in machines where friction needs to be reduced.

Conduction

What causes the handle of a spoon to get hot even though the handle is outside the cup of hot water? Will the handle of a spoon remove some of the heat from hot soup? The temperature can be taken of two cups of hot soup over five- and ten-minute intervals to see how the hot soup containing the spoon cools faster. At the same time pupils should feel how the handle of the spoon becomes warmer.

In providing an explanation children should question what happens to the molecules in the metallic spoon. Some pupils will reply that the hot molecules in the spoon moved rapidly because of heat to the handle. Some children may or may not use the term conduction to explain this phenomenon. Pans and kettles become hot on the stove by conduction. A discussion will help develop this concept, which is experienced daily.

From the concept of conduction a logical question frequently arises that is related to insulation. Children will deduce from discussion that handles on pans, cookers, and kettles are usually made of wood or other types of insulated material so that they will not burn themselves when touching the handle. Questions should be encouraged such as, "Where else are insulating materials used in the home?" Heating pipes and systems and air conditioning can serve as good illustrations in the use of insulation.

Which metals are better conductors of heat? Make available equal-sized strips of copper, aluminum, and iron. Display wax and tacks with a burner and a stand. Attempt to have the children propose the design of the experiment as illustrated in fig. 20.1. By simultaneously applying the burner to the edges of the three metals, the pupils can observe which tack falls off first. The pupils will infer that the wax melted, causing the tack to fall. They will also discover which of the metals is the best conductor of heat.

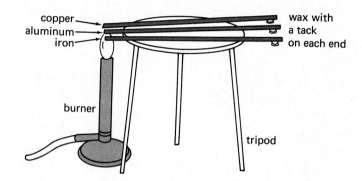

Fig. 20.1. Simultaneous heating of three different metals.

Metals Expand on Heating

A simple experiment is to wrap a wire around the head of a nail and suspend the wire as shown in fig. 20.2. The observation will be made that the wire sags as it expands. Let it cool and rub an ice cube along the wire until the wire becomes taut, indicating its contraction.

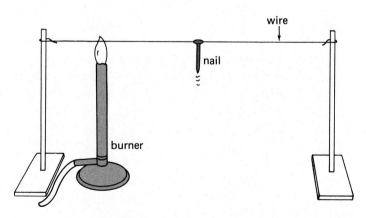

Fig. 20.2.   Wire expands upon heating.

Air Expands on Heating

A bottle or a flask, a balloon, and a burner are displayed. Ask the pupils to design a demonstration to show what happens when air is heated (see fig. 20.3). The discussion of warmer air compared with cooler air can be related to weather phenomena. The concept that warmer air rises can be reinforced at this time.

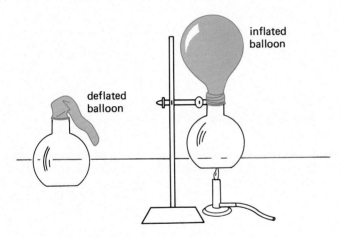

deflated balloon

inflated balloon

Fig. 20.3. Comparing the effect of heating air.

An enjoyable demonstration is the making of popcorn. Follow the directions on the package. Because there is moisture in each kernel and heat changes the moisture to steam, a vapor pressure is developed that causes the corn to expand and pop.

Anecdote: "On a freezing winter day, Susan's mother stepped outside of the house to bring in the bottle of milk that the milkman had left several hours ago. The milk bottle was cracked."

Problem Solving

This anecdote was written on the chalkboard, and the teacher asked, "What is the problem?" The first youngster in the sixth grade replied, "What caused the crack in the milk bottle?"

The teacher asked for hypotheses and the following were stated:

1. "The milkman accidentally dropped the bottle on the floor."
2. "The expansion of the freezing water in the milk made the bottle crack."
3. "During transportation, the milk bottle was cracked."

The pupils suggested the experiments to test these hypotheses:

1. Several milk bottles were filled with equal volumes of water and were marked to show the level of water at room temperature.
2. Dry ice (not to be handled by bare hands) was used around the milk bottles to freeze the water.
3. It was observed that those bottles containing water showed an increase in volume because of expansion on freezing.
4. Two other bottles containing no-calorie soda pop and sugared soda pop, respectively, did not exhibit freezing conditions or an increase in volume.

Heat in Solutions

To a glass of water add a tablespoonful of sugar. Take the temperature of the water for three minutes before adding the sugar. Continue to read the temperature for another three minutes after the sugar is added. Repeat the procedure, substituting ammonium nitrate for the sugar. Repeat the experiment, but substitute calcium oxide. Was heat given off or absorbed when each solid chemical dissolved in the solution?

When a chemical change occurs, heat is either given off or absorbed. Take a wad of steel wool that has been soaked in water. Drain the water, and place the steel wool in a thermos bottle. Pupils should record the temperature every two minutes for fifteen minutes. What happens when all the oxygen in the thermos bottle is used up as it combines with the steel wool? Will the temperature continue to rise? How can you find out? This suggests removing the cork, allowing air to enter, sealing the thermos with the thermometer, and continuing to take readings of temperature changes.

Refer to chapter 13 for concepts on air, water, and weather in relation to changing the liquid water to either a gas or a solid. Heat is the energy responsible for this change in the state of matter. Also, see chapter 17 on changing matter and energy.

Everyday Problem

Obtain a glass jar with a metal cover that is difficult to unscrew. Place the cover under hot water and unscrew the cap. Discuss the effect of hot water on the metal screw cap after the anecdote is presented as a problem. Some children will suggest using a towel to get a firm grip. The children may recommend a lever or a can opener. All of these suggestions should be tried along with the use of heat in hot water. Although the topic for discussion at the moment is heat, other correct solutions to the problem should be received favorably.

Convection

Air and liquids are heated through convection. To observe convection currents in water place shredded bits of newspaper or blotting paper in a beaker of heated water. Move the beaker over to the side of the hot plate. Observe the convection current produced in the water by the motion of the shredded newspaper or blotting paper.

Convection currents of air are frequently responsible for heating homes. We can see the smoke leaving the chimney or the incinerator. The warm air rises and the heavier cool air sinks. For this reason, it is recommended that windows in a home be opened slightly at the bottom and at the top. The cool air rushes in at the bottom and is warmed by radiation and/or convection. The warmer air rises to the top, and some of it leaves the room through the opening at the top of the window. Fresh, cool air comes in at the bottom, and the circulation of air in the room continues. See fig. 20.4 for demonstration of convection currents of air.

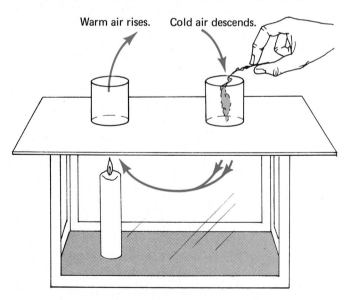

Warm air rises. Cold air descends.

Fig. 20.4. Convection in a box.

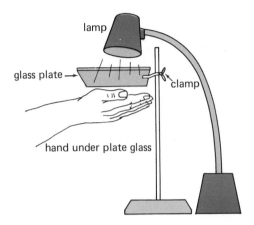

Fig. 20.5. Radiant heat waves pass through glass and heat palm of hand.

Radiation

Place the palm of the hand near an electric bulb (lamp). Turn the lamp on. Note how quickly the heat *radiates* from the bulb to the hand. If convection were at work, it would take longer for the palm to warm, because air is a poor conductor of heat.

Place a transparent glass plate between the bulb and the palm (fig. 20.5). Note that the glass plate is cool although the heat waves radiate from the electric bulb through the glass. The palm of the hand receives the heat. Radiation heats us when we sit near the fireplace or if we face the sun. Heat from the sun passes through a window pane and we feel the heat on our faces. Yet the window pane is cool. This is typical of radiation. Also, if we sit around a campfire or near a radiator we feel heat waves.

In class discussion the lower grades do not necessarily need to know the terms conduction, convection, and radiation. The children can understand the phenomena of how heat is transferred from one object to another. In the upper grades and in intermediate school the terms conduction, convection, and radiation may be introduced with experiments, demonstrations, and personal experiences. Applications of heating the home can be discussed after a survey is made; children can learn if the heating systems in their homes are hot-air, hot-water, or steam.

A Problem-Solving Lesson Plan

Three Steps of Teacher Behavior

1. Provide the situation, anecdote, or demonstration.

   Lately, Mr. Smith, who owns a luncheonette, has received complaints from his customers. They say that his coffee turns cold by the time they arrive at work in the morning. A salesman shows Mr. Smith several new coffee take-out containers.

2. Display the material that suggests experiments.

   The following are displayed: thermometers, water, beakers, Bunsen burners, graduated cylinders, and containers made of styrofoam, glass, heat-resistant plastic, paper, metal, and two-layer thermal cups.

3. The specific principle to be taught: Trapped air is an efficient insulator of heat energy.

Five Steps of Pupil Behavior

Note: In the days previous to this experience the students had had some calorimetry work, and it is assumed that they now know the difference between heat and

SOURCE: Developed by Michael Keany, science teacher at Manhasset Junior-Senior High School, New York.

temperature. The students have also been asked to do outside reading on the work of Count Rumford and the caloric fluid theory of heat. The day before this lesson, the students had a debate based upon their past observations as to whether or not heat is actually a fluid. No conclusive results were reached.

1. Students identify the problem.

    "Which type of container will keep the coffee the warmest for the longest time?"

2. Students state hypotheses. Actual responses follow.

    a. "Since I believe that heat is actually a fluid, it makes sense to me that the densest material would keep the heat fluid from leaking out because the particles are closest together. I say the metal container would be the best."
        ° (Three people in the class agreed with this point of view.)
    b. "Heat is not a fluid! I think a dense material would lead the heat away the fastest. It's like when you grab the metal handle of a pot on the stove. I think something light (not very dense) would be the best container. I say that the stryofoam container will hold heat for the longest time."
        ° (The vast majority of people agreed with this person. They said that it made sense because styrofoam containers are used to keep ice from melting.)
    c. "The ski jackets have air pockets in them. I think that air is the least dense material. It should keep the heat in the best. I would say that the 'cup inside the cup' would be the best."

° (Only one other person agreed.)

d. No one chose the glass, or the paper, or the plastic container.

3. Design and perform experiments to verify or discard hypotheses.

The class thought that we should test some boiling water in each type of cup. The initial temperature should be noted in each case. The temperature should be noted every thirty seconds. One person suggested that the class should use equal amounts of water in every container. A discussion resulted. Another person thought that it was "unfair" to have the tops uncovered. We discussed this as a variable.

The experiment was carried out. Volunteers measured with the plastic, glass, and paper.

4. Evaluate data.

The resulting data were graphed on the blackboard after similar groups had compared their findings.

5. Formulate the generalization.

The slope of the graph of the styrofoam and the thermal cup indicated that they were the best insulators. The metal and the glass were relatively poor "keepers of heat." The paper cup was somewhere in between the two groups.

The generalization that the class made was that:

"Substances with low densities are effective when they are used to keep in heat energy."

Serious doubt was cast upon the idea that heat was a fluid.

The question arose as to why the plastic cup was a poor insulator and why the plastic cup inside the plastic cup (thermal cup) was a good insulator.

These points were discussed during the beginning of the next class period.

Other Anecdotes That Lead to Problem Solving

Twice a year John's uncle travels to Bermuda for a vacation. When asked why he chooses both the summer and winter, he says, "to escape the heat of the summer and the cold of the winter." (*Problem:* How is it possible for Bermuda to have a mild winter and a comfortable summer?) Hypotheses, experiments, and evaluation of data will lead to the concept that a given amount of energy will raise the temperature of land more than water in arriving at a solution to this problem.

Demonstrations with Cold

The properties of various things change when extremely low temperatures surround them. Pupils are fascinated when items such as frankfurters are dipped into a special frozen mixture in a can. The teacher should exercise caution in performing the following demonstrations using dry ice.

Pour about 2 inches of acetone in a #2 can. Acetone may be purchased at a pharmacy or from a scientific supply company. Obtain some dry ice, wrap a towel, and crack with a mallet into smaller pieces or chips. At first there will be much bubbling when the dry ice chips are added to the acetone. After a few minutes, when bubbling subsides, add some more dry ice. *Use rubber gloves and tongs when handling the dry ice.* The acetone–dry-ice combination in the can is now ready to accept different objects.

Place a frankfurter into the can with the tongs, and wait for about a minute. Remove the frankfurter with the tongs. With rubber gloves on your hands, throw the frankfurter against the chalkboard as though it were a ball. Pupils will observe that the frankfurter is as hard as a rock and breaks into small pieces like glass. Other substances to test at this below-freezing temperature are vegetables such as celery, a piece of lettuce, and a fresh flower. All of these substances will be hard as a rock when removed from the acetone and dry ice. Note that the dry ice is about -103 degrees F.

For another stimulating demonstration prepare a 1-inch cube out of paper and carefully pour some mercury (liquid at room temperature) into this small paper container. Very carefully (with gloves on hands) place the container with mercury into the dry-ice–acetone combination. Hold a pencil upright with one end submerged in the mercury. After about one or two minutes the liquid mercury will turn to a solid. Remove the container of mercury with the pencil tip frozen in it. You may use this as a hammer in driving a nail into a board.

Background Information	I. Historical development

Background Information

I. Historical development

    A. Heat was considered a weightless and separate substance until the early nineteenth century.

    B. Joseph Black (1750) presented the "caloric" theory.

        1. An imaginary substance, called caloric, was found in all objects.

        2. Temperature varied as the amount of caloric found in the object; the more caloric, the higher the temperature.

    C. Benjamin Thompson (known as Count Rumford of Bavaria) disproved the "caloric" theory as a result of the following experience:

        1. In supervising the boring of cannon holes,

water was added to prevent overheating.

2. Count Rumford observed that as more water was added, it boiled away because of the heat produced by the rotating tool.

3. He suggested that the random movement of the molecules of brass that was cut or scraped caused the heat.

D. Sir Humphry Davy confirmed the kinetic theory of heat.

1. He melted two cakes of ice by rubbing them together in a vessel that was below 0° C.

2. The amount of work accomplished determined the amount of ice melted.

3. Rumford and Davy demonstrated that heat was a form of motion called energy.

E. James Prescott Joule established the law of conservation of energy.

II. Definitions

A. Temperature is a measure of the intensity of heat in degrees Centigrade, Fahrenheit, or Kelvin (absolute scale).

B. Calorie is the quantity of heat needed to raise the temperature of 1 gram of water 1° C.

C. Heat is molecular motion.

1. When liquid water loses its surface molecules as vapor to the atmosphere by evaporation, the average kinetic energy is lowered and the temperature of the liquid is lowered. This is the same as saying evaporation of perspiration is a cooling process.

2. Heat is required to change a liquid to a vapor.

III. Heat is transferred by

A. Conduction

B. Convection

C. Radiation

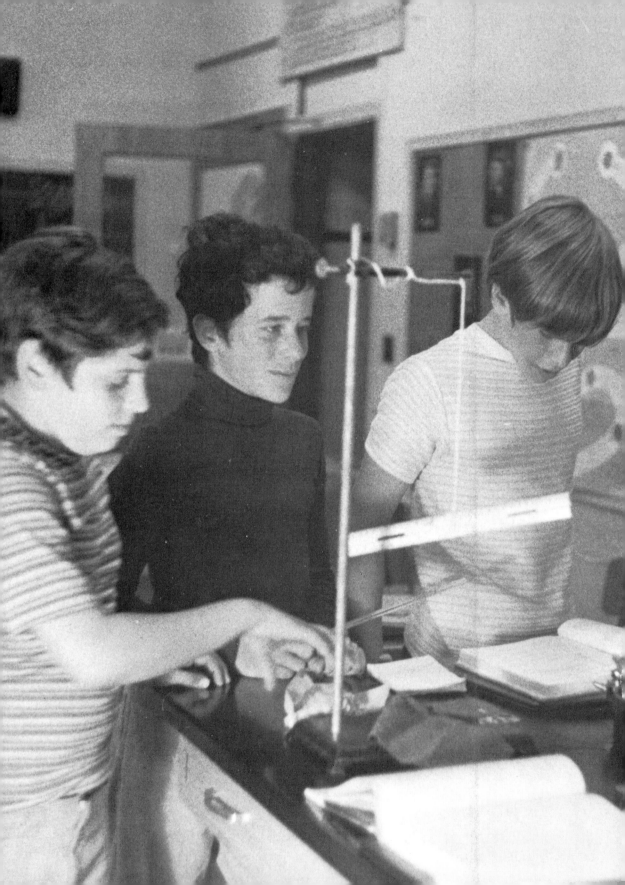

21

SOUND: RADIO, TELEPHONE, TV, AND RADAR

Grades K–2

1. We hear all kinds of sounds.
2. Different things make different sounds.
3. Whistles, bells, and horns are used to send messages.
4. Sounds are made by objects that vibrate or shake.
5. We blow, shake, or hit harder to make louder sounds.

Grades 3–5

6. Sounds travel through air, liquids, and solids.
7. Sounds can be reflected from a surface, producing echoes.

8. Solids are usually better conductors of sound than air.
9. Sounds can be transferred by their vibrations on a record or on tape.
10. Different notes are made by musical instruments when the length of the vibrating object is changed.
11. The ear receives sound vibrations that are converted into messages in the brain.

Grades 6–8

12. Sound travels in longitudinal waves.
13. The frequency of a sound wave is the number of vibrations per second.
14. Sound requires a medium through which it can travel.
15. The properties of sound depend on the characteristics of its waves.

Concept Formation   In the list concepts numbered 1, 2, 6, and 14 are very general ideas about sound. As we go from kindergarten through the upper grades in the intermediate school we can observe the extension of the meanings of these concepts. For example, *we hear all kinds of sounds* is suitable in the lower grades. *Sounds travel through air, liquids, and solids* in grades three to five extends the meaning of *we hear all kinds of sounds*. In grades six through eight, the meaning is extended in depth when we add the concept, *sound requires a medium through which it can travel.*

A normal, healthy child will be aware of the various types of sounds in his environment. A discussion of his experiences at hearing an ambulance, a fire engine, the horn of an auto or ship, records, tapes, crashes, whistles, airplanes, and people talking, and hearing and seeing television will make an awareness of what sounds are desirable compared to noise. It is also possible that what might appear to be good sounds to some people might be considered noise to others. This could initiate a stimulating discussion.

Some teachers prefer to introduce the study of sound through musical instruments or records. With some classes this is very desirable, especially if some of the children play musical instruments. In this situation children can bring their instruments to class and demonstrate playing them. Other children might make various types of instruments from boxes and rubber bands and other equipment.

Illustrations and explanations of sounds are listed in concepts numbered 3, 9, 10, 11, 12, and 15. Again the grade level pattern attempts to extend in depth the meaning for those concepts in the upper grades. Concepts 4, 5, 7, 8, and 13 describe the properties and provide definitions for several aspects of sound.

Lesson Plan—Grade 1

Objectives:

The children will learn that there are many kinds of sounds; sounds are caused by vibrations, and some sounds are loud and others are soft.

Materials:

pop bottle
rubber bands
straws
string telephone
spoon on string
tin and paper plates
nail file and cup

watch and clock

ruler

funnel and hose

Procedures:

At the beginning of the lesson we will ask the children to name some sounds which they think are loud and some sounds which they think are soft. After this brief discussion the children will do the following activities:

1. Hold one end of a ruler down on the table and let the rest of it project over the edge. Push the projecting end downward and let go. As the free end vibrates we hear a sound.

2. Stretch a rubber band over a box and listen to the sound it makes as it vibrates.

3. The children will take turns speaking to each other through a string telephone.

4. Blow across one end of a straw.

5. Blow across one end of an empty pop bottle.

6. Rub a pin across a nail file.

7. Put the pin through the end of a paper cone and again rub the pin across the file.

8. Suspend a spoon from a string and tap the spoon with a pencil. Place the ends of the string close to the ears and again tap the spoon.

9. Listen to the ticking of a watch and clock. Connect a piece of rubber tubing to a funnel and again listen to the clock and watch.

10. Listen to the sounds of two paper plates and two tin plates being struck together.

Evaluation:

After the activities the children will be asked to listen to some sounds and tell which sounds are louder than

SOURCE: Prepared by students in Dr. Phyllis Huff's class at Purdue University, Calumet Campus, Hammond, Indiana.

others and which are softer than others. By doing the activities the children should learn that sounds are caused by vibrations, that some are loud and some are soft, and that there are many kinds of sounds.

Problem Solving

Most of the problem-solving activities were introduced in earlier chapters by means of an anecdote or situation. The following demonstration can serve as a model for introducing a problem-solving activity in class.

Demonstration: While a pupil is blowing into a straw, cut a small piece off at the end of the straw with a scissors. Continue to cut a second piece from the straw while the pupil is blowing. Repeat with cutting a third, and then a fourth, piece of straw at the end while the pupil is blowing. Ask the children what they observe. Repeat the process with other children who blow into the straws. The second group or third group of children can blow into jars with varying amounts of water.

Elicit the problem from the children. Without much direction some children will remark, "What makes the sound change?" In more sophisticated classes some pupils will say, "What makes the pitch change?"

The teacher solicits hypotheses, by asking, "What ideas do you have?" The following hypotheses concerning pitch change were proposed by the pupils:

1. Changing the length of the straw.
2. The kind of material of which the straw is made.
3. The amount of water in the bottle.
4. Changing the diameter of the straw.

In designing the experiments and in testing the hypotheses, the pupils work in groups of two or three. Some

Fig. 21.1. Blowing musical notes into glasses containing different amounts of water.

students will vary the amount of water in the bottles (fig. 21.1) but fail to account for a control. These problems should be discussed in a positive way by asking the pupils to make a comparison of changing conditions. Some pupils will want to use tuning forks to hear the varying notes produced by a change in vibrations and pitch.

In seeking solutions to problems, the concept is reinforced by asking the children to state applications. In learning about the factors that cause a pitch to change, generalizations can be made about how different notes are produced in various musical instruments.

Another problem-solving approach to teaching the concept that the pitch of a string instrument can be changed by changing the tension on the string, the length of the string, or the thickness of the string was developed by introducing the following anecdote: "Laura's class was forming an orchestra with homemade instruments. She wanted to make a banjo. Each instrument had to include a few different notes."

The following materials were displayed: rubber bands of assorted sizes, empty cigar boxes, wooden board with nails and string. In eliciting hypotheses from the children, some favored working with rubber bands and the cigar box. Others preferred using the wooden board with nails (fig. 21.2) and varying the length of string between two nails.

Many hypotheses as to how to obtain different notes were proposed by the children and included the following:

1. Lengthen or shorten the string.
2. Pluck the string harder or softer.
3. Tighten or loosen the string.
4. Use different widths of rubber bands on the cigar box.

Groups of two and three children came to the front of the classroom and performed the experiments. They soon discovered how to change the pitch of notes and made a banjo.

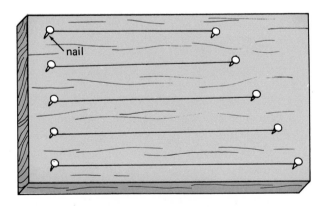

Fig. 21.2.   Varied lengths of string on wooden board.

To demonstrate that sound travels through solids and in all directions, use two yardsticks with four pupils (see fig.   **Demonstrations**

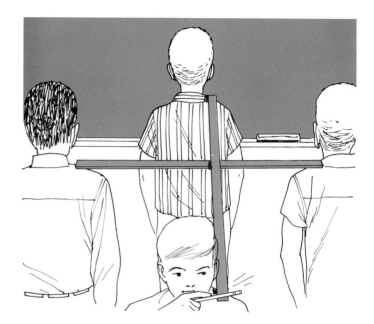

Fig. 21.3. Two yardsticks demonstrate sound travels in all directions.

21.3). If yardsticks are not available, use two long sticks that resemble broomsticks.

Note in the figure that one pupil faces the class and allows the class to watch him tap on the stick, resting on his shoulder, three times with a pencil. As soon as the other three pupils who are supporting the sticks on their shoulders hear the number of taps, they raise their hands holding up the number of fingers to represent the number of taps heard through the sticks. The pupil facing the class repeats this process several times using different numbers of taps and permitting a few seconds for the other three pupils to respond by holding up the correct number of fingers. This game-playing activity will help to develop the concept that sound travels in all directions.

The same procedure can be followed on a desk or large table where two pupils at each end transmit the number of taps on the table while the other students put their ears to the table. This could lead to a discussion of cowboys listening on the ground if other horses are traveling nearby. Could the sound of a railroad train be transmitted through the tracks for a mile or more?

Megaphone

By cupping your hands and putting them to your mouth as you speak, you will hear a difference in the loudness of your sounds (voice). By widening your "megaphone" effect with your hands to your mouth and closing your hands while you speak, you will hear a variation of loudness as you vary the positions of your hands. This is the basis for cheerleaders' use of megaphones (fig. 21.4) or horns at football

Sound for Communication

Fig. 21.4. Megaphone or horn makes sound louder.

games so that their cheers will be louder. As a result of these demonstrations, a major concept should evolve that a sound or a note is made by a vibrating body in air. Perhaps the simplest demonstration is to take a 12-inch ruler and have about 9 or 10 inches of it hang over the edge of a desk. While holding down the ruler with one hand on the desk, pluck the other end to show how it vibrates. The vibrations of the ruler against the desk set the molecules of air in motion and thus produce sounds.

It is believed that many animals communicate with each other by sound. The singing of birds, some scientists believe, constitutes a means of communication. For long-distance communication before electricity and sound waves were known, smoke signals and drums were used to transmit messages. With additional knowledge of sound waves, radio waves, and electricity, new means of efficient communication systems were developed.

Telegraph

The telegraph, the telephone, radio, air-to-ground networks using satellites, and research developments make for a worldwide communications system. It is possible to communicate with, locate, and navigate ships, aircraft, and satellites as a result of radar research. Perhaps one of the earliest means of using electrical energy for communication was achieved by Samuel Morse more than 130 years ago.

The Morse telegraph consisted of a sending key that opened and closed the electric circuit. As the sending key was closed, the current passed through the wire to the electromagnet at the opposite end, resulting in dots and dashes being heard. A bell-type buzzer can be substituted for the original dot-dash sounder. Pupils may wish to set up this buzzer system as a means of relating sound to electricity.

Telephone

Sound waves travel at about 1,100 feet or about 1/5 mile per second. When sound waves are converted to electrical waves, they travel long distances at almost the speed of light (186,000 miles per second). Alexander Graham Bell (1847–1922) invented the telephone in which the speech (sound) waves were changed into electrical vibrations (see fig. 21.5).

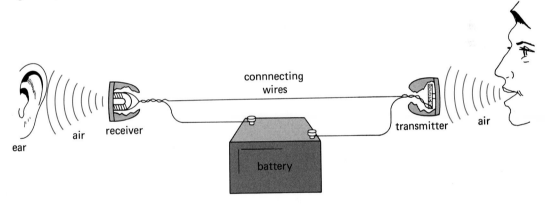

Fig. 21.5. Simple telephone circuit (Courtesy of the American Telephone and Telegraph Company).

The telephone along with the radio and teletypewriters has had very great impact daily activities. The stock market, many business transactions, emergency information related to disasters, and contact of distant friends and relatives were made possible because of these communication systems.

In grades three to five, children are interested in making homemade telephones by using two fruit juice cans connected by a long string of about 25 or more feet. A small hole is made in the bottom of each can, and a knot keeps the string attached to each can. By stretching the string tightly two children can talk and hear through the juice cans. The sound vibrations of air resulting from speaking into the can continue to vibrate through the string if it is taut. Children will ask about using metal wire and electricity in real telephones. A discussion of this question will lead to the understanding that, over great distances and bends, mountains, tall buildings, and other interferences, sound waves must be converted to electrical vibrations or impulses in order to be amplified. Later, when these electrical impulses come through the receiver or a speaker, they are changed back again into the original sound waves.

Radio

Basically this explanation applies to a public address system, to a modified degree to a radio transmitter set (or walkie-talkie), and to recordings which have the electrical

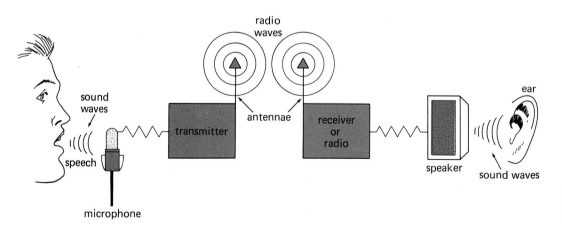

Fig. 21.6.   Model diagram of transmitting radio station.

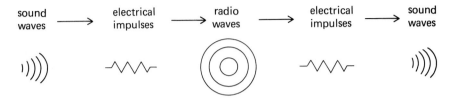

Fig. 21.7. Energy changes in radio transmission.

vibrations changed into the original sound waves of speech and music. In the case of the radio, another important conversion occurs (see fig. 21.6). The electrical impulses are changed to radio waves that travel in space and are received by the antennae of a radio receiver, which change the radio waves back again to electrical impulses and finally through the loudspeaker where the original sound waves are heard. The sequence of energy changes is shown in fig. 21.7.

Television

In television the principles of radio described above are applied. In addition, light energy is converted into electrical energy. The iconoscope contains the sensitive screen of the television camera in the broadcast studio. The intensity of light from the object or person being televised falls on the iconoscope. These dark and light "spots" on the screen become voltage impulses, and the electrical energy is transmitted by electromagnetic waves either in space or through coaxial cables. In the television receiver at home a cathode-ray tube (picture tube or kinescope) receives the electrical impulses and changes them back into light vibrations or the picture viewed on the TV screen.

Many years ago radios and television sets used radio (vacuum) tubes to help to transmit, receive, amplify, and convert electromagnetic vibrations and light energy. Recently transistors have replaced radio tubes and are found in solid-state sets. A transistor is usually a small piece of metal (germanium) to which wires are connected. Solid transistors permit radio and radar sets in aircraft to be bounced in space without breaking. The transistor is also much smaller than the radio tube.

Radar

The word "radar" is an acronym for radio detection and ranging. Through the use of radio waves (electromagnetic waves with frequencies above 100 megahertz or megacycles per second), an object such as a car, airplane, or ship can be located on a screen. This is shown as a "blip," which resembles the dot of light on the TV screen that is formed momentarily when the set is turned off. On the radar screen scales show distance and compass direction of the "blip" that represents the solid object. This calibration is the result of the time it takes for the signal to strike the object and to return as an "echo" or reflected electromagnetic wave. This wave is picked up by a powerful antennae, which resembles a huge saucer, and is fed into the radar screen as the "blip."

Radar is used to locate lost airplanes or ships at sea. It can be used to prevent collisions during bad weather. Weather forecasting is easier with radar detection of cloud formations, storms, and precipitation.

Laboratory Problem Solving

It is not necessary to do the following problem on a stormy day. Hypothetical situations can be furnished to any of the classes in sixth to eighth grades. However, a more realistic laboratory approach can be done if assigned during a storm.

Anecdote: "Tom and Lou were watching the flashes of light and listening to the thunder of a summer storm some distance from their home. Lou said, 'That storm is probably very close to us—maybe less than a mile.' Tom disagreed and said, 'It must be at least five miles away.' "

Statement of the problem: How far away is the storm?

Suggested hypotheses:

1. Distance is estimated by observing the brightness of the light given off by lightning.

2. Distance is estimated by the loudness of thunder.

3. Measure the time interval between the observation of lightning and the sound of thunder.

Laboratory—actual or theoretical:

1. Using stopwatches, pupils clock the time interval from the moment they see the flash of lightning until they hear the first thunder.

2. The number of seconds during this interval determines the distance of the lightning (note that sound travels about 1,100 feet per second in air), which is multiplied by the number of seconds noted on the stopwatch.

3. Assuming that most of the pupils clocked the same storm at the same time, the results can be listed in class and an average time obtained.

This laboratory situation may be used initially or later for reinforcement of the following concepts:

1. Sound travels through air at about 1,100 feet per second.

2. Sound travels fastest through solid substances, slower through liquids, and slowest through gases.

3. Sound is produced by the vibration of molecules and therefore cannot travel through a vacuum.

I. Sound waves
    A. Are longitudinal waves with air molecules providing the back-and-forth or vibrating motion (see fig. 21.8).

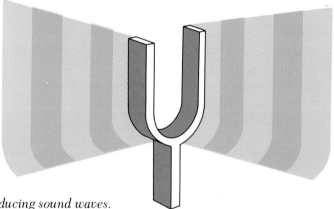

Fig. 21.8.   Tuning fork producing sound waves.

B. Longitudinal waves exhibit a series of compressions (pressed together) and rarefactions (stretched apart) such as in a coiled metal spring suspended vertically.
    1. One complete vibration or sound wave consists of one compression and one rarefaction.
    2. Sound waves travel in all directions because of air molecules vibrating and pushing against one another.
        a. Amplitude is a measure of energy carried by the wave (from the norm to the crest or from the norm to the trough).

b. Wavelength of a sound wave is the distance from the compression to the next compression (crest) or the distance between two adjacent crests.

c. The greater the amplitude, the greater is the loudness of sound.

d. Compressions and rarefactions produce vibrations against the eardrum.

e. These vibrations are transmitted to three small bones in the middle ear and finally to the auditory nerve and brain for sensation of sound.

II. Characteristics of sound

A. Pitch is the number of vibrations or sound waves per second. It is also called the frequency; each complete wave is known as a cycle. Thus the frequency is the number of cycles per second, especially noted in radio waves.

1. The higher the pitch, the greater is the frequency or the greater is the number of vibrations per second.

2. The lower the pitch, the smaller is the frequency or the fewer are the vibrations per second.

3. The human ear detects frequencies in the range from about 20 cycles per second to about 20,000 cycles per second (hertz).

B. Intensity is the amount of energy in sound waves and depends on:

1. Amplitude of vibration

2. Area of the vibrating body

3. Distance from the source of sound

4. Density of the medium through which the sound waves travel

C. Quality or timbre can be distinguished as the

sounds of same pitch and intensity but from different musical instruments. We can distinguish a G on a violin from one on a piano, even though they both have the same pitch and intensity.

III. Uses of sound in instruments

A. Echo sounder transmits sound waves from a ship to the seabed and receives back the echo from the seabed. Depth of seabed is calculated using knowledge of the speed of sound in water and the time it takes for the signal to return after it reaches the seabed.

B. Geophones (seismic shooting) measure depth of rock layers far below the ground. A series of microphones called geophones receive echoes from below the ground where measurements are taken. A series of explosions create underground echoes, which are then picked up and located.

IV. Television—many thousands of spots (light and dark areas) make up the transmission of thirty pictures per second.

A. Iconoscope is a special tube in camera located in the broadcast studio.

1. Contains a screen with millions of tiny photocells.

2. Image of person or object in studio falls on these photocells that give off electrons in proportion to the intensity of the light striking it.

3. This causes scanning; the beam of electrons scans across the image like reading a printed page from left to right, down a line, and repeat. It is similar to reading a page containing about 525 lines at the rate of 30 pages per second.

4. These impulses appear in very rapid succes-

sion. They are amplified and broadcast at the same time the sound is broadcast from the microphones.

5. The TV receiver in the home picks up the electrical impulses from the antenna and converts them back into the original picture and sound.

    a. Cathode-ray tube, kinescope, or also known as TV picture tube, has an "electric gun."

    b. This varies the intensity of the electron beam or light and dark areas to produce the picture on the fluorescent screen.

    c. Sound is received simultaneously on a radio receiver.

V. Radar is an acronym for radio detecting and ranging.

    A. Radar uses a transmitter of ultrahigh frequency waves that concentrates a powerful beam in a single direction (like a radio searchlight).

       1. Beam penetrates fog, clouds, and storms.

       2. Beam is reflected back to transmitter after striking an object such as ship, plane, or building.

       3. Reflected beam is recorded on the screen of a cathode-ray tube with markings that show distance (range) and direction. It appears as a "pip," which looks like the light dot, on a TV tube just after it is turned off.

    B. Various radar instruments are available for searching landing fields, other ships or planes, and weather conditions. Collisions with other aircraft or solid objects are avoided with the help of radar.

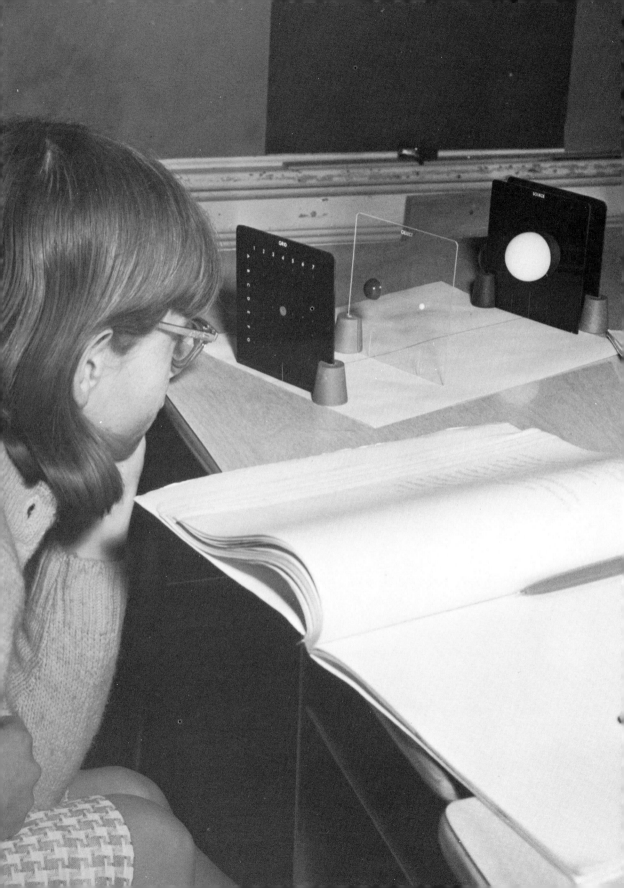

22

LIGHT AND
ITS BEHAVIOR

Grades K–2

1. Light comes from the sun, electric bulbs, and things that burn.
2. Light bounces off a mirror like a ball bounces off a wall.
3. Light makes it possible for us to see objects.
4. Sunlight contains many colors.

Grades 3–5

5. Water droplets in the air separate sunlight into its rainbow colors.
6. Sometimes light seems to behave like waves and other times like packets of energy.
7. Light is bent (refracted) by lenses.

8. Colored objects absorb all the colors of light except the color it reflects.

Grades 6–8

9. After striking a surface, some light is absorbed, some is reflected, and some is transmitted.
10. The angle of incidence of a light wave is equal to the angle of reflection.
11. Light rays, like other electromagnetic waves, travel at 186,000 miles per second.
12. Light passes through transparent objects and only some light goes through a translucent object.
13. No light passes through opaque (solid) objects.
14. Refraction of light occurs with a change in the speed of light as it passes from one type of substance like air into another like water.

Concept Formation

The general, descriptive properties of light are concepts numbered 1, 3, 8, 9, and 11. Concepts 2, 4, 5, 7, 10, 12, 13, and 14 deal with the behavior and properties of light in more specific terms. Concept 6 can be assigned as a theoretical concept in the case of wave theory or quantum theory.

In introducing the concepts that evolve from discussion, play, demonstration, or laboratory activity, children in the lower grades can bring in toys that contain lenses, prisms, bulbs, and any form of light, such as special lamps. Because children have had experience with these toys and other materials related to light, they can ask questions so that other children may discuss them. Many of these questions may take the form such as:

What makes the sky blue?

Why does my pencil look bent when I place it in a glass of water?

How does a magnifying glass make a piece of paper burn?

Do some people really have to wear glasses in order to see?

How does a periscope work?

How does a prism make a rainbow?

Do light bulbs give off heat all the time?

Most pupils at all grade levels will have had either some direct experience in answering these questions or they can be invited to speculate about their explanations. Inquiry procedures will evolve, and laboratory experiences can be provided according to the available materials. Some of the brief explanations that frequently occur in answer to some of the above questions are:

Refraction

Clouds contain droplets of water that act like prisms. The sunlight strikes the prism and some of the blue color of light coming through the "tiny prisms" is scattered by dust particles and reflected to the eye as blue.

A pencil in a glass of water looks as though it is bent because of refraction. In the upper grades and middle school, the pupils will explain that the speed of light is slowed when it enters the water in the glass. Light travels faster in air than in a solid crystal. Because of the difference in the speed with which light travels through different substances, the appearance is given that the pencil is bent. Stepping into a bathtub or a pool, does your foot look straight both in air and in water? (These explanations were offered by fourth and fifth graders.)

A piece of paper burns after a magnifying lens brings

together a group of the sun's rays into a spot of concentrated sunlight on the paper. If this experiment or demonstration is done in class, fire precautions should be taken, because the paper may flare up spontaneously on a sunny day. (Do not try this on a cloudy day.)

Vision and Corrective Lenses

Many people wear glasses because the image of light rays from an object are reflected either in front of (fig. 22.1) or too far behind (fig. 22.2) the exact location required for normal vision (fig. 22.3) in the eye.

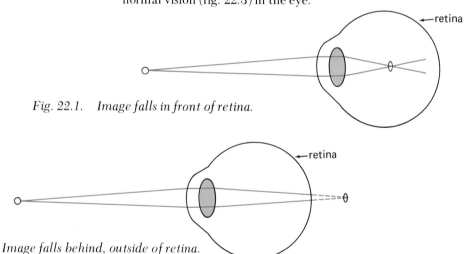

Fig. 22.1.   *Image falls in front of retina.*

Fig. 22.2.   *Image falls behind, outside of retina.*

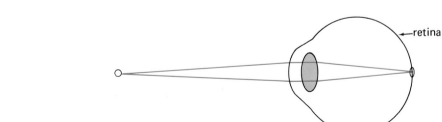

Fig. 22.3.   *Normal vision, image falls on retina.*

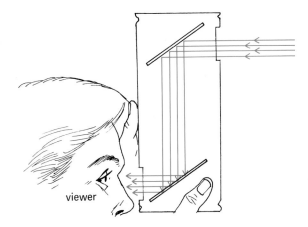

Fig. 22.4.   Constructing a periscope from a milk container.

Periscope

In discussing how a periscope works, it may be more effective to have pupils design and construct their individual periscopes. Milk cartons and two small mirrors are sufficient to construct a periscope (see fig. 22.4). Cardboard can be substituted for milk cartons, and both mirrors would be used to emphasize the reflection of light from one mirror to the other. Where should the openings in the container be located to permit light (image) to enter the periscope so that the viewer can see it? This problem should be solved experimentally along with a discussion on the behavior of light.

Prism and Rainbow

Pupils enjoy playing with a prism to obtain the rainbow effect of colors on a wall or ceiling. When the prism is held in the sunlight and moved at an angle that permits the prism to refract the sunlight, the spectrum of colors will be observed. Pupils should experiment with the change in the position of the prism when sunlight strikes it. Does the arrangement of the order of colors from red to violet remain the same in each instance when sunlight enters the prism?

Some pupils may have touched a light bulb and felt how hot it becomes immediately after it lights up. The electrical energy is converted to light energy and heat energy. Usually where there is light, there is also heat energy. Pupil experiences about light and heat should be discussed and may lead to experiments and ultimate abstractions.

Problem Solving   One concept related to light and heat energy such as *dark-colored surfaces absorb heat* and *light-colored surfaces reflect heat* can be developed from the following problem:

Anecdote: "Sylvia wants to buy a dress that will keep her cool on hot summer days. She saw two beautiful, identical dresses that she liked; one is black and the other is white."

Problem: Which color dress will keep her cooler?

Materials: Samples of black and white cloth, a white lamp, thermometers.

Hypotheses:
1.   The black dress will keep Sylvia cooler.
2.   The white dress will keep Sylvia cooler.
3.   The color of dress has no effect on temperature.

Experiments:
1.   Pupils can wear dresses of selected colors and discuss what controls are being used, if any.

2. Sample pieces of cloth are exposed to a white lamp, and temperatures are recorded every two minutes for a period of ten minutes.

3. Sylvia can hold samples of cloth to the sun and react to the degree of heat.

Observation: The white cloth was 3 degrees cooler.

Discussion: Because of this demonstration, Sylvia found that she could keep cooler in the white dress. The teacher should stimulate a discussion when an abstraction evolves from a specific concept. Although pupils will learn that some objects reflect while others absorb light, this problem should lead to the suggestion that light-colored objects reflect and dark-colored objects absorb light.

The following demonstration in a transparent, deep **Demonstration** saucer or cup shows refraction (fig. 22.5) and should invite the following types of questions by pupils:

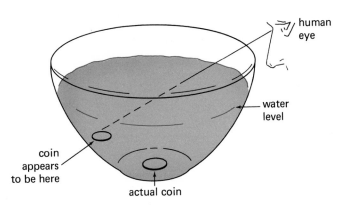

Fig. 22.5. *Refraction using a coin.*

1. Compare the speed of light as it travels through air, water, and glass.

2. What causes the "bending" of light?

3. Does the depth of the water have any effect on refraction?

4. Would the same amount of refraction occur if oil were used in place of water?

Lenses

The magnifying lens can be used to study the magnification of an object as well as refraction. The image of the candle appears larger through the lens. Move the lens back and forth between the eye and the candle, and observe the variation in appearance of the size of the image and the clarity of the object.

Pupils have telescopes, microscopes, cameras, projectors, and eyeglasses. They could bring these objects to class and discuss the applications of lenses in these instruments. Demonstrations of how they operate will reinforce the concept of light and its behavior through lenses. The children discover that the lenses magnify objects because of refraction.

An interesting laboratory situation has each pupil exchange a magnifying lens with his neighbor. Assuming that the thickness of these lenses vary, the children can draw the magnified image of an insect of a printed letter on a piece of paper. The distance of the object from the lens and the distance from the lens to the eye should be measured and compared with the size of the magnified image. Neighboring students should compare their results in terms of the thickness of the lens.

The Eye

The eye is the important organ that responds to intensity of light. As we enter a movie theater on a bright, sunny day, a minute may pass before we can see in the darkness. The pupil in the eye (fig. 22.6) automatically adjusts in size to permit more light to enter the eye in the darkened theater. When you leave a theater and go into direct sunlight, the pupil in your eye acts like a shutter in a camera, and less light will enter into your eye. This action makes the pupil look smaller.

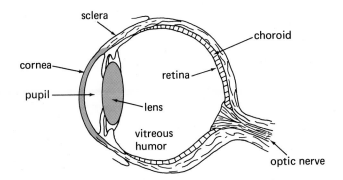

Fig. 22.6. The eye.

It is suggested that health care and safety of the eye be discussed in class. Specific questions concerning enough light when reading and writing, will focus attention on health care of the eye. Other questions are: "Do you avoid eyestrain by resting eyes or shutting them after long periods of intensive use?" "Do you avoid rubbing your eyes and irritating them with your hands?" "If eyeglasses are prescribed, do you wear them?" "Do you wear safety glasses in a laboratory?" "Do you have eye examinations regularly?"

I. Historical data
    A. Pythagoras, around 500 B.C., suggested that light consists of particles projected from luminous bodies.
    B. Isaac Newton in the seventeenth century reiterated the same idea in his explanation that light travels in straight lines and casts shadows. He also believed that light is composed of small particles, known as the corpuscular theory.
    C. Ancient Greeks
        1. Ancient Greeks knew the inverse square law that the intensity or brightness of light decreases as the square of the distance.
        2. They were also aware that the angle of incidence is equal to the angle of reflection.
        3. They explained refraction as the bending of light.
    D. Wave theory of light
        1. Thomas Young observed that darkness can be produced by combining two beams of light, which is known as interference. This was a demonstration of the wave theory.
        2. James Clerk Maxwell (1831–79) developed the mathematical theory of wave propagation, better known as electromagnetic oscillations.
    E. Both theories are used to explain different properties of light.
        1. Light energy or radiant energy and other electromagnetic waves consist of tiny packets of energy called quanta.
        2. The quanta or packets of energy travel in a wavelike motion.
II. Nature of light
    A. Measurements

1. Light travels at about 186,000 miles per second or more than 660 million miles per hour.
2. Light travels from the sun to the earth (93 million miles) in about eight minutes.
3. Candlepower and foot-candle are two commonly used units for measuring light.
   a. Candlepower measures intensity of light given off by an object.
   b. Foot-candle measures the amount of illumination or light in a room.
   c. Engineers use the unit "lumen" in place of candlepower.
4. Light meters indicate the amount of light striking it.
   a. In the photoelectric cell, light is converted into electricity; its amount is indicated on the ammeter. The more light that falls on the meter, the greater is the electric current.
   b. Cadmium sulfide is another type of light meter; because this chemical is very sensitive to light, it behaves like a photoelectric cell by controlling the amount of electricity flowing from a dry cell.

B. Properties of light
   1. Most light will pass through transparent and translucent objects, although some light is absorbed and reflected.
   2. Light does not pass through opaque materials; instead they absorb and/or reflect light.
   3. Smooth, shiny objects reflect more light than rough, dull surfaces.
   4. On smooth surfaces such as mirrors, the angle of incidence is equal to the angle of reflection.

5. Light rays are bent or refracted when they pass from one medium such as air to another medium such as water or glass; if the light rays enter one substance at an angle of 90° (perpendicularly), the rays go through without being bent.

6. The speed of light depends on the density of material; the more dense the transparent object, the slower will light travel through it.

7. A triangular, transparent glass or prism breaks up sunlight into the spectrum: violet, indigo, blue, green, yellow, orange, and red.

   a. Each color has its own wavelength.

   b. Red light has the longest wavelength; violet has the shortest visible wavelength.

   c. The shortest waves (violet) light are bent the most and the longest waves (red) are bent the least.

III. Electromagnetic radiations

   A. Radiant energy spectrum consists of electromagnetic waves.

      1. Radio waves
      2. Infrared waves
      3. Light rays (visible spectrum)
      4. Ultraviolet rays
      5. X rays
      6. Gamma rays
      7. Cosmic rays

   B. Electromagnetic waves travel at a speed of 186,000 miles per second.

   C. Electromagnetic waves differ in frequency and in wavelength.

      1. They are measured in cycles or hertz and frequently contain a prefix kilo (thousand) or mega (million).

2.   One cycle represents one complete wave from one crest to another.
3.   If the frequency of a wave is 100 cycles or 100 hertz, it means that 100 waves occur in 1 second.

BIBLIOGRAPHY

Appendix A
Professional Publications for Teachers

Part I

American Association for the Advancement of Science. *The Science Book List for Children*. 1515 Massachusetts Ave., N.W., Washington, D.C., 20005.

Arey, Charles K. *Science Experiments for Elementary Schools*. New York: Teachers College Press, Columbia University, 1961.

Association for Childhood Education International. *Science for the Eights to Twelves*. Membership Science Bulletin no. 13-A. Washington, D.C.: 1964–65.

Association for Childhood Education International. *Young Children and Science*. Membership Science Bulletin no. 12-A. Washington, D.C.: 1964–65.

Aylesworth, T. G. *Planning For Effective Science Teaching*.

Columbus, Ohio: American Education Publications, 1964.

Baker, Tunis. *Baker Science Packets*. 650 Concord Drive, Holland, Mich. 49423.

Blackwood, Paul E. *Science Teaching in the Elementary Schools: A Survey of Practices*. Washington, D.C.: U.S. Government Printing Office, 1965.

Blough, Blenn O., and Schwartz, Julius. *Elementary School Science and How to Teach It*. New York: Holt, Rinehart & Winston, 1969.

Burnett, R. W. *Teaching Science in the Elementary School*. New York: Holt, Rinehart & Winston, 1960.

Carin, Arthur, and Sund, Robert B. *Teaching Science Through Discovery*. Columbus, Ohio: Merrill, 1970.

Challand, Helen J., and Brandt, Elizabeth. *Science Activities from A to Z*. Chicago: Children's Press, 1963.

Craig, Gerald S. *Science for the Elementary School Teacher*. Waltham, Mass.: Blaisdell, 1966.

Freeman, Kenneth; Dowling, Thomas I.; Lacy, Nan; and Tippet, James S. *Helping Children Understand Science*. New York: Holt, Rinehart & Winston, 1958.

Gega, Peter C. *Science in Elementary Education*. New York: John Wiley, 1966.

Greenlee, Julian. *Teaching Science to Children*. Dubuque, Iowa: William C. Brown, 1955.

Hennessy, David E. *Elementary Teachers' Classroom Science Demonstrations and Activities*. Englewood Cliffs, N.J.: Prentice-Hall, 1964.

Hubler, Clark. *Working with Children in Science*. Boston: Houghton Mifflin, 1957.

Hurd, Paul De Hart, and Gallagher, James J. *New Directions in Elementary Science Teaching*. Belmont, Calif. Wadsworth, 1968.

Jacobson, Willard L., and Tannenbaum, Harold E. *Modern Elementary School Science: A Recommended Sequence*. New York: Teachers College Press, Columbia University, 1961.

Kambly, Paul E., and Suttle, John E. *Teaching Elementary School Science.* New York: Ronald Press, 1963.

Karplus, Robert, and Thier, Herbert D. *A New Look at Elementary School Science.* Chicago: Rand McNally, 1967.

Kuslan, Louis I., and Stone, Harris A. *Teaching Children Science: An Inquiry Approach.* Belmont, Calif.: Wadsworth, 1968.

Kuslan, Louis I., and Stone, Harris A. *Readings on Teaching Children Science.* Belmont, Calif.: Wadsworth, 1969.

Lewis, June E., and Potter, Irene. *The Teaching of Science in the Elementary School.* Englewood Cliffs, N.J.: Prentice-Hall, 1970.

Mills, Lester C., and Dean, Peter M. *Problem Solving Methods in Science Teaching.* Science Manpower Monographs. New York: Teachers College Press, Columbia University, 1960.

Munzer, Martha E., and Brandwein, Paul F. *Teaching Science Through Conservation.* New York: McGraw-Hill, 1960.

National Science Teachers Association. Washington, D.C. Request the list of publications that pertain to the teaching of science in the elementary and secondary schools.

Navarra, John G., and Zafforoni, Joseph. *Science Today for the Elementary School Teacher.* New York: Harper & Row, 1960.

Piltz, Albert. *Creative Teaching of Science in the Elementary School.* Boston: Allyn & Bacon, 1968.

Renner, John W., and Reagan, William B. *Teaching Science in the Elementary School.* New York: Harper & Row, 1968.

Schmidt, Victor E., and Rockcastle, Verne. *Teaching Science with Everyday Things.* New York: McGraw-Hill, 1968.

Suchman, Richard J. *The Elementary School Training Program in Scientific Inquiry.* U.S. Office of Education, NDEA Title VII, project no. 216.

Tannenbaum, Harold E., and Stillman, Nathan. *Science Education for Elementary School Teachers.* Boston: Allyn & Bacon, 1960.

Tannenbaum, Harold E., and Piltz, A. *Evaluation in Elementary School Science.* Washington, D.C.: U.S. Government Printing Office, Office of Education OE 29057, circular no. 757, 1964.

U.S. Department of Health, Education and Welfare, Office of Education. *A Suggested Check-List for Assessing a Science Program.* Washington, D.C.: Department of Public Documents, U.S. Government Printing Office, 1964.

Victor, Edward. *Science for the Elementary School.* New York: Crowell-Collier Macmillan, 1970.

Victor, Edward, and Lerner, Marjorie S. *Readings in Science Education for the Elementary School.* New York: Crowell-Collier Macmillan, 1967.

Appendix B
Science Periodicals for Teachers and Children

(*Note*: An asterisk denotes that the periodical is intended primarily for teachers.)

°*American Biology Teacher.* The National Association of Biology Teachers, 19 S. Jackson St., Danville, Ill. 61832

°*American Forests.* The American Forestry Association, 919 17th St., N.W., Washington, D.C.

°*The American Journal of Physics.* American Association of Physics Teachers, 57 E. 55th St., New York, N.Y. 10022

°*The Aquarium.* Innes Publishing Co., Philadelphia, Pa. 19107

° *Audubon Magazine.* National Audubon Society, 950 Third Ave., New York, N.Y. 10022

°*Chemistry.* Science Service, 1719 16th St., N.W., Washington, D.C. 20009

°*Cornell Rural School Leaflets*. New York State College of Agriculture, Ithaca, N.Y. 14850

Current Science and Aviation. American Education Publications, Education Center, Columbus, Ohio 43216

°*Geotimes*. American Geological Institute, 1515 Massachusetts Ave., N.W., Washington, D.C.

°*Grade Teacher*. Educational Publishing Company, Darien, Conn. 06820

°*Journal of Chemical Education*. Business and Publication Office, 20th and Northampton Streets, Easton, Pa. 18042

°*Journal of Research in Science Teaching*. John Wiley and Sons, 605 Third Ave., New York, N.Y. 10016

Junior Astronomer. Benjamin Adelman, 4211 Colie Drive, Silver Spring, Md. 20906

Junior Natural History. American Museum of Natural History, Central Park West at 79th St., New York, N.Y. 10024

My Weekly Reader. American Education Publications, Education Center, Columbus, Ohio 43216

National Geographic. National Geographic Society, 1146 16th St., N.W., Washington, D.C.

Natural History. American Museum of Natural History, Central Park West at 79th St., New York, N.Y. 10024

Nature Magazine. American Nature Association, 1214 15th Street, N.W., Washington, D.C.

Outdoors Illustrated. National Audubon Society, 950 Third Avenue, New York, N.Y. 10022

°*Physics Today*. American Institute of Physics, 335 E. 45 St., New York, N.Y. 10017

Popular Science Monthly. Popular Science Publishing Co., 335 Lexington Avenue, New York, N.Y. 10016

°*School Science and Mathematics*. School Science and Mathematics Association, P.O. Box 48, Oak Park, Ill. 60305

°*Science.* American Association for the Advancement of Science, 1515 Massachusetts Ave., N.W. Washington, D.C. 20025

Science and Children. National Science Teachers Association, Washington, D.C. 20036

°*Science Digest.* 959 Eighth Ave., New York, N.Y. 10019

°*Science Education.* John Wiley and Sons, 605 Third Ave., New York, N.Y. 10016

°*Science News Letter.* Science Service, 1719 N St., N.W., Washington, D.C. 20036

°*Science Teacher.* National Science Teachers Association, 1201 16th St., N.W., Washington, D.C. 20036

Science World. Scholastic Magazines, 50 West 44 St., New York, N.Y. 10036

°*Scientific American.* 415 Madison Ave., New York, N.Y. 10017

Sky and Telescope. Sky Publishing Corp., Harvard College Observatory, Cambridge, Mass. 02138

Space Science. Benjamin Adelman, 4211 Colie Drive, Silver Spring, Md. 20906

°*Tomorrow's Scientists.* National Science Teachers Association, 1201 16th St., N.W., Washington, D.C. 20036

°*UNESCO Courier.* The Unesco Publications Center, 801 Third Ave., New York, N.Y. 10022

°*Weatherwise.* American Meteorological Society, 3 Joy Street, Boston, Mass. 02108

Part II   Appendix C
Publications for Children

Chapter 10   Living Plants

Adler, Irving, and Adler, Ruth. *Tree Products.* New York: John Day, 1966.

Billington, Elizabeth T. *Adventures with Flowers.* New York: Frederick Warne, 1966.

Blough, Glenn O. *Discovering Plants.* New York: McGraw-Hill, 1966.

Blough, Glenn O. *Plants Round the Year.* New York: Harper & Row, 1967.

Blough, Glenn O. *Useful Plants and Animals.* New York: Harper & Row, 1967.

Brown, Douglas G. *Exploring and Understanding Plant Structure.* Westchester, Ill.: Benefic Press, 1968.

Comstock, Anna B. *Handbook of Nature Study.* Ithaca, N.Y.: Comstock Publishing Associates, 1947.

Cosgrove, Margaret. *Plants in Time.* New York: Dodd, Mead, 1967.

Darling, Lois, and Darling, Louis. *A Place in the Sun.* New York: Morrow, 1968.

Gulcher, J. M., and Noailles, R. H. *A Fruit Is Born.* New York: Sterling, 1966.

Hammond, Winifred C. *The Riddle of Seeds.* New York: Coward McCann Geogahan, 1965.

Hoffman, Melita. *A Trip to the Pond: An Adventure in Nature.* New York: Doubleday, 1966.

Hutchins, Ross E. *Plants Without Leaves: Lichens, Fungi, Mosses, Liverworts, Slime-Molds, Algae, Horsetails.* New York: Dodd, Mead, 1966.

Klein, Stanley. *A World in a Tree.* New York: Doubleday, 1968.

Lemmon, Robert S. *Parks and Gardens: Community of Living Things.* Mankato, Minn.: Creative Educational Society in cooperation with the National Audubon Society, 1967.

Living World of Nature Series. New York: McGraw-Hill.
The Desert. 1966.
The Seashore. 1966.
The Great Plains. 1967.
The Pond. 1967.
The Mountain. 1968.

McCormick, Jack. *The Life of the Forest.* New York: McGraw-Hill, 1966.

North, Sterling. *Hurray Spring!* New York: Dutton, 1966.

Parker, Bertha M. *Adaptation to Environment.* New York: Harper & Row, 1967.

Parker, Bertha M. *Flowers, Fruits, Seeds.* New York: Harper & Row, 1967.

Parker, Bertha M. *The Garden and Its Friends.* New York: Harper & Row, 1967.

Parker, Bertha M. *The Garden Indoors.* New York: Harper & Row, 1967.

Parker, Bertha M. *Leaves.* New York: Harper & Row, 1967.

Parker, Bertha M. *Living Things.* New York: Harper & Row, 1967.

Parker, Bertha M. *Plants and Animal Partnerships.* New York: Harper & Row, 1967.

Parker, Bertha M. *Plant Factories.* New York: Harper & Row, 1967.

Parker, Bertha M. *Trees.* New York: Harper & Row, 1967.

Parker, Bertha M., and Buchsbaum, Ralph. *Balance in Nature.* New York: Harper & Row, 1967.

Parker, Bertha M., and Podendorf, Illa. *Domesticated Plants.* New York: Harper & Row, 1967.

Peterson, Roger Tory, and McKenny, Margaret. *A Field Guide to Wild Flowers of Northeastern and North Central North America.* Boston: Houghton Mifflin, 1968.

Ress, Etta Schneider. *Field and Meadow: Community of Living Things.* Mankato, Minn.: Creative Educational Society in cooperation with the National Audubon Society, 1967.

Schwartz, George I., and Schwartz, Bernice S. *Life in a Log.* New York: Doubleday, 1972.

Selsam, Millicent E. *Plants That Heal.* New York: Morrow, 1966.

Shuttleworth, Floyd S., and Zim, Herbert. *Non-Flowering Plants.* New York: Golden Press, 1967.

Slaton, William, and Slayton, Nellie. *Bacteria and Viruses: Friends or Foes?* Englewood Cliffs, N. J.: Prentice-Hall, 1965.

Sterling, Dorothy. *Fall Is Here*. Garden City, N.Y.: Doubleday, 1966.

Stone, A. Harris, and Leskowitz, Irving. *Plants Are Like That*. Englewood Cliffs, N.J.: Prentice-Hall, 1968.

Chapter 11   Animals and Their Surroundings

Bailey, John. *Our Wild Animals*. New York: Nelson, 1965.

Barry, Robert. *Animals Around the World*. New York: McGraw-Hill, 1967.

Bendick, Jeanne. *The First Book of Fishes*. New York: Franklin Watts, 1965.

Blough, Glenn O. *Animals and Their Young*. New York: Harper & Row, 1967.

Blough, Glenn O. *Animals Round the Year*. New York: Harper & Row, 1967.

Blough, Glenn O. *Animals That Live Together*. New York: Harper & Row, 1967.

Blough, Glenn O. *An Aquarium*. New York: Harper & Row, 1967.

Blough, Glenn O. *The Birds in the Big Woods*. Harper & Row, 1967.

Blough, Glenn O. *Discovering Dinosaurs*. New York: McGraw-Hill, 1967.

Blough, Glenn O. *Discovering Insects*. New York: McGraw-Hill, 1967.

Blough, Glenn O. *The Insect Parade*. New York: Harper & Row, 1967.

Blough, Glenn O. *The Pet Show*. New York: Harper & Row, 1967.

Blough, Glenn O. *Useful Plants and Animals*. New York: Harper & Row, 1967.

Brevoort, Harry F., and Fanning, Eleanor I. *Insects from Close Up*. New York: T. Y. Crowell, 1965.

Brouillette, Jeanne S. *Moths*. Chicago: Follett, 1966.

Conklin, Gladys. *The Bug Club Book*. New York: Holiday House, 1966.

Cosgrove, Margaret. *Eggs—and What Happens Inside Them*. New York: Dodd, Mead, 1966.

Costello, David F. *The World of Ants*. Philadelphia: Lippincott, 1968.

Darling, Lois, and Darling, Louis. *Before and After the Dinosaurs*. New York: William Morrow, 1965.

Dupre, Ramona S. *Spiders*. Chicago: Follett, 1967.

Earle, Olive L. *Strange Companions in Nature*. New York: William Morrow, 1966.

Feilen, John. *Deer*. Chicago: Follett, 1967.

Feilen, John. *Squirrels*. Chicago: Follett, 1967.

Friendly, Natalie. *Miraculous Web*. Englewood Cliffs, N.J.: Prentice-Hall, 1968.

Gannon, Robert. *What's Under a Rock?* New York: Dutton, 1971.

Gendron, Val, and McGill, David A. *Whales*. Chicago: Follett, 1965.

George, Jean C. *Spring Comes to the Ocean*. New York: T. Y. Crowell, 1965.

Guthrie, Esther L. *Home Book of Animal Care*. New York: Harper & Row, 1966.

Hogner, Dorothy Childs. *A Book of Snakes*. New York: T. Y. Crowell, 1966.

Holden, Raymond. *Famous Fossil Finds*. New York: Dodd, Mead, 1966.

Hoover, Helen. *Animals at My Door Step*. New York: Parents Magazine Press, 1966.

Hoyt, Murray. *The World of Bees*. New York: Coward McCann Geogahan, 1965.

Hutchins, Ross E. *The Travels of Monarch X*. New York: Rand McNally, 1966.

Inger, Robert F. *Reptiles*. Chicago: Follett, 1966.

Jennings, Gary. *The Shrinking Outdoors*. Philadelphia: Lippincott, 1972.

Kohn, Bernice. *Fireflies*. Englewood Cliffs, N.J.: Prentice-Hall, 1966.

Lubell, Cecil, and Lubell, Winifred. *In a Running Brook*. Skokie, Ill.: Rand McNally, 1968.

Mason, George F. *Animals Appetites*. New York: William Morrow, 1966.

Mason, Edwin A. *Robins*. Chicago: Follett, 1966.

McClung, Robert M. *Moths and Butterflies and How They Live*. New York: William Morrow, 1966.

McClung, Robert M. *Honker*. New York: William Morrow, 1965.

McCormick, Jack. *The Life of the Forest*. New York: McGraw-Hill, 1966.

McCoy, J. J. *Our Captive Animals*. New York: Seabury, 1971.

Meeks, Esther. *Mammals*. Chicago: Follett, 1965.

Newman, L. H. *Man and Insects*. Garden City, N.Y.: Natural History Press, 1966.

Otto, George R. *Exploring and Understanding Amphibians and Reptiles*. Westchester, Ill.: Benefic Press, 1968.

Parker, Bertha M. *Adaptation to Environment*. New York: Harper & Row, 1967.

Parker, Bertha M. *Animal Travels*. New York: Harper & Row, 1967.

Parker, Bertha M. *Animals of the Seashore*. New York: Harper & Row, 1967.

Parker, Bertha M. *Animals of Yesterday*. New York: Harper & Row, 1967.

Parker, Bertha M. *Animals We Know*. New York: Harper & Row, 1967.

Parker, Bertha M. *Birds*. New York: Harper & Row, 1967.

Parker, Bertha M. *Birds in Your Backyard*. New York: Harper & Row, 1967.

Parker, Bertha M. *Fishes*. New York: Harper & Row, 1967.

Parker, Bertha M. *How Animals Get Food.* New York: Harper & Row, 1967.

Parker, Bertha M. *Insects and Their Ways.* New York: Harper & Row, 1967.

Parker, Bertha M. *Life Through the Ages.* New York: Harper & Row, 1967.

Parker, Bertha M. *Living Things.* New York: Harper & Row, 1967.

Parker, Bertha M. *Plant and Animal Partnerships.* New York: Harper & Row, 1967.

Parker, Bertha M. *Reptiles.* New York: Harper & Row, 1967.

Parker, Bertha M. *Saving Our Wildlife.* New York: Harper & Row, 1967.

Parker, Bertha M. *Six Legged Neighbors.* New York: Harper & Row, 1967.

Parker, Bertha M. *Spiders.* New York: Harper & Row, 1967.

Parker, Bertha M. *Toads and Frogs.* New York: Harper & Row, 1967.

Parker, Bertha M., and Buchsbaum, Ralph. *Balance in Nature.* New York: Harper & Row, 1967.

Parker, Bertha M., and Emerson, Alfred E. *Insect Societies.* New York: Harper & Row, 1967.

Parker, Bertha M., and Gregg, Robert E. *Insect Friends and Enemies.* New York: Harper & Row, 1967.

Parker, Bertha M., and Podendorf, Illa. *Animal World.* New York: Harper & Row, 1967.

Parker, Bertha M., and Weichert, William S. *Domesticated Animals.* New York: Harper & Row, 1967.

Pfadt, Robert E. *Animals Without Backbones.* Chicago: Follett, 1967.

Raskin, Edith. *The Pyramid of Living Things.* New York: McGraw-Hill, 1967.

Ress, Etta Schneider. *Field and Meadow: Community of Living Things.* Mankato, Minn.: The Creative Educational Society in cooperation with the National Audubon Society, 1967.

Russell, Solveig P. *Which Is Which?* Englewood Ciffs, N.J.: Prentice-Hall, 1966.

Selsam, Millicent E. *Benny's Animals: How He Put Them in Order.* New York: Harper & Row, 1966.

Selsam, Millicent E. *How Animals Tell Time.* New York: William Morrow, 1967.

Selsam, Millicent E. *When an Animal Grows.* New York: Harper & Row, 1966.

Shapp, Martha, and Shapp, Charles. *Let's Find Out About Birds.* New York: Franklin Watts, 1967.

Shuttlesworth, Dorothy. *Animal Camouflage.* Garden City, N.Y.: Natural History Press, 1966.

Shuttlesworth, Dorothy, and Swain, Suzan. *All Kinds of Bees.* New York: Random House, 1967.

Simon, Hilda. *Insect Masquerades.* New York: Viking, 1968.

Simon, Seymour. *Animals in Field and Laboratory.* New York: McGraw-Hill, 1968.

Sullivan, Navin. *Animal Time Keepers.* Englewood Cliffs, N.J.: Prentice-Hall, 1966.

Sutton, Myron, and Sutton, Ann. *Animals on the Move.* Skokie, Ill.: Rand McNally, 1965.

Tee Van, Helen Damrosch. *Small Mammals Are Where You Find Them.* New York: Alfred A. Knopf, 1966.

Van Gelder, Richard. *Bats.* Chicago: Follett, 1967.

Vessel, Matthew F., and Wong, Herbert H. *Seashore Life of Our Pacific Coast.* Palo Alto, Calif.: Fearon, 1965.

Vevers, Gwynne. *Ants and Termites.* New York: McGraw-Hall, 1966.

Wheeler, Ruth L. *The Story of Birds of North America.* Irvington-on-Hudson, N.Y.: Harvey House, 1965.

Chapter 12   The Human Body and Good Health

Adler, Irving, and Adler, Ruth. *Taste, Touch and Smell.* New York: John Day, 1966.

Elgin, Kathleen. *Read About the Eye*. New York: Franklin Watts, 1967.

Froman, Robert. *The Many Human Senses*. Boston: Little, Brown, 1966.

Keen, Martin. *The Wonders of the Human Body*. New York: Grosset & Dunlap, 1966.

Kelly, Patricia M. *The Mighty Human Cell*. New York: John Day, 1967.

Levine, Milton, and Seligman, Jean. *The Wonder of Life*. New York: Simon & Shuster, 1968.

Parker, Bertha M. *Community Health*. New York: Harper & Row, 1967.

Parker, Bertha M. *Foods*. New York: Harper & Row, 1967.

Parker, Bertha M. *You as a Machine*. New York: Harper & Row, 1967.

Power, Jules. *How Life Begins*. New York: Simon & Shuster, 1965.

Schneider, Leo. *Microbes in Your Life*. New York: Harcourt Brace Jovanovich, 1966.

Showers, Paul. *Your Skin and Mine*. New York: T. Y. Crowell, 1965.

White, Anne Terry, and Lietz, Gerald M. *Man the Thinker*. Champaign, Ill.: Garrard, 1967.

Chapter 13   Our Changing Environment: Air, Water, and Weather

Blough, Glenn O. *Water Appears and Disappears*. New York: Harper & Row, 1967.

Carona, Philip B. *Water*. Chicago: Follett, 1966.

Fellger, Merrill C. *Exploring and Understanding Water*. Westchester, Ill.: Benefic Press, 1968.

Knight, David C. *Let's Find Out About Weather*. London: C. A. Watts, 1967.

Lehr, Paul E. *Storms*. New York: Golden Press, 1966.

May, Julian. *Weather*. Chicago: Follett, 1966.

Parker, Bertha M. *Ask the Weatherman.* New York: Harper & Row, 1967.

Parker, Bertha M. *Clouds, Rain, and Snow.* New York: Harper & Row, 1967.

Parker, Bertha M. *Water.* New York: Harper & Row, 1967.

Parker, Bertha M. *Water Supply and Sewage Disposal.* New York: Harper & Row, 1967.

Parker, Bertha M. *Ways of the Weather.* New York: Harper & Row, 1967.

Pine, Tillie, and Levine, Joseph. *Weather All Around.* New York: McGraw-Hill, 1966.

Rosenfeld, Sam. *Ask Me a Question About the Weather.* New York: Harvey House, 1966.

Spar, Jerome. *The Way of the Weather.* Mankato, Minn.: Creative Educational Society in cooperation with the American Museum of Natural History, 1967.

Stambler, Irwin. *Weather Instruments: How They Work.* New York: Putnam, 1968.

Tresselt, Alvin. *Hide and Seek Fog.* New York: Lothrup, Lee and Shepard, 1965.

Wyler, Rose. *The First Book of Weather.* New York: Franklin Watts, 1965.

Zim, Herbert S. *Waves.* New York: Morrow, 1967.

Chapter 14   The Changing Earth's Surface

Bendick, Jeanne. *The Shape of the Earth.* Chicago: Rand McNally, 1965.

Carlisle, Norman. *Riches of the Sea: The New Science of Oceanology.* New York: Sterling, 1967.

Carona, Philip B. *Our Planet Earth.* Chicago: Follett, 1967.

Carona, Philip B. *Earth Through the Ages.* Chicago: Follett, 1968.

Carr, Albert B., and Hopkins, Robert S. *Islands of the Deep Sea.* New York: John Day, 1967.

Carson, Rachel. *The Sea Around Us.* New York: Golden Press, 1958.

Cartwright, Sally. *The Tide.* New York: Coward McCann Geogahan, 1970.

Coombs, Charles. *Deep Sea World: The Story of Oceanography.* New York: William Morrow, 1966.

Cromer, Richard. *Soil.* Chicago: Follett, 1967.

Fenton, Carollane, and Fenton, Mildred Adams. *The Land We Live On.* New York: Doubleday, 1966.

Gallant, Roy A., and Schuberth, Christopher J. *Discovering Rocks and Minerals.* New York: Natural History Press, 1967.

Goetz, Delia. *Grasslands.* New York: Morrow, 1966.

Goldin, Augusta. *The Bottom of the Sea.* New York: T. Y. Crowell, 1967.

Howell, Ruth Rea. *Everything Changes.* New York: Atheneum, 1968.

Hungerford, Harold, and Knapp, Clifford. *Exploring and Understanding Our Changing Earth.* Westchester: Ill.: Benefic Press, 1968.

Keene, Melvin. *The Beginner's Story of Minerals and Rocks.* New York: Harper & Row, 1966.

Ladyman, Phyllis. *Inside the Earth.* Reading, Me.: Scott, 1969.

Lauber, Patricia. *Junior Science Book of Volcanoes.* Champaign, Ill.: Garrard, 1965.

Lauber, Patricia. *This Restless Earth.* New York: Random House, 1970.

Ley, Willy. *Inside the Orbit of the Earth.* New York: McGraw-Hill, 1968.

MacFall, Russell P. *Gem Hunters Guide.* New York: T. Y. Crowell, 1969.

Matthews, William H. *The Story of the Earth.* New York: Harvey House, 1968.

May, Julian. *The Land Beneath the Sea.* New York: Holiday House, 1971.

McCue, George. *Desert*. New York: Benziger, 1971.

McCue, George. *Ecology*. New York: Benziger, 1971.

McCue, George. *Forests*. New York: Benziger, 1971.

McCue, George. *Grasslands*. New York: Benziger, 1971.

McCue, George. *Mountains*. New York: Benziger, 1971.

McCue, George. *Oceans*. New York: Benziger, 1971.

McFall, Christie. *Wonders of Sand*. New York: Dodd, Mead, 1966.

Parker, Bertha M. *The Earth, a Great Storehouse*. New York: Harper & Row, 1967.

Parker, Bertha M. *The Earth's Changing Surface*. New York: Harper & Row, 1967.

Parker, Bertha M. *Pebbles and Seashells*. New York: Harper & Row, 1967.

Parker, Bertha M. *Soil*. New York: Harper & Row, 1967.

Parker, Bertha M. *Stories Read from Rocks*. New York: Harper & Row, 1967.

Pétrie, Jean. *The Earth*. New York: Franklin Watts, 1968.

Pine, Tillie S., and Levine, Joseph. *Rocks and How We Use Them*. New York: McGraw-Hill, 1967.

Pringle, Laurence. *This Is a River*. New York: Macmillan, 1972.

Ravielli, Anthony. *The World Is Round*. New York: Viking, 1970.

Rosenfeld, Sam. *Ask Me a Question About the Earth*. New York: Harvey House, 1966.

Rothman, Joel. *At Last to the Ocean: The Story of an Endless Cycle of Water*. New York: Crowell-Collier Macmillan, 1971.

Sherman, Diane. *You and the Oceans*. Chicago: Children's Press, 1965.

Stephens, William M. *Science Beneath the Sea*. New York: G. P. Putnam, 1966.

Stone, Harris A., and Ingmanson, Dale. *Rocks and Rills:*

A Look at Geology. Englewood Cliffs, N.J.: Prentice-Hall, 1967.

Talcott, Emogene. *Glacier Tracker.* New York: Lothrop, Lee, and Shepard, 1970.

Tangborn, Wendel U. *Glaciers.* New York: Crowell-Collier Macmillan, 1965.

Waters, John, and Waters, Barbara. *Salt Water Aquariums.* New York: Holiday House, 1968.

Chapter 15   The Solar System

Alter, Dinsmore. *Pictorial Guide to the Moon.* New York: T. Y. Crowell, 1967.

Asimov, Isaac. *What Makes the Sun Shine?* Boston: Little, Brown, 1971.

Azimov, Isaac. *Galaxies.* Chicago: Follett, 1968.

Azimov, Isaac. *Mars.* Chicago: Follett, 1966.

Azimov, Isaac. *The Moon.* Chicago: Follett, 1967.

Azimov, Isaac. *Stars.* Chicago: Follett, 1968.

Bergaust, Erik. *Mars—Planet for Conquest.* New York: G. P. Putnam, 1967.

Blough, Glenn O. *How The Sun Helps Us.* New York: Harper & Row, 1967.

Bonestell, Chesley. *The Solar System.* Chicago: Children's Press, 1967.

Branley, Franklyn M. *A Book of Mars for You.* New York: T. Y. Crowell, 1968.

Branley, Franklin M. *A Book of Outer Space for You.* New York: T. Y. Crowell, 1970.

Branley, Franklin M. *A Book of Stars for You.* New York: T. Y. Crowell, 1967.

Branley, Franklin M. *The Milky Way.* New York: T. Y. Crowell, 1969.

Branley, Franklin M. *The Moon.* New York: T. Y. Crowell, 1972.

Freeman, Mae B. *Do You Know About Stars?* New York: Random House, 1970.

Gallant, Roy A. *Exploring the Moon.* Garden City, N.Y.: Doubleday, 1966.

Gallant, Roy A. *Exploring the Planets.* Garden City, N.Y.: Doubleday, 1967.

Gamow, George. *The Moon.* New York: Abelard Schuman, 1971.

Heintze, Carl. *Search Among the Stars.* New York: Van Nostrand Reinhold, 1966.

Holmes, David C. *The Search for Life on Other Worlds.* New York: Sterling, 1966.

Hyde, Margaret O. *Exploring Earth and Space.* New York: McGraw-Hill, 1967.

King, Henry C. *The World of the Moon.* New York: T. Y. Crowell, 1966.

Knight, David C. *The First Book of the Sun.* New York: Franklin Watts, 1968.

Knight, David C. *Let's Find Out About Earth.* New York: Franklin Watts, 1968.

Knight, David C. *Let's Find Out About Mars.* New York: Franklin Watts, 1966.

Konan, Colin A. *The Stars.* New York: McGraw-Hill, 1966.

Land, Barbara. *The Telescope Makers.* New York: T. Y. Crowell, 1968.

Maisak, Lawrence. *Survival on the Moon.* New York: Crowell-Collier Macmillan, 1966.

Milgrom, Harry. *First Experiments with Gravity.* New York: E. P. Dutton, 1966.

Moore, Patrick, and Brinton, Henry. *Exploring Other Planets.* New York: Hawthorn, 1967.

Page, Thornton, and Page, Lou Williams. *Telescopes: How to Make Them and Use Them.* New York: Crowell-Collier Macmillan, 1966.

Parker, Bertha M. *Beyond the Solar System.* New York: Harper & Row, 1967.

Parker, Bertha M. *The Earth's Nearest Neighbor.* New York: Harper & Row, 1967.

Parker, Bertha M. *Gravity.* New York: Harper & Row, 1967.

Parker, Bertha M. *The Sky Above Us.* New York: Harper & Row, 1967.

Parker, Bertha M. *The Sun and Its Family.* New York: Harper & Row, 1967.

Polgreen, John, and Polgreen, Cathleen. *The Stars Tonight.* New York: Harper & Row, 1967.

Posin, Daniel Q. *Exploring and Understanding the Solar System.* Westchester, Ill.: Benefic Press, 1968.

Rosenfeld, Sam. *Ask Me a Question About the Heavens.* New York: Harvey House, 1966.

Shapp, Martha, and Shapp, Charles. *Let's Find Out About the Moon.* New York: Franklin Watts, 1965.

Shapp, Martha, and Shapp, Charles. *Let's Find Out About the Sun.* New York: Franklin Watts, 1965.

Zim, Herbert S. *The Universe.* New York: William Morrow, 1966.

Chapter 16   *Space Travel: Airplanes, Jets, Rockets, Space Vehicles*

Blough, Glenn O. *Masters of the Air.* Washington, D.C.: The Smithsonian Institution, 1965.

Coombs, Charles. *Project Apollo Mission to the Moon.* New York: Morrow, 1965.

Corbett, Scott. *What Makes a Plane Fly?* Boston: Little, Brown, 1967.

Freeman, Mae. *When Air Moves.* New York: McGraw-Hill, 1968.

Gardner, Martin. *Space Puzzles: Curious Questions and Answers About the Solar System.* New York: Simon and Shuster, 1971.

Hyde, Margaret O. *Off into Space! Science for Younger Space Travelers.* New York: McGraw-Hill, 1966.

Jaffe, Leonard. *Communications in Space.* New York: Holt, Rinehart & Winston, 1966.

Lauber, Patricia. *Big Dreams and Small Rockets.* New York: T. Y. Crowell, 1965.

Ley, Willy. *Rockets, Missiles, and Men in Space.* New York: Viking, 1967.

Lukashok, Alvin. *Communications Satellites: How They Work.* New York: G. P. Putnam, 1967.

May, Julian. *Astronautics.* Chicago: Follett, 1968.

May, Julian. *Rockets.* Chicago: Follett, 1967.

McFarland, Kenton G. *Airplanes—How They Work.* New York: G. P. Putnam, 1966.

Newell, Homer E. *Space Book for Young People.* New York: McGraw-Hill, 1968.

Parker, Bertha M. *Rockets and Missiles.* New York: Harper & Row, 1967.

Parker, Bertha M. *Satellites and Space Travel.* New York: Harper & Row, 1967.

Posin, Dan Q. *Exploring and Understanding Rockets and Satellites.* Westchester, Ill.: Benefic Press, 1967.

Sonnenborn, Ruth A. *The Question and Answer Book of Space.* New York: Random House, 1965.

Victor, Edward. *Airplanes.* Chicago: Follett, 1966.

Victor, Edward. *Planes and Rockets.* Chicago: Follett, 1965.

Young, Richard S. *Extraterrestrial Biology.* New York: Holt, Rinehart & Winston, 1966.

Chapter 17   Matter and Energy

Adler, Irving. *Atom Energy.* New York: John Day, 1971.

Adler, Irving, and Adler, Ruth. *Atoms and Molecules.* New York: John Day, 1966.

Bronowski, J., and Selsam, Millicent E. *Biography of an Atom.* New York: Harper & Row, 1965.

Harrison, George R. *First Book of Energy.* New York: Franklin Watts, 1965.

Hyde, Margaret O. *Atoms Today and Tomorrow.* New York: McGraw-Hill, 1966.

Jones, Claire. *Pollution: The Dangerous Atom.* Minneapolis, Minn.: Lerner Publications, 1972.

Palder, Edward L. *Magic With Chemistry.* New York: Grosset & Dunlap, 1966.

Parker, Bertha M. *Matter, Molecules, and Atoms.* New York: Harper & Row, 1967.

Parker, Bertha M. *What Things Are Made Of.* New York: Harper & Row, 1967.

Pearl, Richard M. *The Wonder World of Metals.* New York: Harper & Row, 1966.

Potter, Robert D., and Potter, Robert C. *Young People's Book of Atomic Energy.* New York: Dodd, Mead, 1967.

Woodburn, John H. *Excursions into Chemistry.* Philadelphia: Lippincott, 1965.

Woodbury, David O. *The New World of the Atom.* New York: Dodd, Mead, 1965.

Chapter 18   Magnetism and Electricity

Adler, Irving. *Electricity in Your Life.* New York: John Day, 1965.

Adler, Irving, and Adler, Ruth. *Magnets.* New York: John Day, 1966.

Clark, Mary Lou. *You and Electronics.* Chicago: Children's Press, 1967.

Corbett, Scott. *What Makes T.V. Work?* Boston: Little, Brown, 1965.

Epstein, Sam, and Epstein, Beryl. *The First Book of Electricity.* New York: Franklin Watts, 1965.

Knight, David C. *Let's Find Out About Magnets.* New York: Franklin Watts, 1967.

Lieberg, Owen S. *Wonders of Magnets and Magnetism.* New York: Dodd, Mead, 1967.

Parker, Bertha M. *Electricity.* New York: Harper & Row, 1967.

Parker, Bertha M. *Magnets.* New York: Harper & Row, 1967.

Ruchlis, Hy. *The Wonder of Electricity.* New York: Harper & Row, 1965.

Sachs, Raymond. *Magnets.* New York: Coward McCann Geogahan, 1967.

Seeman, Bernard. *The Story of Electricity and Magnetism.* Irvington-on-Hudson, N.Y.: Harvey House, 1967.

Stone, A., and Siegel, B. *Turned On: A Look at Electricity.* Englewood Cliffs, N.J.: Prentice-Hall, 1970.

Sootin, Harry. *Experiments with Electric Currents.* New York: W. W. Norton, 1969.

Sootin, Harry. *Experiments with Static Electricity.* New York: W. W. Norton, 1969.

Victor, Edward. *Electricity.* Chicago: Follett, 1967.

Victor, Edward. *Exploring and Understanding Magnets and Electromagnets.* Westchester, Ill.: Benefic Press, 1967.

Chapter 19   Machines At Work

Blackwood, Paul E. *Push and Pull: The Story of Energy.* New York: McGraw-Hill, 1966.

Blough, Glenn O. *Doing Work.* New York: Harper & Row, 1967.

Goldwater, Daniel. *Bridges.* New York: Scott, 1965.

Harrison, George R. *The First Book of Energy.* New York: Franklin Watts, 1965.

Hoke, John. *Solar Energy.* New York: Franklin Watts, 1968.

Miller, Lisa. *Levers.* New York: Coward McCann Geogahan, 1968.

Parker, Bertha M. *Machines; Toys.* New York: Harper & Row, 1967.

Pine, Tillie S., and Levine, Joseph. *Simple Machines and How We Use Them*. New York: McGraw-Hill, 1965.

Ross, Frank, Jr. *The World of Power and Energy*. New York: Lothrup, Lee, and Shepard, 1967.

Saunders, F. Wenderoth. *Machines for You*. Boston: Little, Brown, 1967.

Valens, Evans G. *Motion*. Cleveland: World, 1965.

Victor, Edward. *Exploring and Understanding Machines*. Westchester, Ill.: Benefic Press, 1969.

Chapter 20   Heat And Its Behavior

Adler, Irving, and Adler, Ruth. *Heat*. New York: John Day, 1964.

Barr, George. *Young Scientist and the Fire Department*. New York: McGraw-Hill, 1966.

Branley, Franklyn. *Solar Energy*. New York: T. Y. Crowell, 1957.

Feravolo, Rocco. *Easy Physics Projects: Air, Water, and Heat*. Englewood Cliffs, N.J.: Prentice-Hall, 1966.

Holden, Raymond. *All About Fire*. New York: Random House, 1964.

Lieberg, Owen S. *Wonders of Heat and Light*. New York: Dodd, Mead, 1966.

Parker, Bertha M. *Fire*. New York: Harper & Row, 1967.

Parker, Bertha M. *Fire, Friend and Foe*. New York: Harper & Row, 1967.

Parker, Bertha M. *Heat*. New York: Harper & Row, 1967.

Parker, Bertha M. *Thermometers, Heat, and Cold*. New York: Harper & Row, 1967.

Pine, Tillie S., and Levine, Joseph. *Heat All Around*. New York: Whittlesey House, 1963.

Stone, A. H., and Siegel, B. M. *The Heat's On*. Englewood Cliffs, N.J.: Prentice-Hall, 1970.

Victor, Edward. *Heat*. Chicago: Follett, 1967.

Chapter 21   Sound: Radio, Telephone, TV, and
               Radar

Anderson, Dorothy S. *Junior Science Book of Sound.* Champaign, Ill.: Garrard, 1962.

Beeler, Nelson. *Experiments in Sound.* New York: Crowell-Collier Macmillan, 1961.

Branley, Franklyn M. *High Sounds—Low Sounds.* New York: T. Y. Crowell, 1967.

Kohn, Bernice. *Echoes.* New York: Coward McCann Geogahan, 1965.

Meyer, Jerome S. *Sound and Its Reproduction.* Cleveland: World, 1964.

Miller, Lisa. *Sound.* New York: Coward McCann Geogahan, 1965.

Olney, Ross. *Sound All Around: How Hi-Fi and Stereo Work.* Englewood Cliffs, N.J.: Prentice-Hall, 1967.

Parker, Bertha M. *Sound.* New York: Harper & Row, 1967.

Showers, Paul. *How You Talk.* New York: T. Y. Crowell Company, 1967.

Stone, Harris A. *Take a Balloon.* Englewood Cliffs, N.J.: Prentice-Hall, 1967.

Victor, Edward. *Exploring and Understanding Sound.* Westchester, Ill.: Benefic Press, 1969.

Chapter 22   Light and Its Behavior

Adler, Irving, and Adler, Ruth. *Shadows.* New York: John Day, 1968.

Alexenberg, Melvin L. *Light and Sight.* Englewood Cliffs, N.J.: Prentice-Hall, 1969.

Branley, Franklyn M. *North, South, East, and West.* New York: T. Y. Crowell, 1966.

Brewer, A. C. *Exploring and Understanding Light.* Westchester, Ill.: Benefic Press, 1969.

Campbell, Ann. *Let's Find Out About Color*. New York: Franklin Watts, 1966.

Freeman, Ira M. *Light and Radiation*. New York: Random House, 1968.

Hellman, Hal. *The Art and Science of Color*. New York: McGraw-Hill, 1967.

Hoke, John. *The First Book of Photography*. New York: Franklin Watts, 1964.

Kohn, Bernice. *Light*. New York: Coward McCann Geogahan, 1965.

Kohn, Bernice. *Light You Can See*. Englewood Cliffs, N.J.: Prentice-Hall, 1965.

Mason, George F. *Animal Vision*. New York: William Morrow, 1968.

Parker, Bertha M. *Light*. New York: Harper & Row, 1967.

Polgreen, John, and Polgreen, Cathleen. *Sunlight and Shadows*. Garden City, N.Y.: Doubleday, 1967.

Simon, Seymour. *Let's-Try-It-Out—Light and Dark*. New York: McGraw-Hill, 1970.

Ubell, Earl. *The World of Candle and Color*. New York: Atheneum, 1969.

Appendix D

Directory of Science Equipment Companies

Allied Radio Corp., 833 N. Jefferson Boulevard, Chicago, Ill. 60610 (radio and electronic materials)

America Basic Science Club, 501 E. Crockett, San Antonio, Texas 78202 (science kits)

American Optical Instrument Division, Eggert and Sugar Roads, Buffalo, N.Y. 14215 (microscopes)

Atomic Corporation of America, 14725 Arminita St., Panorama City, Calif. 91402 (atomics)

Baker Science Packets, 650 Concord Drive, Holland, Mich. 49423 (science experiments)

Bausch & Lomb, Inc., 85737 Bausch Street, Rochester, N.Y. 14602 (microscopes)

Bioscope Manufacturing Company, Box 1492, Tulsa, Okla. 74101 (microprojectors)

Cambosco Scientific Company, 37 Antwerp St., Brighton, Mass. 02135 (general supplies)

Carolina Biological Supply Co., 2700 York Road, Burlington, N.C., 27215 (biological supplies)

Central Scientific Compay, 2600 South Kostner Road, Chicago, Ill, 60613; 79 Amherst St., Cambridge, Mass. 02143; 6446 Telegraph Road, Los Angeles, Calif. 90022 (general supplies)

Clay-Adams Co., 141 E. 25th St., New York, N.Y. 10010 (charts)

Corning Glass Works, Building 8, 4th floor, Corning, N.Y., 14830 (glassware)

Creative Playthings, P.O. Box 1100, Princeton, N.J. 08540 (general kits for science activities)

Denoyer-Geppert Co., 5235–39 Ravenswood Avenue, Chicago, Ill. 60640 (biology and astronomy charts & models)

Difco Laboratories, 920 Henry St., Detroit, Mich. 48201 (culture media)

Edmund Scientific Co., 555 Edscorp Building, Barrington, Mass. 08007 (optical equipment)

Educational Services, 108 Water St., Watertown, Mass. 02172 (science supplies)

Fisher Scientific Company, 711 Forbes St., Pittsburgh, Pa. 15219; 635 Greenwich St., New York, N.Y. 10014 (general)

General Biological Supply House, 8200 South Hoyne Ave., Chicago, Ill. 60620 (biological materials)

A. C. Gilbert Co., New Haven, Conn. (science toys)

C. S. Hammond, Maplewood, N.J. 07040 (science kits)

Heath Co., Benton Harbor, Mich. 49022 (electronic kits)

La Pine Scientific Co., 6001 South Knox Ave., Chicago, Ill. 60629 (general)

Los Angeles Biological Laboratories, 2977 West 14th St., Los Angeles, Calif. 90006 (biological supplies)

Macalaster-Bicknell Co., 253 Norfolk St., Cambridge, Mass. 02139 (general equipment)

Models of Industry, 2100 5th St., Berkeley, Calif. 94710 (handbooks with equipment)

National Audubon Society, 950 Third Ave., New York, N.Y. 10022 (nature charts, birds)

Nature Games, 8339 West Dry Creek Road, Healdsburg, Calif. 95448 (games using pictures)

A. J. Nystrom & Co., 3333 Elston Ave., Chicago, Ill. 60618 (biological models and charts)

Product Design Co., 2769 Middlefield Road, Redwood City, Calif. 94063 (kits for student experiments)

Sargent-Welch Co., 4647 Foster Ave., Chicago, Ill. 60630 (general)

Science Kit, Box 69, Tonowanda, N.Y. 04150

Stansi Scientific Co., 1231 N. Honore St., Chicago, Ill. 60622 (science kits and general equipment)

Taylor Instrument Co. 95 Ames St., Rochester, N.Y. 14601 (weather instruments)

Things of Science, Science Service, 1719 N. Street, N.W. Washington, D.C. 20036 (monthly kits)

Ward's Natural Science Establishment, P.O. Box 24, Beechwood Station, Rochester, N.Y. 14609 (teaching aids and general)

Appendix E

Distributors of Films, Film Loops, and Slides

(*Note:* Many of the science supply companies listed in Appendix C also distribute films and slides in addition to cassettes and phonograph records.)

Academy Films, 748 North Seward, Hollywood, Calif. 90028

American Cancer Society, 219 East 42 Street, New York, N.Y. 10017

American Dental Association, Bureau of AV Services, 222 East Superior Street, Chicago, Ill. 60614

American Heart Association, Film Library, 267 West 25 St., - New York, N.Y. 10001

American Museum of Natural History, Central Park West at 79th Street, New York, N.Y. 10024

Association Films, 347 Madison Avenue, New York, N.Y. 10017

Bell Telephone System (call local office for film information)

Brandon Films, 221 West 57 St., New York, N.Y. 10019

Churchill Films, 622 North Robertson Boulevard, Los Angeles, Calif. 90069

Coronet Films, Coronet Building, Chicago, Ill. 60601

Educational Services, 47 Galen Street, Watertown, Mass. 02172

Educational Testing Service, 20 Nassau St., Princeton, N.Y. 08540

Encyclopedia Brittanica Films, 425 North Michigan Ave., Chicago, Ill. 60601

Eye Gate House, 146-01 Archer Ave., Jamaica, N.Y. 11435

Filmstrip House, 432 Park Ave. South, New York, N.Y. 10016

Ford Motor Company, Film Library, 3000 Schaefer Rd., Dearborn, Mich. 48122

Gateway Productions, 1859 Powell St., San Francisco, Calif. 94133

General Electric Educational Films, 60 Washington Ave., Schenectady, N.Y. 12305

General Motors Corp., Film Library, 3044 West Grand Boulevard, Detroit, Mich. 48202

Handel Film Corp., 8730 Sunset Boulevard, Los Angeles, Calif. 90069

Harper & Row, 10 East 53 St., New York, N.Y. 10022

D. C. Heath & Co., 285 Columbia Ave., Boston, Mass. 02116

Hubbard Scientific Co., P.O. Box 105, Northbrook, Ill. 60062

International Film Bureau, 332 S. Michigan Ave., Chicago, Ill. 60604

Jam Handy Organization, 2821 E. Grand Boulevard, Detroit, Mich. 48211

Kaydee Films, National Instructional Films, 58 E. Route 59, Nanuet, N.Y. 10954

McGraw-Hill Text Films, 1221 Avenue of the Americas, New York, N.Y. 10020

Charles E. Merrill Books, 1300 Alum Creek Drive, Columbus, Ohio 43216

Modern Learning Aids, 1212 Avenue of the Americas, New York, N.Y. 10036

Moody Institute of Science, 1200 East Washington Boulevard, Whittier, Calif. 90606

Martin Moyer Productions, 900 Federal Ave., Seattle, Wash. 98102

National Aeronautics and Space Administration, Washington, D.C. 20546

National Audubon Society, Photo and Film Dept., 950 Third Ave., New York, N.Y. 10022

National Dairy Council, Chicago, Ill. 60606

National Education Association, 1201 16th St., N.W., Washington, D.C. 20036

National Film Board of Canada, 680 Fifth Avenue, New York, N.Y. 10019

Popular Science Publishing Co., AV Division, 355 Lexington Ave. New York, N.Y. 10017

Science Research Associates, 259 E. Erie St., Chicago, Ill. 60611

Sierra Club, 1050 Mills Tower, 220 Bush Street, San Francisco, Calif. 94104

Standard Oil Co. 39 Rockefeller Plaza, New York, N.Y. 10020

Sterling Educational Films 241 E. 34 St., New York, N.Y. 10016

Society for Visual Education, 1345 Diversey Parkway, Chicago, Ill. 60614

Thorne Films, 1229 University Ave., Boulder, Colorado 80302

Universal Education and Visual Arts, 221 Park Ave., New York, N.Y. 10003

U.S. Atomic Energy Commission, Division of Public Information, Washington, D.C. 20545

U.S. Bureau of Mines, 4800 Forbes Ave., Pittsburgh, Pa. 15213

U.S. Department of Agriculture, Motion Picture Services, Washington, D.C. 20250

U.S. Department of Agriculture, Soil Conservation Service, South Building, Washington, D.C. 20250

INDEX